## BOULDER (Including Foothills and Mountains)

1. Betasso Preserve: Canyon Loop Trail
2. Boulder: Boulder Creek Path
3. Boulder: Heil Valley Ranch
4. Boulder: South Boulder Creek Trail
5. Boulder: Walden Ponds
6. Chautauqua Park: First Flatiron
7. Eldorado Canyon: Eldorado Springs Trail
8. Gregory Canyon: Green Mountain Loop
9. Indian Peaks Wilderness: Devil's Thumb Lake
10. Indian Peaks Wilderness: Glacier Rim Trail
11. Indian Peaks Wilderness: Mount Audubon
12. James Peak Wilderness: Heart Lake
13. Walker Ranch: Meyers Homestead Trail
14. Walker Ranch: Walker Ranch Loop

## DENVER (Including Foothills and Mountains)

15. Alderfer Three Sisters Open Space Park: Ponderosa Sisters Loop
16. Barr Lake State Park: Lake Perimeter Trail
17. Bear Creek Lake Park: Bear Creek Trail
18. Deer Creek Open Space Park: Meadowlark Plymouth Creek Loop
19. Denver: Washington Park
20. Elk Meadow Open Space Park: Sleepy S Loop
21. Evergreen: Evergreen Lake
22. Golden Gate Canyon State Park: Mountain Lion Trail
23. Lakewood: Green Mountain Trail
24. Meyer Ranch Open Space Park: Lodgepole Loop
25. Mount Evans Wilderness: Hell's Hole Trail
26. Mount Evans Wilderness: Mount Bierstadt
27. Mount Evans Wilderness: Mount Evans
28. Mount Falcon Park: Castle and Parmalee Trail Loop
29. Red Rocks: Trading Post Trail
30. Rocky Mountain Arsenal National Wildlife Refuge: Lakes Loop
31. Westminster: Colorado Hills Trail
32. White Ranch Park: Belcher Hill

## NORTH OF DENVER (Including Fort Collins and Rocky Mountain National Park)

33. Button Rock Preserve: Sleepy Lion Trail
34. Cathy Fromme Prairie: Fossil Creek Trail
35. Fort Collins: Poudre River Trail
36. Glen Haven: Crosier Mountain Trail
37. Horsetooth Mountain Park: Horsetooth Falls and Horsetooth Rock
38. Larimer County: Devil's Backbone Trail
39. Lory State Park: Arthur's Rock
40. Rabbit Mountain: Eagle Wind Trail
41. Rocky Mountain National Park: Gem Lake
42. Rocky Mountain National Park: Lily Mountain
43. Rocky Mountain National Park: Longs Peak
44. Rocky Mountain National Park: Storm Pass Trail to Estes Cone
45. Rocky Mountain National Park: Twin Sisters
46. Round Mountain: Summit Adventure Trail

## SOUTH OF DENVER (Including Colorado Springs)

47. Bear Creek Cañon Park: Palmer Red Rock Loop
48. Blodgett Peak Open Space: Water Tank Trail
49. Castlewood Canyon State Park: Inner Canyon Loop
50. Colorado Trail: Little Scraggy Trail
51. Douglas County: Glendale Farm Trail
52. Douglas County: Greenland Trail
53. Garden of the Gods: Perkins Central Garden Trail
54. North Cheyenne Cañon Park: Lower Columbine Trail
55. Pike National Forest: Devil's Head Fire Lookout
56. Pike National Forest: Wigwam Trail
57. Pine Valley Ranch Park: Pine Valley Ranch Loop
58. Reynolds Open Space Park: Raven's Roost Oxen Draw Loop
59. Roxborough State Park: South Rim Trail
60. Waterton Canyon Recreation Area: Waterton Canyon

# 60 Hikes within 60 MILES

## DENVER AND BOULDER

### INCLUDING COLORADO SPRINGS, FORT COLLINS, AND ROCKY MOUNTAIN NATIONAL PARK

## Kim Lipker

**MENASHA RIDGE PRESS**
Birmingham, Alabama

Copyright © 2006 Kim Lipker
All rights reserved
Printed in the United States of America
Published by Menasha Ridge Press
Distributed by Publishers Group West
First edition, second printing 2008

Library of Congress Cataloging-in-Publication Data

Lipker, Kim, 1969–
    60 hikes within 60 miles, Denver: including Colorado Springs, Fort Collins,
    and Rocky Mountain National Park/Kim Lipker.—1st ed.
        p. cm.
    ISBN 10: 0-89732-627-X
    ISBN 13: 978-0-89732-627-8
    1. Hiking—Colorado—Denver Region—Guidebooks. 2. Denver Region
    (Colo.)—Guidebooks. I. Title. II. Title: Sixty hikes within sixty miles, Denver.

GV199.42.C62D474 2006
796.5109788´83—dc22

                                                                    2006044897

Cover design by Grant M. Tatum
Text design by Karen Ocker
Cover photo copyright Kim Lipker
All other photos by Kim Lipker, Bruce Becker, and Michael Bollinger
Maps by Kim Lipker and Ben Pease

Menasha Ridge Press
P.O. Box 43673
Birmingham, AL 35243
www.menasharidge.com

For Anna and Alex and Bruce
Let the music of the mountains dance within your heart.

# TABLE OF CONTENTS

# TABLE OF CONTENTS

# ACKNOWLEDGMENTS

I am most thankful for the fact that I was born in Colorado and that my kids are sixth-generation natives of the state. It's hard to think of living anywhere else. I would also like to thank the following for helping me write this book:

My husband, Bruce, has an enduring enthusiasm for hiking and the outdoors, come rain or shine. He was there through the entire process of mapping out the hikes, going on the hikes, and staying home to babysit. He is my biggest fan.

My parents are wonderful and helped with the grandkids when I needed time to write. They didn't mind when the children tore up their new beach house for a week or two at a time while I hid out and wrote. Karen, my sister, fits here too, somewhere between superaunt and hiking pal.

My hiking buddies, Renee, Diane, and Shannon, kept me company and provided a guest room between travels. Michael Bollinger, one of the nicest people you will ever know, went above and beyond his offer to assist. You will see some of his photos in this book.

The women of the Old Town Writing Group—Laura, Sarah, and Leslie—keep me on my toes.

The babysitters extraordinaire, Leslie, Jenni, and Darcy, chased after the kids while Mommy was "at work."

My Menasha Ridge Press editor, Russell Helms, is my personal Obi-Wan Kenobi. His guidance, patience, and encouragement were, and still are, empowering. His sense of humor matches my own, and I look forward to many more years of friendship.

The other Menasha Ridge Press folks are just as amazing. Thanks, Molly, for the opportunities.

Thank you to all the land stewards in Colorado who volunteer to make the hiking here some of the best in the world. There are too many to name. Your tireless efforts make the trails safe and keep them preserved for generations to come.

And finally, special thanks are due to Suellen May. She is simply one of the most extraordinary people I have ever known.

—Kim Lipker

# FOREWORD

Welcome to Menasha Ridge Press's *60 Hikes within 60 Miles,* a series designed to provide hikers with information needed to find and hike the very best trails surrounding cities usually underserved by good guidebooks.

Our strategy was simple: First, find a hiker who knows the area and loves to hike. Second, ask that person to spend a year researching the most popular and very best trails around. And third, have that person describe each trail in terms of difficulty, scenery, condition, elevation change, and all other categories of information that are important to hikers. "Pretend you've just completed a hike and met up with other hikers at the trailhead," we told each author. "Imagine their questions; be clear in your answers."

An experienced hiker and writer, author Kim Lipker has selected 60 of the best hikes in and around the Denver metropolitan area. From the urban paths of Washington Park to the glaciers of the Indian Peaks Wilderness to the prairies of Rocky Mountain Arsenal National Wildlife Refuge, Lipker provides trekkers of all abilities with a great variety of hikes—and all within roughly 60 miles of Denver.

You'll get more out of this book if you take a moment to read the introduction explaining how to read the trail listings. The Topographic Maps section will help you understand how useful topos will be on a hike, and will also tell you where to get them. And though this is a "where-to," not a "how-to" guide, those of you who have hiked extensively will find the introduction of particular value.

As much for the opportunity to free the spirit as well as to free the body, let these hikes elevate you above the urban hurry.

*All the best,*
*The Editors at Menasha Ridge Press*

# ABOUT THE AUTHOR

Kim Lipker grew up in Colorado doing most of the hikes featured in this book, never imagining that her frolics through the forest would ever land themselves in print. Kim is the author of *The Unofficial Guide to Bed and Breakfasts and Country Inns in the Rockies*. She writes a regular parenting column and other features for *Rocky Mountain Parent* magazine, along with a host of other writing projects.

Her first news article was published at age 12 in a special edition of the *Rocky Mountain News*, so she's been at the writing thing for a while. Kim received her Bachelor of Journalism degree from the University of Missouri–Columbia.

She's lived within 60 miles of Denver most of her life and presently lives in Fort Collins with her two kids Anna and Alex, and her husband, Bruce.

# PREFACE

## ▶ WRITING A HIKING GUIDEBOOK

Hiking books are tough work. Just kidding! This project enabled me to do two of my favorite things: hike and write. When I came on board for this project, there were three camps of people. First, there were the friends and writing buddies who were so excited about my book that they offered whatever support I needed. They braved the good, bad, and ugly on the trails and jumped when I pointed the GPS in their direction. They were the good friends who huffed and puffed with me when I knew they'd rather curse me and my inability to get a shopping-guide book contract: *60 Malls within 60 Miles: Denver and Boulder.*

Then there were the friends who couldn't believe that I'd narrow down the hikes into 60 feasible, well-rounded hikes. They know that Boulder County alone has more than 100 hikes to its name. These were the folks that talk, talk, talked about all the hikes, but never did the walk. Although discouraging, they kept me always mindful of the experienced crowd of hikers in Colorado.

Last, there were the relatives who calculated that from the time I signed my book contract to the deadline, I'd have to do *at least* one hike a week and didn't I have a family to raise and where were we going to find the time and blah, blah, blah. Well, the hikes are done, and if we can tour 300 bed-and-breakfasts across three states with a newborn (my last book), then we can easily hike 60 hikes in one region of one state with two toddlers running wild (and we did).

So, now that you know that we hiked every single trail in this book, let me assure you that every hike was chosen for its own unique merits. I am the type of person who chooses a wine by how the bottle's label design or wine name pops out at me. Although some of the hiking trails have peculiar names, like Devil's Backbone Trail in Loveland, I had a more scientific approach to their inclusion. Every trail in Colorado was previewed, narrowed down, and then balanced by skill and region. I consulted hiking clubs and then made final cuts. Every trail is one that I would recommend to my editor if he visited Denver.

## ▶ COLORADO FRONT RANGE

Denver is a world-class city with an amazing independent pioneer spirit. Critics have often called Denver a cow town, but rest assured that I've never seen a cow there, save for an old Mr. Steak costume in a St. Patrick's Day parade. Denver's appeal has everything to do with the unique blend of recreational activities available to Colorado's residents and visitors. Where else can you hike a glacier in the morning and go to a Broadway production of *Wicked* downtown in the evening?

For readers unfamiliar with the geography or terminology specific to Denver, here is a quick primer. Denver basically sits in the middle of Colorado at the base of the Rocky Mountains. The state is split in half: To the west are the mountains, to the east

Alex Lipker shields his eyes from the Colorado sun along the shores of Barr Lake.

are the plains. Fort Collins and Boulder are north of Denver and Colorado Springs is south. These four cities make a line called the Colorado Front Range.

Weather in this area is usually ten degrees warmer than in the mountains. Summer can be hot and winter cold, but on average, the weather is quite mild, pleasant, and the blue sky blazes with a bright sun almost every day. Don't be surprised if some of the Front Range and Foothill towns are windy. Their location on the map leads to some mighty gusts in winter.

Tourist season tends to vary from town to town, but summer is the high season in Estes Park and Rocky Mountain National Park. In the fall, Boulder (home to University of Colorado) and Fort Collins (home to Colorado State University) bustle with college students.

Colorado Springs is the land of "America the Beautiful." The famous song, written by Pikes Peak native Katharine Lee Bates more than a century ago, still speaks volumes about the area, the state, and our country's breathtaking beauty. *Spacious skies, amber waves of grain, purple mountains' majesty above the fruited plain.* You will understand why this is such an inspiring place when you visit its attractions, from Pikes Peak to the Garden of the Gods.

The Eastern Colorado prairie is one of the largest regions in Colorado and one of the least populated. Nothing is hidden in a land that is every bit as dramatic as its mountain-peak cousins. Here are rolling hills, golden fields of wheat, fierce thunderstorms, and threats of tornadoes.

## ▶ DENVER, COLORADO

This capital city sits at 1 mile above the sea, 5,280 feet to be exact (hence the name mile-high city, because there are 5,280 feet in a mile). Recent economic growth and population increases have made Denver quite a cosmopolitan city. You'll find new

Renee Putman gets a few yards ahead on the Bear Creek Trail.

sporting complexes, renovated cultural centers, talented chefs, top-notch shopping, and activities for all ages. This area is home to the state's largest concentration of population and its center of government, commerce, and culture. For the purpose of this book, we have defined Greater Denver as the downtown area and the metropolitan area immediately surrounding it.

While Denver is a city looking toward the future, it is also a great place to learn about Colorado's rich history. A host of museums and landmarks pay homage to this wonderful Western heritage: the Denver Art Museum, the Denver Museum of Natural History, the Colorado History Museum, the Buffalo Bill Museum, the Black American West Museum, and the Molly Brown House are just a few places to visit during your stay.

You can explore both the world and other areas of Colorado in the Greater Denver area. A wonderful new aquarium, Downtown Aquarium, features sharks, stingrays, and unique exhibits such as the Indonesian River Journey. More than 3,000 animals call the Denver Zoo home, and Denver Botanic Gardens boasts a wide variety of flowering plants from around the world.

Denver averages 300 days of sunshine a year. That's more days of annual sun than in San Diego or Miami Beach. Visitors come to Denver for business and pleasure all year.

Dining, theater, special events, and festivals round out a hearty helping of things to do and enjoy in Denver. Perhaps that is why one of four people living in the metro area moved to Denver in the past decade. The city has essentially doubled its population since 1960.

## ▶ ROCKY MOUNTAIN NATIONAL PARK

The crowning jewel of the 60 hikes is Rocky Mountain National Park. If you travel too far into the park, you miss the 60-mile mark, but you can still find plenty of perimeter hikes to whet your appetite for day and overnight hikes in Rocky Mountain National Park. These hikes include Longs Peak, Gem Lake, Lily Mountain, Storm Pass Trail to Estes Cone, and Twin Sisters.

Visitors to the Front Range will most likely join thousands of others who make their way to Rocky Mountain National Park every year (3 million to be exact). It is truly an experience not to be missed. It is said that more than 110 mountain peaks tower over the 415 square miles of hiking trails, picnic spots, waterfalls, cold lakes, and bountiful wildlife. I recommend visiting the area in the fall, when the elk are in the valleys for their bugling, or mating, season. Crowds are waning, the colors are changing, and the weather is still quite pleasant.

# PREFACE

## ▶ HISTORY AND A PERSONAL TOUCH

During the research for this book, my husband really liked doing the glacier hikes again, while I grew to be a bigger fan of the loop and balloon trails. I became a born-again hiker in Boulder County and Jefferson County, and am so happy at the progress made there, in my old stomping grounds. The trails here are constantly upgraded and acquiring open space is a priority in both counties.

Lesser-known hikes, like the urban hikes, were nice to revisit. These urban hikes tend to be easier and less crowded and are a great way to get novice hikers interested in the sport. Washington Park in downtown Denver is a great place to spend a Saturday morning, and the Poudre River Trail in Fort Collins is a paved wonder.

The best way to explore the history of Denver and the surrounding area is to visualize those people who have walked the trails before you. Pioneers who just crossed the prairie may have stopped in their wagons to fill water jugs at Barr Lake State Park. A gold miner down on his luck may have found hope near Eldorado Springs Trail. Native American children may have climbed Arthur's Rock every day. In the 1930s, women who climbed Longs Peak for recreation sometimes had to camp separately from the men and cook their camp dinner. (My grandma was one of them.)

If you are hiking in Estes Park, be sure to stop at the Stanley Hotel. My aunt has waitressed there for many years and it is rich with stories; they say that Stephen King found the inspiration for *The Shining* while staying there.

There is always the bad with the good, and the biggest bad goes to the little boy who hit my pregnant friend in the stomach while passing us in Meyer Ranch Open Space. It was also annoying to see so many hikers with their dogs off the leash and not picking up their dog's poop. Be warned, many places ticket hikers if they don't follow the rules, which are there for a reason. A friend of a friend got a heavy fine for having her dog off of the leash on the Meyers Homestead Trail.

In the time that it took me to research and write this book, a forest ranger died while hiking in Rocky Mountain National Park, another experienced hiker was lost and then found in the same park, and a man was allegedly mugged at a Jefferson County Trailhead. Please be careful on the trail and always hike with a buddy. At the very least, let someone know where you are going and when you expect to be back.

Thank you for picking up this book. Be assured that I had you, the reader, in mind during every one of my hikes.

# HIKING RECOMMENDATIONS

## ▶ HIKES 1 TO 3 MILES

Alderfer Three Sisters Open Space Park:
  Ponderosa Sisters Loop
Blodgett Peak Open Space: Water Tank Trail
Boulder: Walden Ponds
Castlewood Canyon State Park:
  Inner Canyon Loop
Deer Creek Open Space Park:
  Meadowlark Plymouth Creek Loop
Denver: Washington Park
Douglas County: Glendale Farm Trail
Elk Meadow: Sleepy S Loop
Evergreen: Evergreen Lake

Garden of the Gods:
  Perkins Central Garden Trail
Meyer Ranch Open Space Park:
  Lodgepole Loop
North Cheyenne Cañon Park:
  Lower Columbine Trail
Pike National Forest:
  Devil's Head Fire Lookout
Red Rocks: Trading Post Trail
Rocky Mountain Arsenal National Wildlife
  Refuge: Lakes Loop
Westminster: Colorado Hills Trail

## ▶ HIKES 3 TO 6 MILES

Bear Creek Cañon: Palmer Red Rock Loop
Bear Creek Lake Park: Bear Creek Trail
Betasso Preserve: Canyon Loop Trail
Boulder: Boulder Creek Path
Button Rock Preserve: Sleepy Lion Trail
Cathy Fromme Prairie: Fossil Creek Trail
Chautauqua Park: First Flatiron
Lakewood: Green Mountain Trail
Larimer County: Devil's Backbone Trail
Lory State Park: Arthur's Rock
Pine Valley Ranch Park:
  Pine Valley Ranch Loop

Rabbit Mountain:
  Eagle Wind Trail
Reynolds Open Space Park: Raven's Roost
  Oxen Draw Loop
Rocky Mountain National Park:
  Gem Lake
Rocky Mountain National Park:
  Lily Mountain
Roxborough State Park: South Rim Trail
Walker Ranch: Meyers Homestead Trail
White Ranch Park: Belcher Hill

## ▶ HIKES 6 TO 9 MILES

Barr Lake State Park: Lake Perimeter Trail
Boulder: Heil Valley Ranch
Boulder: South Boulder Creek Trail
Douglas County: Greenland Trail
Eldorado Canyon: Eldorado Springs Trail
Fort Collins: Poudre River Trail
Glen Haven: Crosier Mountain Trail
Golden Gate Canyon: Mountain Lion Trail
Gregory Canyon: Green Mountain Loop
Horsetooth Mountain Park:
  Horsetooth Falls and Horsetooth Rock

Indian Peaks Wilderness: Mount Audubon
James Peak Wilderness: Heart Lake
Mount Evans Wilderness:
  Mount Bierstadt
Mount Evans Wilderness: Mount Evans
Rocky Mountain National Park:
  Storm Pass Trail to Estes Cone
Rocky Mountain National Park: Twin Sisters
Walker Ranch: Walker Ranch Loop
Waterton Canyon Recreation Area:
  Waterton Canyon

# HIKING RECOMMENDATIONS

## ▶ HIKES LONGER THAN 9 MILES

Colorado Trail: Little Scraggy Trail
Indian Peaks Wilderness: Devil's Thumb
  Lake
Indian Peaks Wilderness: Glacier Rim Trail
Mount Evans Wilderness: Hell's Hole Trail
Mount Falcon Park:
  Castle and Parmalee Trail Loop
Pike National Forest:
  Wigwam Trail
Rocky Mountain National Park:
  Longs Peak
Round Mountain: Summit Adventure Trail

## ▶ TRAILS WHERE AT LEAST A PORTION IS GOOD FOR CHILDREN, NOVICES, AND THE OLDER SET

Bear Creek Lake Park:
  Bear Creek Trail
Blodgett Peak Open Space: Water Tank Trail
Boulder: Boulder Creek Path
Boulder: South Boulder Creek Trail
Boulder: Walden Ponds
Castlewood Canyon State Park:
  Inner Canyon Loop
Cathy Fromme Prairie: Fossil Creek Trail
Denver: Washington Park
Douglas County: Glendale Farm Trail
Evergreen: Evergreen Lake
Fort Collins: Poudre River Trail
Garden of the Gods:
  Perkins Central Garden Trail
Larimer County: Devil's Backbone Trail
Meyer Ranch Open Space Park:
  Lodgepole Loop
North Cheyenne Cañon Park:
  Lower Columbine Trail
Red Rocks: Trading Post Trail
Rocky Mountain Arsenal National Wildlife
  Refuge: Lakes Loop
Waterton Canyon Recreation Area:
  Waterton Canyon
Westminster: Colorado Hills Trail

## ▶ HIKES FOR KIDS

Alderfer Three Sisters Open Space Park:
  Ponderosa Sisters Loop
Barr Lake State Park: Lake Perimeter Trail
Bear Creek Lake Park: Bear Creek Trail
Betasso Preserve: Canyon Loop Trail
Blodgett Peak Open Space: Water Tank Trail
Boulder: Boulder Creek Path
Boulder: South Boulder Creek Trail
Boulder: Walden Ponds
Button Rock Preserve: Sleepy Lion Trail
Castlewood Canyon State Park:
  Inner Canyon Loop
Cathy Fromme Prairie: Fossil Creek Trail
Deer Creek Open Space Park:
  Meadowlark Plymouth Creek Loop
Denver: Washington Park
Douglas County: Glendale Farm Trail
Douglas County: Greenland Trail
Elk Meadow: Sleepy S Loop
Evergreen: Evergreen Lake
Fort Collins: Poudre River Trail
Garden of the Gods:
  Perkins Central Garden Trail
Larimer County: Devil's Backbone Trail
Meyer Ranch Open Space Park:
  Lodgepole Loop
North Cheyenne Cañon Park:
  Lower Columbine Trail
Pike National Forest:
  Devil's Head Fire Lookout

# HIKING RECOMMENDATIONS

## ▶ HIKES FOR KIDS (CONTINUED)

Pine Valley Ranch Park:
  Pine Valley Ranch Loop
Rabbit Mountain: Eagle Wind Trail
Red Rocks: Trading Post Trail
Reynolds Open Space Park:
  Raven's Roost Oxen Draw Loop
Rocky Mountain Arsenal National Wildlife
  Refuge: Lakes Loop

Rocky Mountain National Park:
  Gem Lake
Rocky Mountain National Park:
  Lily Mountain
Waterton Canyon Recreation Area:
  Waterton Canyon
Westminster: Colorado Hills Trail

## ▶ TRAILS FOR HARD-CORE HIKERS

Golden Gate Canyon: Mountain Lion Trail
Gregory Canyon: Green Mountain Loop
Indian Peaks Wilderness: Devil's Thumb Lake
Indian Peaks Wilderness: Glacier Rim Trail
Indian Peaks Wilderness: Mount Audubon
James Peak Wilderness: Heart Lake
Lakewood: Green Mountain Trail

Mount Evans Wilderness: Hell's Hole Trail
Mount Evans Wilderness: Mount Bierstadt
Mount Evans Wilderness: Mount Evans
Rocky Mountain National Park: Longs Peak
Round Mountain: Summit Adventure Trail
Walker Ranch: Walker Ranch Loop
White Ranch Park: Belcher Hill

## ▶ TRAILS WHERE AT LEAST A PORTION IS CONCRETE OR ASPHALT

Barr Lake State Park:
  Lake Perimeter Trail
Bear Creek Lake Park:
  Bear Creek Trail
Boulder: Boulder Creek Path
Boulder: South Boulder Creek Trail
Castlewood Canyon State Park:
  Inner Canyon Loop

Cathy Fromme Prairie: Fossil Creek Trail
Denver: Washington Park
Evergreen: Evergreen Lake
Fort Collins: Poudre River Trail
Garden of the Gods:
  Perkins Central Garden Trail
Red Rocks: Trading Post Trail

## ▶ TRAILS GOOD FOR DOGS

Alderfer Three Sisters Open Space Park:
  Ponderosa Sisters Loop
Bear Creek Lake Park: Bear Creek Trail
Betasso Preserve: Canyon Loop Trail
Blodgett Peak Open Space: Water Tank Trail
Boulder: Boulder Creek Path
Boulder: Walden Ponds
Castlewood Canyon State Park:
  Inner Canyon Loop

Colorado Trail: Little Scraggy Trail
Deer Creek Open Space Park: Meadowlark
  Plymouth Creek Loop
Denver: Washington Park
Douglas County: Glendale Farm Trail
Douglas County: Greenland Trail
Eldorado Canyon: Eldorado Springs Trail
Elk Meadow: Sleepy S Loop
Evergreen: Evergreen Lake

# HIKING RECOMMENDATIONS

## ▶ TRAILS GOOD FOR DOGS (CONTINUED)

Fort Collins: Poudre River Trail

Garden of the Gods:
  Perkins Central Garden Trail

Glen Haven: Crosier Mountain Trail

Golden Gate Canyon: Mountain Lion Trail

Gregory Canyon: Green Mountain Loop

Horsetooth Mountain Park: Horsetooth Falls
  and Horsetooth Rock

Indian Peaks Wilderness: Devil's Thumb
  Lake

Indian Peaks Wilderness: Glacier Rim Trail

Indian Peaks Wilderness: Mount Audubon

James Peak Wilderness: Heart Lake

Lakewood: Green Mountain Trail

Larimer County: Devil's Backbone Trail

Lory State Park: Arthur's Rock

Meyer Ranch Open Space Park:

Lodgepole Loop

Mount Evans Wilderness: Hell's Hole Trail

Mount Falcon Park:
  Castle and Parmalee Trail Loop

North Cheyenne Cañon Park:
  Lower Columbine Trail

Pike National Forest:
  Devil's Head Fire Lookout

Pine Valley Ranch Park:
  Pine Valley Ranch Loop

Rabbit Mountain: Eagle Wind Trail

Red Rocks: Trading Post Trail

Reynolds Open Space Park:
  Raven's Roost Oxen Draw Loop

Walker Ranch: Meyers Homestead Trail

Westminster: Colorado Hills Trail

White Ranch Park: Belcher Hill

## ▶ FLATLAND HIKES

Barr Lake State Park: Lake Perimeter Trail

Bear Creek Lake Park: Bear Creek Trail

Boulder: Boulder Creek Path

Boulder: South Boulder Creek Trail

Boulder: Walden Ponds

Cathy Fromme Prairie: Fossil Creek Trail

Denver: Washington Park

Douglas County: Glendale Farm Trail

Douglas County: Greenland Trail

Fort Collins: Poudre River Trail

Garden of the Gods:
  Perkins Central Garden Trail

Larimer County: Devil's Backbone Trail

Rocky Mountain Arsenal National Wildlife
  Refuge: Lakes Loop

Waterton Canyon Recreation Area:
  Waterton Canyon

Westminster: Colorado Hills Trail

## ▶ HIKES WITH STEEP SECTIONS

Alderfer Three Sisters Open Space Park:
  Ponderosa Sisters Loop

Bear Creek Cañon: Palmer Red Rock Loop

Chautauqua Park: First Flatiron

Deer Creek Open Space Park: Meadowlark
  Plymouth Creek Loop

Elk Meadow: Sleepy S Loop

Glen Haven: Crosier Mountain Trail

Golden Gate Canyon: Mountain Lion Trail

Gregory Canyon: Green Mountain Loop

Indian Peaks Wilderness: Devil's Thumb Lake

Indian Peaks Wilderness: Glacier Rim Trail

Indian Peaks Wilderness:
  Mount Audubon

James Peak Wilderness: Heart Lake

Lakewood: Green Mountain Trail

Lory State Park: Arthur's Rock

Mount Evans Wilderness: Hell's Hole Trail

# HIKING RECOMMENDATIONS

## ▶ HIKES WITH STEEP SECTIONS (CONTINUED)

Mount Evans Wilderness: Mount Bierstadt
Mount Evans Wilderness: Mount Evan
Mount Falcon Park:
  Castle and Parmalee Trail Loop
Pike National Forest:
  Devil's Head Fire Lookout
Pike National Forest: Wigwam Trail
Pine Valley Ranch Park:
  Pine Valley Ranch Loop
Reynolds Open Space Park:

Raven's Roost Oxen Draw Loop
Rocky Mountain National Park: Longs Peak
Rocky Mountain National Park:
  Storm Pass Trail to Estes Cone
Rocky Mountain National Park: Twin Sisters
Round Mountain:
  Summit Adventure Trail
Roxborough State Park: South Rim Trail
Walker Ranch: Walker Ranch Loop
White Ranch Park: Belcher Hill

## ▶ ALPINE HIKES

Button Rock Preserve: Sleepy Lion Trail
Glen Haven: Crosier Mountain Trail
Golden Gate Canyon: Mountain Lion Trail
Indian Peaks Wilderness: Devil's Thumb Lake
Indian Peaks Wilderness: Glacier Rim Trail
Indian Peaks Wilderness: Mount Audubon
James Peak Wilderness: Heart Lake
Mount Evans Wilderness: Hell's Hole Trail
Mount Evans Wilderness: Mount Bierstadt
Mount Evans Wilderness: Mount Evans

Rocky Mountain National Park: Gem Lake
Rocky Mountain National Park:
  Lily Mountain
Rocky Mountain National Park: Longs Peak
Rocky Mountain National Park:
  Storm Pass Trail to Estes Cone
Rocky Mountain National Park: Twin Sisters
Round Mountain: Summit Adventure Trail
Walker Ranch: Walker Ranch Loop
White Ranch Park: Belcher Hill

## ▶ HIKES ALONG WATER

Barr Lake State Park: Lake Perimeter Trail
Bear Creek Lake Park: Bear Creek Trail
Boulder: Boulder Creek Path
Boulder: South Boulder Creek Trail
Boulder: Walden Ponds
Button Rock Preserve: Sleepy Lion Trail
Castlewood Canyon State Park:
  Inner Canyon Loop
Colorado Trail: Little Scraggy Trail
Deer Creek Open Space Park: Meadowlark
  Plymouth Creek Loop
Denver: Washington Park
Evergreen: Evergreen Lake
Fort Collins: Poudre River Trail
Golden Gate Canyon: Mountain Lion Trail

Indian Peaks Wilderness:
  Devil's Thumb Lake
James Peak Wilderness: Heart Lake
Mount Evans Wilderness: Mount Bierstadt
Mount Evans Wilderness: Mount Evans
North Cheyenne Cañon Park:
  Lower Columbine Trail
Pine Valley Ranch Park:
  Pine Valley Ranch Loop
Rocky Mountain Arsenal National Wildlife
  Refuge: Lakes Loop
Walker Ranch: Walker Ranch Loop
Waterton Canyon Recreation Area:
  Waterton Canyon
Westminster: Colorado Hills Trail

# HIKING RECOMMENDATIONS

## ▶ PLENTIFUL-WILDLIFE HIKES

Alderfer Three Sisters Open Space Park:
  Ponderosa Sisters Loop
Barr Lake State Park: Lake Perimeter Trail
Bear Creek Cañon: Palmer Red Rock Loop
Bear Creek Lake Park: Bear Creek Trail
Betasso Preserve: Canyon Loop Trail
Blodgett Peak Open Space: Water Tank Trail
Boulder: Heil Valley Ranch
Boulder: Walden Ponds
Button Rock Preserve: Sleepy Lion Trail
Castlewood Canyon State Park:
  Inner Canyon Loop
Cathy Fromme Prairie: Fossil Creek Trail
Colorado Trail: Little Scraggy Trail
Douglas County: Glendale Farm Trail
Douglas County: Greenland Trail
Eldorado Canyon: Eldorado Springs Trail
Elk Meadow: Sleepy S Loop
Fort Collins: Poudre River Trail
Glen Haven: Crosier Mountain Trail
Golden Gate Canyon: Mountain Lion Trail
Indian Peaks Wilderness:
  Devil's Thumb Lake
Indian Peaks Wilderness: Glacier Rim Trail
Indian Peaks Wilderness: Mount Audubon
James Peak Wilderness: Heart Lake
Lory State Park: Arthur's Rock

Meyer Ranch Open Space Park:
  Lodgepole Loop
Mount Evans Wilderness: Hell's Hole Trail
Mount Evans Wilderness: Mount Bierstadt
Mount Evans Wilderness: Mount Evans
Mount Falcon Park:
  Castle and Parmalee Trail Loop
Pike National Forest:
  Devil's Head Fire Lookout
Pike National Forest: Wigwam Trail
Pine Valley Ranch Park:
  Pine Valley Ranch Loop
Rabbit Mountain: Eagle Wind Trail
Reynolds Open Space Park:
  Raven's Roost Oxen Draw Loop
Rocky Mountain Arsenal National Wildlife
  Refuge: Lakes Loop
Rocky Mountain National Park: Gem Lake
Rocky Mountain National Park:
  Lily Mountain
Rocky Mountain National Park:
  Storm Pass Trail to Estes Cone
Rocky Mountain National Park: Twin Sisters
Walker Ranch: Meyers Homestead Trail
Walker Ranch: Walker Ranch Loop
Waterton Canyon Recreation Area:
  Waterton Canyon

## ▶ GOOD WINTER HIKES

*(Remember to check weather conditions first;
winters in Colorado are fickle.)*
Alderfer Three Sisters Open Space Park:
  Ponderosa Sisters Loop
Barr Lake State Park: Lake Perimeter Trail
Bear Creek Lake Park: Bear Creek Trail
Blodgett Peak Open Space: Water Tank Trail
Boulder: Boulder Creek Path
Boulder: Heil Valley Ranch
Boulder: South Boulder Creek Trail
Boulder: Walden Ponds

Castlewood Canyon State Park: Inner Canyon
  Loop
Cathy Fromme Prairie: Fossil Creek Trail
Chautauqua Park: First Flatiron
Deer Creek Open Space Park: Meadowlark
  Plymouth Creek Loop
Denver: Washington Park
Douglas County: Glendale Farm Trail
Douglas County: Greenland Trail
Eldorado Canyon: Eldorado Springs Trail
Elk Meadow: Sleepy S Loop

# HIKING RECOMMENDATIONS

## ▶ GOOD WINTER HIKES (CONTINUED)

Fort Collins: Poudre River Trail
Garden of the Gods:
  Perkins Central Garden Trail
Horsetooth Mountain Park: Horsetooth Falls
  and Horsetooth Rock
Lakewood: Green Mountain Trail
Larimer County: Devil's Backbone Trail
Lory State Park: Arthur's Rock
Meyer Ranch Open Space Park:
  Lodgepole Loop
North Cheyenne Cañon Park: Lower
  Columbine Trail
Pine Valley Ranch Park:
  Pine Valley Ranch Loop

Rabbit Mountain: Eagle Wind Trail
Red Rocks: Trading Post Trail
Reynolds Open Space Park:
  Raven's Roost Oxen Draw Loop
Rocky Mountain Arsenal National Wildlife
  Refuge: Lakes Loop
Rocky Mountain National Park: Gem Lake
Roxborough State Park:
  South Rim Trail
Walker Ranch: Meyers Homestead Trail
Waterton Canyon Recreation Area:
  Waterton Canyon
Westminster: Colorado Hills Trail
White Ranch Park: Belcher Hill

## ▶ FOOT-TRAFFIC-ONLY HIKES

*(This usually means no bikes, no horses, and no motorized vehicles.)*
Button Rock Preserve: Sleepy Lion Trail
Chautauqua Park: First Flatiron
Evergreen: Evergreen Lake
Indian Peaks Wilderness: Devil's Thumb Lake
Indian Peaks Wilderness: Glacier Rim Trail
Indian Peaks Wilderness: Mount Audubon
James Peak Wilderness: Heart Lake
Mount Evans Wilderness: Hell's Hole Trail
Mount Evans Wilderness: Mount Bierstadt
Mount Evans Wilderness: Mount Evans
Pike National Forest:
  Devil's Head Fire Lookout

Pike National Forest: Wigwam Trail
Red Rocks: Trading Post Trail
Reynolds Open Space Park:
  Raven's Roost Oxen Draw Loop
Rocky Mountain Arsenal National Wildlife
  Refuge: Lakes Loop
Rocky Mountain National Park: Gem Lake
Rocky Mountain National Park:
  Lily Mountain
Rocky Mountain National Park: Longs Peak
Rocky Mountain National Park:
  Storm Pass Trail to Estes Cone
Rocky Mountain National Park: Twin Sisters
Roxborough State Park: South Rim Trail

## ▶ GEOLOGICAL HIKES

Alderfer Three Sisters Open Space Park:
  Ponderosa Sisters Loop
Blodgett Peak Open Space: Water Tank Trail
Chautauqua Park: First Flatiron
Eldorado Canyon: Eldorado Springs Trail
Garden of the Gods:
  Perkins Central Garden Trail

Horsetooth Mountain Park:
  Horsetooth Falls and Horsetooth Rock
Indian Peaks Wilderness: Glacier Rim Trail
Larimer County: Devil's Backbone Trail
Mount Evans Wilderness: Hell's Hole Trail
Mount Evans Wilderness: Mount Bierstadt
Mount Evans Wilderness: Mount Evans

# HIKING RECOMMENDATIONS

## ▶ GEOLOGICAL HIKES (CONTINUED)

Pike National Forest:
  Devil's Head Fire Lookout
Red Rocks: Trading Post Trail
Rocky Mountain National Park: Longs Peak

Rocky Mountain National Park: Storm Pass
  Trail to Estes Cone
Roxborough State Park: South Rim Trail

## ▶ TRAILS THAT ARE PARTLY HANDICAP-ACCESSIBLE

Barr Lake State Park: Lake Perimeter Trail
Boulder: Boulder Creek Path
Boulder: South Boulder Creek Trail
Boulder: Walden Ponds
Button Rock Preserve: Sleepy Lion Trail
Castlewood Canyon State Park:
  Inner Canyon Loop
Cathy Fromme Prairie: Fossil Creek Trail
Denver: Washington Park
Evergreen: Evergreen Lake

Fort Collins: Poudre River Trail
Garden of the Gods:
  Perkins Central Garden Trail
Pine Valley Ranch Park:
  Pine Valley Ranch Loop
Rocky Mountain Arsenal National Wildlife
  Refuge: Lakes Loop
Waterton Canyon Recreation Area:
  Waterton Canyon

## ▶ TRAILS THAT BAN DOGS

Barr Lake State Park: Lake Perimeter Trail
Boulder: Heil Valley Ranch
Boulder: South Boulder Creek Trail
Button Rock Preserve:
  Sleepy Lion Trail
Rocky Mountain Arsenal National Wildlife
  Refuge: Lakes Loop
Rocky Mountain National Park:
  Gem Lake

Rocky Mountain National Park:
  Lily Mountain
Rocky Mountain National Park: Longs Peak
Rocky Mountain National Park:
  Storm Pass Trail to Estes Cone
Rocky Mountain National Park: Twin Sisters
Roxborough State Park: South Rim Trail
Waterton Canyon Recreation Area:
  Waterton Canyon

## ▶ HIKES THAT I'D TAKE MY 91-YEAR-OLD GRANDPA ON AT LEAST A PORTION

Barr Lake State Park: Lake Perimeter Trail
Bear Creek Lake Park: Bear Creek Trail
Boulder: Boulder Creek Path
Boulder: South Boulder Creek Trail
Boulder: Walden Ponds
Castlewood Canyon State Park: Inner Canyon
  Loop
Cathy Fromme Prairie: Fossil Creek Trail
Denver: Washington Park
Douglas County: Glendale Farm Trail

Evergreen: Evergreen Lake
Fort Collins: Poudre River Trail
Garden of the Gods: Perkins Central Garden
  Trail
North Cheyenne Cañon Park:
  Lower Columbine Trail
Rocky Mountain Arsenal National Wildlife
  Refuge: Lakes Loop
Waterton Canyon Recreation Area: Waterton
  Canyon

# INTRODUCTION

Welcome to *60 Hikes within 60 Miles: Denver and Boulder*. If you're new to hiking or even if you're a seasoned trailsmith, take a few minutes to read the following introduction. We explain how this book is organized and how to use it.

## ▶ HIKE DESCRIPTIONS

Each hike contains eight key items: a locator map, an "In Brief" description of the trail, a key at-a-glance information box, directions to the trail, a trail map, an elevation profile, a trail description, and a description of nearby activities. Combined, the maps and information provide a clear method to assess each trail from the comfort of your favorite reading chair.

### IN BRIEF

A "taste of the trail." Think of this section as a snapshot focused on the historical landmarks, beautiful vistas, and other sights you may encounter on the trail.

### KEY AT-A-GLANCE INFORMATION

The information in the key at-a-glance boxes gives you a quick idea of the specifics of each hike. There are 13 basic elements covered.

**LENGTH** The length of the trail from start to finish. There may be options to shorten or extend the hikes, but the mileage corresponds to the described hike. Consult the hike description to help decide how to customize the hike for your ability or time constraints.

**CONFIGURATION** A description of what the trail looks like from overhead. Trails can be loops, out-and-backs (trails on which one enters and leaves along the same path), figure eights, or balloons (trails on which one enters and leaves on the same path with a loop in between).

**DIFFICULTY** The degree of effort an "average" hiker should expect on a given hike. For simplicity, difficulty is described as "easy," "moderate," or "difficult."

**SCENERY** A rating of the overall environs of the hike and what to expect in terms of plant life, wildlife, streams, and historic buildings.

**EXPOSURE** A quick check of how much sun you can expect on your shoulders during the hike. Descriptors used include terms such as "shady," "exposed," and "sunny."

**TRAFFIC** Indicators of how busy the trail might be on an average day, and if you might be able to find solitude out there. Trail traffic, of course, varies from day to day and season to season.

**SURFACE** A description of the trail surface, be it paved, rocky, dirt, or a mixture of elements.

**HIKING TIME** The length of time it takes to hike the trail. A slow but steady hiker will average 2 to 3 miles an hour, depending on the terrain. Most of the estimates in this

# INTRODUCTION

book reflect a speed of about 2 miles per hour. Take the miles of the hike and divide by two and this will give a rough estimate of hiking time. For example, an 8-mile hike should take the average hiker four hours.

**SEASON** The best months to hike the trail determined by access and weather conditions.

**ACCESS** A notation of fees or permits needed to access the trail (if any) and whether the trail has specific hours.

**FACILITIES** What to expect in terms of restrooms, phones, water, and other amenities available at the trailhead or nearby.

**MAPS** Which maps are the best, or easiest, for this hike and where to get them.

**SPECIAL COMMENTS** These comments cover little extra details that don't fit into any of the above categories. Here you'll find information on trail-hiking options and facts, or tips on how to get the most out of your hike.

## DIRECTIONS TO THE TRAIL

The detailed directions will lead you to each trailhead. If you use GPS technology, provided UTM coordinates allow you to navigate directly to the trailhead.

## TRAIL DESCRIPTIONS

The trail description is the heart of each hike. Here, the author provides a summary of the trail's essence and highlights any special traits the hike offers. Ultimately, the hike description will help you choose which hikes are best for you.

## NEARBY ACTIVITIES

Look here for information on nearby hikes.

## ▶ WEATHER

I must stress that the weather in Colorado can change every ten minutes. Be prepared for anything: sun, snow, flash flood, lightning, and hail. Start by knowing the weather forecast and the road conditions, and pack smart. It can be quite a lovely day in Denver, but a trailhead may be inaccessible due to blizzard conditions. You must be prepared, and you should consider carrying a hiking card (CORSAR, discussed below). If you need to be rescued, these hiking cards can save your life and your pocketbook.

## ROAD CONDITIONS

Colorado Traffic Management Center of CDOT
**www.cotrip.org**; (877) 315-7623

Colorado Avalanche Information Center
**www.geosurvey.state.co.us/avalanche**; (303) 499-9650

# INTRODUCTION

## CLIMATE OVERVIEW:

Semiarid                          Short springs
Dry summers                       Mild winters, except in the mountains

### AVERAGE HIGHS AND LOWS IN DENVER (degrees Fahrenheit)

|      | JAN | FEB | MAR | APR | MAY | JUN |
|------|-----|-----|-----|-----|-----|-----|
| HIGH | 43° | 47° | 52° | 62° | 71° | 81° |
| LOW  | 16° | 20° | 26° | 35° | 44° | 52° |

|      | JUL | AUG | SEP | OCT | NOV | DEC |
|------|-----|-----|-----|-----|-----|-----|
| HIGH | 88° | 86° | 77° | 66° | 53° | 45° |
| LOW  | 52° | 57° | 48° | 36° | 25° | 17° |

It is hard to generalize the climate and the altitude throughout Colorado, but I can say that what you pack and how you deal with altitude can make or break a hiking trip.

The Rockies' rugged and varied geography creates a number of weather zones. Whatever the region, whatever the season, be sure to dress in layers. In the summer, expect warm days and cool evenings. Bring shorts, hiking boots, a sweater, and a weatherproof jacket. In the winter, bring snow gear for the mountains and warm outerwear for elsewhere.

Denver and most of the hikes in this book sit on the Eastern Slope of the Continental Divide. The prairie region reaches 4,000 feet above sea level. The tundra and the regions closest to the Continental Divide can reach elevations above 14,000 feet. Keep this in mind when planning your trip.

## ▶ ALTITUDE SICKNESS

Nothing ruins a hiking trip more often than the body's resistance to altitude adjustment. The illness is usually characterized by vomiting, loss of breath, extreme headache, lightheadedness, sleeplessness, and overall flulike aches. My advice: Take it easy. When traveling to a higher altitude, give your body a day or two to adjust to where there is less oxygen, hotter sun, and less air pressure. Drink plenty of water and lay off the alcohol and cigarettes. Wear sunglasses and sunscreen. It is that easy. (As always, if serious symptoms persist, locate the nearest emergency room or call 911.)

## ▶ HIKING CARD (CORSAR)

The Colorado Outdoor Recreation Search and Rescue Card (CORSAR) may be purchased at most outdoors shops, such as Recreational Equipment, Inc. (REI). You can buy them for a year for $3 or spend $12 and buy a five-year card. The card is not

View of southwest Denver from
Lakewood: Green Mountain Trail.

insurance. It does not pay medical transport, which may include helicopter flights or ground ambulance. The card will allow reimbursement to county sheriffs for costs included on a mission. These costs can include mileage, meals, equipment, gasoline, and rental fees (horses, ATV, aircraft) for vehicles used in the search. By purchasing the card, the CORSAR information says, "you have helped ensure that trained and well-equipped search and rescue teams will respond should you become lost or in need of rescue and they will not have to incur undue expense due to your emergency."

## ▶ ALLOCATING TIME

On flat or lightly undulating terrain, I averaged 2 miles per hour when hiking. That speed drops in direct proportion to the steepness of a path, and it does not reflect the many pauses and forays off-trail in pursuit of yet another view or place to stop for a snack. Give yourself plenty of time. Few people enjoy rushing through a hike, and fewer still take pleasure in hiking after dark. Remember, too, that your pace naturally slackens over the back half of a long trek.

## ▶ MAPS

The maps in this book have been produced with great care and, used with the hiking directions, will direct you to the trail and help you stay on course. However, you will find superior detail and valuable information in the United States Geological Survey's 7.5-minute series topographic maps. Topo maps are available online in many locations. The easiest single Web resource is located at **terraserver.microsoft.com.** You can view and print topos of the entire United States there, and view aerial photographs of the same area. The downside to topos is that most of them are outdated, having been created 20 to 30 years ago. But they still provide excellent topographic detail.

# INTRODUCTION

If you're new to hiking, you might be wondering, "What's a topographic map?" In short, a topo indicates not only linear distance but elevation as well, using contour lines. Contour lines spread across the map like dozens of intricate spider webs. Each line represents a particular elevation, and at the base of each topo, a contour's interval designation is given. If the contour interval is 200 feet, then the distance between each contour line is 200 feet. Follow five contour lines up on the same map, and the elevation has increased by 1,000 feet.

Let's assume that the 7.5-minute series topo reads "Contour Interval 40 feet," that the short trail we'll be hiking is two inches in length on the map, and that it crosses five contour lines from beginning to end. What do we know? Well, because the linear scale of this series is 2,000 feet to the inch (roughly two and three-quarters inches representing 1 mile), we know our trail is approximately four-fifths of a mile long (2 inches are 2,000 feet). But we also know we'll be climbing or descending 200 vertical feet (5 contour lines are 40 feet each) over that distance. And the elevation designations written on occasional contour lines will tell us if we're heading up or down.

In addition to outdoor shops and bike shops, you'll find topos at major universities and some public libraries, where you might try photocopying the ones you need to avoid the cost of buying them. But if you want your own and can't find them locally, visit the United States Geological Survey Web site at **topomaps.usgs.gov.** I also recommend **www.topozone.com** and others mentioned in the appendix as resources for topographic maps and software.

## GPS TRAILHEAD COORDINATES

To collect accurate map data, each trail was hiked with a handheld GPS unit (Garmin Etrex). Data collected was then downloaded and plotted onto a digital USGS topo map. In addition to rendering a highly specific trail outline, this book also includes the GPS coordinates for each trailhead. More accurately known as UTM coordinates, the numbers index a specific point using a grid method. The survey datum used to arrive at the coordinates is NAD27. For readers who own a GPS unit, whether handheld or onboard a vehicle, the UTM coordinates provided on the first page of each hike may be entered into the GPS unit. Just make sure your GPS unit is set to navigate using the UTM system in conjunction with NAD27 datum. Now you can navigate directly to the trailhead.

Most trailheads, which begin in parking areas, can be navigated to by car. However, some hikes still require a short walk to reach the trailhead from a parking area. In those cases, a handheld unit would be necessary to continue the GPS navigation process. That said, however, readers can easily access all trailheads in this book by using the directions given, the overview map, and the trail map, which shows at least one major road leading into the area. But for those who enjoy using the latest GPS technology to navigate, the necessary data has been provided. A brief explanation of the UTM coordinates follows.

# INTRODUCTION

## UTM COORDINATES: ZONE, EASTING, AND NORTHING

Within the UTM coordinates box on the first page of each hike, there are three numbers labeled zone, easting, and northing. Here is an example from the Eldorado Springs Trail on page 35:

**UTM Zone (WGS84)   13T**

**Easting   474939**

**Northing   4419936**

The zone number (13) refers to one of the 60 longitudinal zones (vertical) of a map using the Universal Transverse Mercator (UTM) projection. Each zone is 6 degrees wide. The zone letter (T) refers to one of the 20 latitudinal zones (horizontal) that span from 80° South to 84° North.

The easting number (474939) references in meters how far east the point is from the zero value for eastings, which runs north-south through Greenwich, England. Increasing easting coordinates on a topo map or on your GPS screen indicate you are moving east. Decreasing easting coordinates indicate you are moving west. Since lines of longitude converge at the poles, they are not parallel as lines of latitude are. This means that the distance between Full Easting Coordinates is 1,000 meters near the equator but becomes smaller as you travel farther north or south. The difference is small enough to be ignored, but only until you reach the polar regions.

In the northern hemisphere, the northing number (4419936) references in meters how far you are from the equator. Above the equator, northing coordinates increase by 1,000 meters between each parallel line of latitude (east-west lines). On a topo map or GPS receiver, increasing northing numbers indicate you are traveling north.

In the southern hemisphere, the northing number references how far you are from a latitude line that is 10 million meters south of the equator. Below the equator, northing coordinates decrease by 1,000 meters between each line of latitude. On a topo map, decreasing northing coordinates indicate you are traveling south.

## ▶ TRAIL ETIQUETTE

Whether you're on a city, county, state, or national park trail, always remember that great care and resources (from nature as well as from your tax dollars) have gone into creating these trails. Treat the trail, wildlife, and fellow hikers with respect.

- Hike on open trails only. Respect trail and road closures (ask if not sure), avoid possible trespassing on private land, and obtain all permits and authorization as required. Also, leave gates as you found them or as marked.

- Leave only footprints. Be sensitive to the ground beneath you. This also means staying on the existing trail and not blazing any new trails. Be sure to pack out what you pack in. No one likes to see the trash someone else has left behind.

# INTRODUCTION

- Never spook animals. An unannounced approach, a sudden movement, or a loud noise startles most animals. A surprised snake or skunk can be dangerous to you, to others, and to themselves. Give animals extra room and time to adjust to your presence.
- Plan ahead. Know your equipment, your ability, and the area where you are hiking—and prepare accordingly. Be self-sufficient at all times; carry necessary supplies for changes in weather or other conditions. A well-executed trip is a satisfaction to you and to others.
- Be courteous to other hikers, bikers, or equestrians you meet on the trails.

## ▶ WATER

"How much is enough? One bottle? Two? Three?! But think of all that extra weight!" Well, one simple physiological fact should convince you to err on the side of excess when it comes to deciding how much water to pack: A hiker working hard in 90-degree heat needs approximately ten quarts of fluid every day. That's two and a half gallons—12 large water bottles or 16 small ones. In other words, pack along one or two bottles even for short hikes.

For most people, the pleasures of hiking make carrying water a relatively minor price to pay to remain healthy. If you're tempted to drink "found water," do so only if you understand the risks involved. Probably the most common waterborne "bug" that hikers face is giardia, which may not hit until one to four weeks after ingestion. It will have you passing noxious rotten-egg gas, vomiting, shivering with chills, and living in the bathroom. But there are other parasites to worry about, including E. coli and cryptosporidium (and they are harder to kill than giardia). Better yet, hydrate prior to your hike, carry (and drink) six ounces of water for every mile you plan to hike, and hydrate after the hike.

## ▶ WHAT TO PACK: FIRST-AID KIT AND HIKER'S ESSENTIALS

Be sure each hiker has the Forest Service "ten essentials" which include: map, compass, water, knife, waterproof matches, high-energy food, suitable extra clothing (such as raingear), mirror, first-aid kit, and whistle. A first-aid kit may contain more items than you might think. These are just the basics:

Ace bandages or Spenco joint wraps
Antibiotic ointment (Neosporin or the generic equivalent)
Aspirin or acetaminophen
Band-Aids

Benadryl or the generic equivalent—diphenhydramine (an antihistamine, in case of allergic reactions)
Butterfly-closure bandages

# INTRODUCTION

Epinephrine in a prefilled syringe (for those known to have severe allergic reactions to such things as bee stings—available by prescription)

Gauze (one roll)

Gauze compress pads (a half-dozen 4-inch × 4-inch)

Hydrogen peroxide or iodine

Insect repellent

Matches or pocket lighter

Moleskin/Spenco "Second Skin"

Snakebite kit

Sunscreen

Whistle (more effective for signaling rescuers than your voice)

The following items are optional, but worth their weight:

Aluminum foil

Bandanna

Cellular phone (emergencies only)

Digital camera

Disinfectant wipes

Doggie pick-up bags

Extra batteries

Flashlight

Foam pad (for lightning strikes)

Garbage bag

Gloves (for warmth)

GPS receiver

High-energy food and drinks

Leash

Lip balm

Long pants

Plastic bags with zip closure

Rain coat and rain pants

Shorts

Socks

Sunglasses

Toilet paper

Watch

## ▶ HIKING WITH CHILDREN

Hiking with children can be a great way to introduce the young to insects, leaves, pine cones, and wind. It's also wonderful exercise and an even better family-bonding experience. It's time away from laundry, cell phones, and dishes—just you and the kids and nature.

### PLANNING AND PACING

It is not advisable to take newborns out in the wild, but short walks in a stroller or a baby carrier are wonderful sensory and bonding opportunities. When my babies cried, I'd walk around our yard and point out leaves, trees, flowers, and birds. It calmed them and was a great way to build up to longer jaunts.

For children up to age 2, plan to pick them up or strap them in. Baby backpacks, baby carriers, strollers, bike trailers, and more all provide baby and parent with ample opportunity to get on the trail. Paved trails and well-maintained gravel trails all provide access to the younger set.

Children ages 2 to 4 can usually hike up to 2 miles. Be sure to plan plenty of extra time and know that you may end up carrying them. Children 5 to 7 can hike 3 to 4 miles over easy terrain. Resting, stopping, and plenty of wandering should be allowed for these age groups. Above age 8, children can easily hike a full day at a slow pace. A full day may include covering 6 miles over variable terrain. Set your entire group or family hiking goals based on the youngest child's ability. Preteens and teenagers may begin to hike more difficult trails if they have had hiking experience.

## WHAT TO BRING

Packing for the kids is much like packing for the parents. Be sure each hiker has the Forest Service "ten essentials," which include: map, compass, water, knife, water-proof matches, high-energy food, suitable extra clothing (such as raingear), mirror, first-aid kit, and whistle. Mom and Dad may want to carry the bulk of the weight and carry obvious things like the knife and matches. However, as kids can carry more, they will enjoy the responsibility. Make a big deal about buying a small backpack for them to carry their own stuff. This gives the kids ownership of the process, and parents don't end up schlepping it all around.

When hiking with a stroller or other apparatus, it's easy to stash extra essentials such as diapers and baby wipes. Consider packing my list of additional "ten kid essentials" for the trail: your child's favorite wholesome snack, juice, sunglasses, sunscreen, baby wipes, kid's trail map, kid's magnifying glass, scavenger hunt cards, lunch, and permanent markers.

Be sure everyone is dressed for the weather. For hot or cold days, the rule is to dress in layers. Start out with more in the winter and less in the summer. All children need to have one proper pair of socks and one proper pair of shoes. Be sure there is no cotton in the socks, since cotton retains moisture and helps create blisters. Instead, buy child-sized wool socks and nylon liners—there are many different weights and variations for any condition. Good tennis shoes are great, and child-sized hiking boots are even better.

## SAFETY CONSIDERATIONS

Children should be taught from the get-go that they must stay within eyesight of an adult. They are to never run ahead on the trail. They are to *never* hike off of the trail. Not only can they get lost or injured, they can cause damage to the trail. Teach your kids to treat the outdoors kindly and the outdoors will repay the favor. Teach children to stay where they are if they get lost. Many children relate to *hugging a tree* when lost. Instruct them to find a tree on the trail, hold on, and blow their whistle. Three whistle blows is the standard distress signal and indicates: I am lost or I need help. Kids are *never* to go near steep cliffs and other drop-off areas. Rules about rivers and other water sources and climbing on accessible rocks must be addressed. My rule is *no!*

Always teach trail etiquette: Leave no trace, pick up after others who do not, the uphill hiker has the right of way, and don't pick or pull anything. And of course, leaves of three, let them be.

# INTRODUCTION

## KEEP IT FUN

Before you leave home, have the kids help make a special kid-friendly map that they can keep in their bag. Making maps helps teach direction and creativity. Create a kid-friendly legend that has items like waterfalls, trails, trees, or rest areas. Draw the route and have the child mark interesting way-points while they are hiking.

Toy stores are home to many hiking or backyard camping things such as kid's magnifying glasses. A magnifying glass can be used to identify plants, insects, minerals in rocks, and flowers.

Make scavenger-hunt cards to use on any hike. A stack of index cards works fine. Have your child cut hiking-related items from used magazines and paste them on each card. If your child can draw, this works as well. Write the name under the item and bring as many as you want on the trail. You can prolong your scavenger-hunt cards throughout the summer by simply marking each item that you see on the back. It's fun to have a trump card that could be tucked away for special sightings: a bull snake, a lost watch, or an abandoned sock. Bring a permanent marker to take notes on your cards—some may even want to laminate their cards.

Play games like "I Spy," try bird-watching, look for animal tracks, or simply count rocks as you hike. The key is to play games that encourage children to observe their surroundings.

Assign a hiking leader (or mountain leader as we call it) and have that child guide the hike. Plan on taking a lot of breaks and at each break, change the hiking leader. Have your child invite a friend, which helps your child see the world from another youngster's perspective.

If the hike is going well, be sure to head home a little early, especially if you have to turn around and trace your steps. It is always better to end early on a positive note than to end with sore feet, a lot of whining, and discouraged hikers.

## ▶ HIKING WITH DOGS

I love hiking with my dog, Bailey. She had a doggy version of ACL surgery during my work on this book, so her mobility was limited. On easy hikes, I'd take her, strap her doggy pack on, and head out. Dogs on trails can lead to some heavy controversy, so use these basic guidelines when taking your hound into the wild.

- Leashing a dog is the only way to prevent it from chasing wildlife and other trail users. Horses have right-of-way around dogs. A six-foot leash will give your dog enough room to tackle the trail without getting tangled in underbrush or other hikers.

- Leashing a dog keeps them from drinking out of streams and other water sources. Harmful bacteria, such as giardia, is a threat to dogs as well as humans. Always pack water for your dog. I use a collapsible doggy bowl and make Bailey carry her own supply of water. A healthy dog should be able to carry up to a third of his weight in a special dog pack.

- Leashing dogs keeps them from getting lost. They are also protected from wildlife attacks when on a leash. Nothing is worse than taking a dog to the veterinarian on a weekend with porcupine quills lodged in its sinuses.

- Dogs must be in shape before undertaking a hike. Start off small, then work up to longer hikes. Make sure that all of your dog's vaccinations and medications are current, including rabies, bordetella, and heartworm. If you are hiking in an area with Lyme disease, ask your vet about vaccinations.

- Keep your dog's paws protected if trails are cold and icy. Bailey has had the hair between her paws become encrusted with ice.

- After a hike, carefully check for ticks and burrs. Prepare for accidents and keep antibiotic cream and self-sticking bandage tape in your first-aid kid.

- It's essential to pack out dog poop rather than leaving it on the trail or even by the side of the trail. Dog poop is not the same as that of other animals, even that of coyotes or wolves. It's dangerous to the environment, especially near water sources, and it makes a bad impression on other hikers—not to mention their boots.

*Special Dog Note:* Pit bulls are not allowed in the City and County of Denver. Owning a pit bull, or bringing one into the city limits, is illegal.

## ▶ LIGHTNING AND TORNADOES

Get an early start on all hikes that go above tree line. Violent storms are common in June, July, and August. Try to reach high-altitude summits by 1 p.m. and turn back when the weather turns bad. If you are caught in a lightning storm above tree line, stay off ridgetops, spread out if you are in a group, and squat or sit on a foam pad with your feet together. Keep away from rock outcroppings and isolated trees. If someone has been struck, be prepared to use CPR to help restore breathing and heartbeat.

In the event of a tornado (they are extremely common in the eastern portion of Colorado), immediately seek shelter. If you are in an open field, lay down in the nearest ditch.

## ▶ HYPOTHERMIA

Hypothermia occurs when your core body temperature is dangerously low. This condition can occur at any time of the year, and cold temperatures, wind, and rain and snow set the stage for complications. Look for signs of shivering, loss of coordination, and loss of judgment. Prevention in the form of preparation is your best defense against getting cold to the core. Remember the mantra "wet is not warm" to prevent hypothermia. Keep your inside layer as dry as possible.

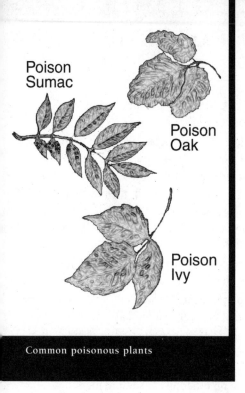

Poison
Sumac

Poison
Oak

Poison
Ivy

Common poisonous plants

Spend some time hiking in Denver and you may be surprised by the variety of snakes in the area. Most snake encounters will be with garter snakes, water snakes, and bull snakes (while not venomous, they are rather large and scary-looking). The only venomous snake in the Denver region is the rattlesnake. Rattler sightings are very common. A good rule of thumb is to give them a wide berth and leave them alone. If you are bitten by a rattlesnake, stay calm and get help immediately.

On a side note, my husband was bitten by a rattlesnake in 1999. He was hiking, *alone*, and felt a slap on his leg. Luckily, hikers found him and a search-and-rescue team was deployed. To this day, the old wives' tale holds true: Mosquito bites do not affect him at all. It has long been told that when a person is bitten by a rattlesnake and the venom enters their system, an antibody is released and is always present. Somehow, this antibody acts as a buffer against mosquito venom. When a mosquito bites a past rattlesnake-bite victim, the mosquito venom does not affect them and thus there is no irritation, bump, or itching.

▶ TICKS

Ticks often wait on brush and tall grass to hitch a ride on a warm-blooded passerby. While they're most visible in the Denver area in early and midsummer, you should be on the lookout for them throughout spring, summer, and fall. Among the local varieties of ticks, deer ticks and dog ticks can transmit diseases. Both of these ticks need several hours of attachment before they can transmit any harbored diseases. Deer ticks, the primary carrier of Lyme disease, are very small, sometimes the size of a poppy seed. You can use several strategies to reduce your chances of ticks getting under your skin. Some people choose to wear light-colored clothing, so ticks can be spotted before they make it to the skin. Insect repellent containing DEET is known as an effective deterrent. Most importantly, though, be sure to check yourself at the end of the hike. And if it's prime tick season, you may want to perform a quick check every hour or so. For ticks that are already embedded, removal with tweezers is best.

▶ POISON IVY

Recognizing and avoiding contact with poison ivy is the most effective way to prevent the painful, itchy rashes associated with this plant. Poison ivy occurs as a vine or ground cover with three leaflets to a leaf. Thus the saying: Leaves of three, let them be. Urushiol, the oil in the sap of these plants, is responsible for the rash. Within 12 to 14 hours of exposure, raised lines and/or blisters will appear, accompanied by a terrible itch. Refrain from scratching, because bacteria under fingernails can cause infection. Wash and dry the rash thoroughly, then apply a calamine lotion to help dry out the rash. If itching or blistering is severe, seek medical attention. If you do come in contact with one of these plants, remember that oil-contaminated clothing, pets, or hiking gear can easily cause an irritating rash on you or someone else, so wash not only any exposed parts of your body but also clothing, gear, and pets if applicable.

## ▶ MOSQUITOES

While not common, humans can become infected with the West Nile virus by an infected mosquito. Culex mosquitoes, the primary variety that can transmit West Nile virus to humans, thrive in urban rather than natural areas. They lay their eggs in stagnant water and can breed in any standing water that remains for longer than five days. Most people infected with West Nile virus have no symptoms of illness, but some may become ill, usually 3 to 15 days after being bitten.

In the Denver area, August and September are the high-risk periods for West Nile virus. At this time of year—and anytime you expect mosquitoes to be buzzing around—you may want to wear protective clothing such as long sleeves, long pants, and socks. Loose-fitting, light-colored clothing is best. Spray clothing with insect repellent. Follow the instructions on the repellent carefully and take extra care with children.

## ▶ CELL PHONES

Do not ever rely on cell phones in the Rockies. Signals and access are very inconsistent. Check with your cellular service provider before leaving home. Many outdoor enthusiasts rely on GPS (Global Positioning Systems) and other forms of communication in the backcountry. Never, never, never make a social call on your cellular phone on a hiking trail.

## ▶ BLACK BEARS

There are no definite rules about what to do if you meet a bear. In most cases, the bear will detect you first and leave. If you do encounter a bear, here are some suggestions from the National Park Service:

- Stay calm.
- Move away, talking loudly to let the bear discover your presence.
- Back away while facing the bear.
- Avoid eye contact.
- Give the bear plenty of room to escape; bears will rarely attack unless they are threatened or provoked.

# INTRODUCTION

- Don't run or make sudden movements; running will provoke the bear, and you cannot outrun a bear.
- Do not attempt to climb trees to escape bears, especially black bears. The bear will pull you down by the foot.
- Fight back if you are attacked. Black bears have been driven away when people have fought back with rocks, sticks, binoculars, and even their bare hands.
- Be grateful it is not a grizzly bear.

## ▶ MOUNTAIN LIONS

Lion attacks on people are rare, with fewer than 12 fatalities in 100 years. Based on observations by people who have come in contact with mountain lions, some patterns are beginning to emerge. Here are more suggestions from the National Park Service:

- Stay calm.
- Talk firmly to the lion.
- Move slowly.
- Back up or stop. Never run, because lions will chase and attack.
- Raise your arms. If you are wearing a sweater or coat, open it and hold it wide.
- Pick up children and make them appear larger.
- If the lion becomes aggressive, throw rocks and large objects at it. This is the time to convince the lion that you are not prey and that you are a danger to it. Never crouch down or turn your back to retrieve said items.
- Fight back and try to remain standing if you are attacked.

# BOULDER
## *Including Foothills and Mountains*

# BETASSO PRESERVE: CANYON LOOP TRAIL

## KEY AT-A-GLANCE INFORMATION

**LENGTH:** 3.2 miles

**CONFIGURATION:** Loop

**DIFFICULTY:** Easy

**SCENERY:** Meadow, forest, views of the Boulder Valley

**EXPOSURE:** Sunny in meadow, shaded in south-facing portions

**TRAFFIC:** Moderate during weekdays, crowded on weekends

**TRAIL SURFACE:** Hard-packed dirt, loose rocks

**HIKING TIME:** 2 hours

**SEASON:** All year (southern-facing portions may be icy during winter months)

**ACCESS:** Free; open sunrise to sunset

**MAPS:** USGS Boulder

**FACILITIES:** Restroom, picnic area

**SPECIAL COMMENTS:** There has been significant conflict between mountain bikers and hikers on this trail, so great lengths have been taken to keep this a multiuse trail. Mountain biking is prohibited on Wednesdays and Saturdays, making these ideal days for hikers. Bikers are required to travel in a single direction on the trail, which changes monthly. Signs posted will indicate the direction, and hikers are advised (but not required) to hike in the opposite direction of bike traffic. Restrooms here are heavily used and can be quite unappealing. Dogs must be leashed.

Betasso Preserve: Canyon Loop Trail

UTM Zone (WGS84)   13T

Easting   470690

Northing   4429330

## IN BRIEF

Canyon Loop Trail is located in Boulder County's historic Betasso Preserve, which was an 1870s mining and sawmill town. This well-maintained hike is easy to find and close to Boulder. Half the trail traverses meadows with Douglas fir trees on north-facing slopes. The rest of the trail is shaded by ponderosa pines and lined with moss-covered boulders.

## DESCRIPTION

At the Canyon Loop Trailhead sign, veer left and head north into a stand of tall ponderosa pines. Pass a group picnic area at the top of the hill where views to the west greet hikers, and head down through a gate, passing an information sign. Climb a small hill, then descend and travel west into the trees. At the trail marker, head north. You'll cross a gully and then climb a slope.

Betasso Preserve is a geology-enthusiast's wonderland, as it lies in the northeast corner of the Colorado mineral belt. Molten material was forced up to the earth's crust 1.7 billion years ago, and instead of bursting through like lava, it settled just beneath the surface and cooled, forming an igneous rock known as The Boulder Creek grandiorite. The slow cooling and hardening of this rock formed visible mineral crystals. Boulder Canyon and Fourmile Canyon surround Betasso

## DIRECTIONS

From Denver, take I-25 north to US 36 toward Boulder. Go west on CO 119, also known as Canyon Boulevard. Travel west for 5 miles to Sugarloaf Road (directly after The Alps Inn). Turn right and be wary of a sharp, blind curve. Follow Sugarloaf Road 1 mile, then turn right on Betasso Road, traveling east. Go 0.5 miles to an open gate on the left. Turn here and follow the road to the Canyon Loop Trail parking area.

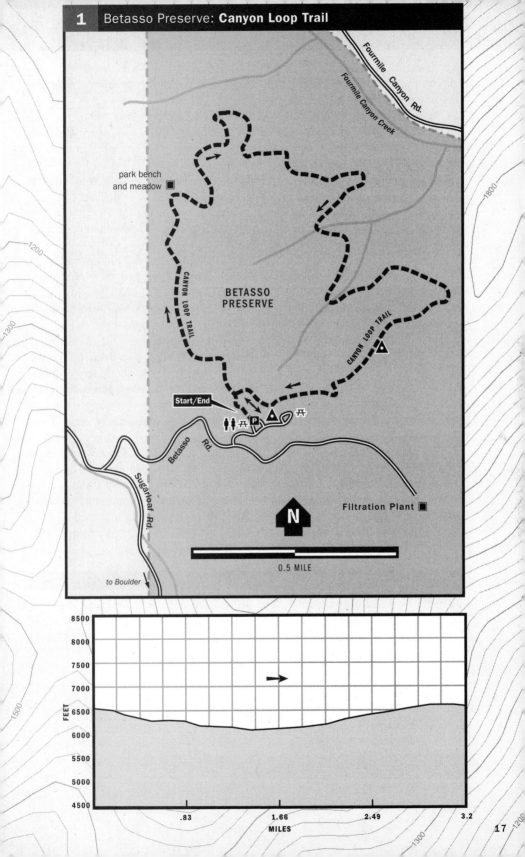

park bench
and meadow

Fourmile Canyon Rd.

Fourmile Canyon Creek

CANYON LOOP TRAIL

BETASSO
PRESERVE

CANYON LOOP TRAIL

Start/End

Betasso Rd.

Sugarloaf Rd.

Filtration Plant

to Boulder

**N**

0.5 MILE

FEET

8500
8000
7500
7000
6500
6000
5500
5000
4500

.83    1.66    2.49    3.2

MILES

Preserve, and the forces of erosion are still visible in the spring when the creeks flow through the preserve.

At the the top of the hill, head east. A small park bench allows you to sit, catch your breath, and enjoy the views of the Boulder Valley and the northern Colorado plains. The meadow blends with the forest and both host gorgeous wildflowers in the spring and summer.

Pine trees line most of the trail, along with shrubs and grasses. Skunk brush is the most common shrub. To understand its name, crush one of its delicate twigs and sniff. Not all of the shrubbery in Betasso Preserve is native; cheatgrass, for example, was introduced to the preserve as a result of cattle grazing and now rapidly outcompetes native grasses.

After the bench, climb onto a little knoll and then begin to head downhill. The trail circles a knob, where there are more wonderful views, and then winds west along a south-facing slope. Here, you are treated to patches of mysteriously cool air, moss-covered rocks, and thick grasses. Hike through a ravine, then head back east into the woods. Round several switchbacks through several gullies. Even in late summer, these gullies may still hold small, full springs to cross.

Although cattle no longer graze here, many mammals live in Betasso Preserve. You may see mule deer, coyotes, rabbits, and a variety of birds. The Albert's squirrel is common near the picnic area. These squirrels feed on pinecones, and unlike other squirrels, do not gather and store food for the winter. Instead, they survive the Colorado winter by feeding on the inner bark of pine twigs, and thus are only found where ponderosa pine trees grow.

The staccato drilling of a woodpecker, common at Betasso Preserve, occasionally jars the subtle sounds of the stream, the forest animals, and the breeze rustling through the pines. Continue as the trail bends to the south and then crests a ridge. The trail ascends gently toward the west. At an unmarked trail crossing, go south where the trail reenters the wooded parkland. Reach another natural trail crossing and continue west. Pass a picnic area and turn right on the road. Pass another, larger picnic area near the trailhead and return to the parking lot.

## ▶ NEARBY ATTRACTIONS

Bummer's Rock Trail, a second trail in Betasso Preserve, and Sugarloaf Mountain Summit Trail. For further information on this area, City of Boulder, Open Space and Mountain Parks: **www.osmp.org.**

# BOULDER: BOULDER CREEK PATH

## ▶ IN BRIEF

The Boulder Creek Path stretches from west Boulder to the eastern end of town near Valmont Reservoir. The trail parallels Boulder Creek as it runs east through the heart of Boulder and out into the plains. Expect a beautiful walk through an equally beautiful urban oasis. Boulder is dreamy and its signature trail never disappoints.

## ▶ DESCRIPTION

Eben G. Fine Park is a fine starting point, with plentiful parking. Leave the parking lot, on the right of the path. An official mile marker, 0, marks the beginning of this hike. Cross the bridge and go east, traveling along Canyon Boulevard. Immediately to the right is an alternate dirt path with picnic tables.

The trail merges with the creek and travels on a parallel path for some time, passing behind the Boulder County Justice Center. The trail continues ever so slightly at a descent that is only noticeable when the hike is traced back to the trailhead from the eastern turnaround point. It is well maintained with level concrete, traffic signs, and painted yellow lines that keep heavy use controlled.

Go under Sixth Street, then pass kid-friendly fishing ponds and head under Ninth Street. Cross under the glass overpass that connects the separate buildings of the Boulder Library over the creek. Continue straight and pass under the concrete bridge at Broadway Avenue, then turn right at the sign marked Boulder Trail East and continue to pass under Boulder roadways. There are a lot of

## ▶ KEY AT-A-GLANCE INFORMATION

**LENGTH:** 5.64 miles

**CONFIGURATION:** One way with out-and-back option

**DIFFICULTY:** Easy

**SCENERY:** Urban, Boulder Creek, river habitat, prairie

**EXPOSURE:** Mostly shaded in creek bed, exposed in prairie portion

**TRAFFIC:** Heavy

**TRAIL SURFACE:** Concrete, wooden bridges

**HIKING TIME:** 3 hours

**SEASON:** All year

**ACCESS:** Free; always open

**MAPS:** USGS Boulder, Niwot

**FACILITIES:** Restrooms, picnic tables at trailhead; plenty of benches and parks along path for a rest stop or picnic

**SPECIAL COMMENTS:** The path is popular with bicyclists, in-line skaters, joggers, and hikers, so don't expect much solitude. The City of Boulder reminds pedestrians to walk to the right and be aware of people on wheels that may be approaching from behind. Dogs and exotic birds are permitted.

## ▶ DIRECTIONS

From Denver, take US 36 toward Boulder. Turn left on Arapahoe Road and travel west through downtown Boulder. Cross Broadway Street, cross Ninth Street, and at Sixth Street begin to pass through traffic circles; reach Eben G. Fine Park and park here.

**Boulder: Boulder Creek Path**

**UTM Zone (WGS84)   13T**

**Easting   474970**

**Northing   4429080**

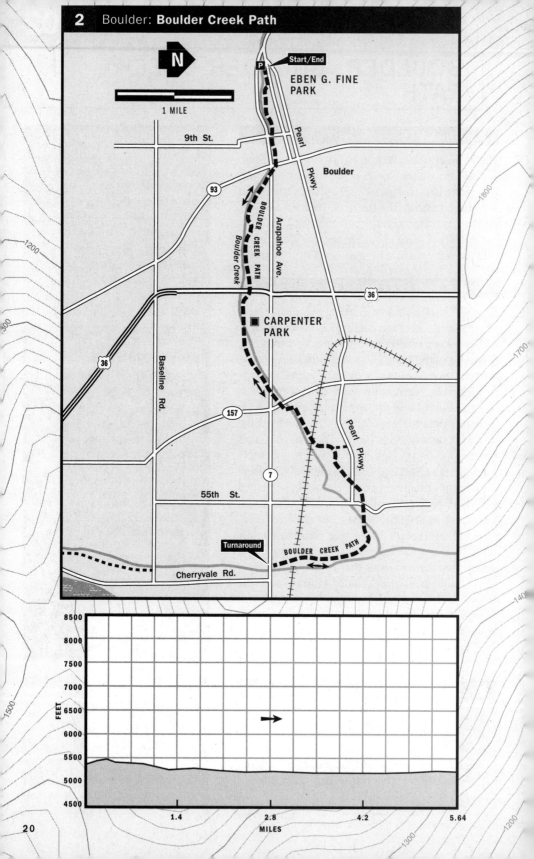

N

1 MILE

Start/End

EBEN G. FINE
PARK

9th St.

Pearl

93

Boulder

BOULDER CREEK PATH

Boulder Creek

Arapahoe Ave.

36

36

CARPENTER
PARK

Baseline Rd.

157

Pearl Pkwy.

7

55th St.

Turnaround

BOULDER CREEK PATH

Cherryvale Rd.

FEET

8500
8000
7500
7000
6500
6000
5500
5000
4500

1.4    2.8    4.2    5.64
MILES

Boulder Creek Path is easy to navigate in every season. Here, the trail is quiet on a weekday, winter morning.

turns off of the trail that access downtown Boulder, residential Boulder, and the University of Colorado.

At this point, you'll pass athletic fields on both sides. Continue under 17th Street with the creek on the right the whole way. Go straight, even though there are numerous side bridges that may tempt you to other routes.

Pass the tennis courts and indoor tennis bubble of the large hotel on the left. Take a right across the bridge near the hotel's outdoor activity area. Go under Folsom Street, then 28th Street, and after about 100 yards, turn left and cross a bridge. The trail skirts along the back of Carpenter Park and crosses the creek on a bridge to the right.

This part of the hike is less crowded and more scenic, with views to the east toward the prairie and west toward the mountains. Up to this point, cottonwood trees and river-basin foliage have lined the trail. Eastern portions of the trail are also home to office parks. Go under Arapahoe Avenue and pass mile marker 3, then go under Foothills Parkway, take a left on a wooden bridge, and pass behind a cluster of office buildings. Follow a short curve and go under the railroad tracks via the railroad bridge. At an obvious T in the trail, take a right. It is here that we saw a large parrot, on a leash, pulling a woman on in-line skates. The trail has opened up more and is prairielike, with tall grasses, short trees, and open fields. Go under 55th Street and bear right at the fork at the lake. The trail has slowly turned and now heads south in back of some office buildings and ends. Stop here and turn around. You can go back to the car or go to your shuttle car parked in one of the office building parking lots (this is around 55th Street and Arapahoe Road).

## ▶ NEARBY ATTRACTIONS

Another parking lot is 200 yards up the road from Eben G. Fine Park. It runs along a popular and crowded kayak course. Two miles of additional trail is available heading west from Eben G. Fine Park to the intersection of Boulder and Fourmile canyons.

Boulder County Open Space: **www.osmp.org**.

Boulder Creek Path is managed by the City of Boulder, and nearby trails can be found at **www.ci.boulder.co.us/goboulder**.

# BOULDER: HEIL VALLEY RANCH

## KEY AT-A-GLANCE INFORMATION

**LENGTH:** 7.12 miles

**CONFIGURATION:** Balloon

**DIFFICULTY:** Moderate

**SCENERY:** Green valley, ponderosa pines, ranch land, yucca plants, seasonal wildflowers; beautiful views of Longs Peak

**EXPOSURE:** Little shade

**TRAFFIC:** Heavy

**TRAIL SURFACE:** Dirt

**HIKING TIME:** 4 hours

**SEASON:** All year

**ACCESS:** Free; open sunrise to sunset

**MAPS:** USGS Lyons

**FACILITIES:** Picnic tables, restrooms, group shelter

**SPECIAL COMMENTS:** The group shelter accommodates up to 25 people on a first-come, first-serve basis. No groups are permitted on the weekend because of limited parking. This area is popular with mountain bikers, hikers, and equestrians. The 1-mile Lichen Loop, which is not part of this hike, is open to pedestrians only. No dogs are allowed on any of the Heil Valley Ranch trails.

Boulder: Heil Valley Ranch

UTM Zone (WGS84)   13T

Easting   474450

Northing   4443920

## ▶ IN BRIEF

Heil Valley Ranch has three trails and is part of Boulder's newest open space: North Foothills Open Space. The longest trail—and the trail featured here—is the Wapiti Trail combined with the Ponderosa Loop. You'll travel through stands of ponderosa pines and open meadows full of prairie grasses and seasonal wildflowers. Heil Valley Ranch is an important winter range for elk that migrate from the Indian Peaks Wilderness—the only herd of elk along the Front Range that migrate from the Continental Divide to the Great Plains. At the turn of the 20th century, elk were eliminated from Boulder County, but they were reintroduced by 1917.

## ▶ DESCRIPTION

Head straight to the end of the parking area and begin the hike at Wapiti Trail. The trail is single-track dirt for only 100 feet and then turns into a wide service road. The trail begins in a big, green valley with a lot of tall ponderosa trees. Start a gentle ascent up the valley. The service road crosses through a creek and continues straight. Pass mountain lion warning signs.

Go through an emergency-services gate; pass a spur of the Lichen Loop and take a left after the spur. Continue along the old ranch fence that parallels the Wapiti Trail and passes an open meadow and prairie dog mounds. Notice foothills to the east. The trail is exposed here, but you soon travel into trees. The trail switches to single-track dirt and crosses a steel-and-wood bridge. Complete one switchback and continue as the trail gets a little rocky.

## ▶ DIRECTIONS

From Denver, take I-25 north to US 36 through Boulder. Head toward Lyons and turn left on Lefthand Canyon Road. Travel 0.5 miles and turn right on Greer Canyon Road. Travel 1.3 miles to the Heil Valley Ranch trailhead.

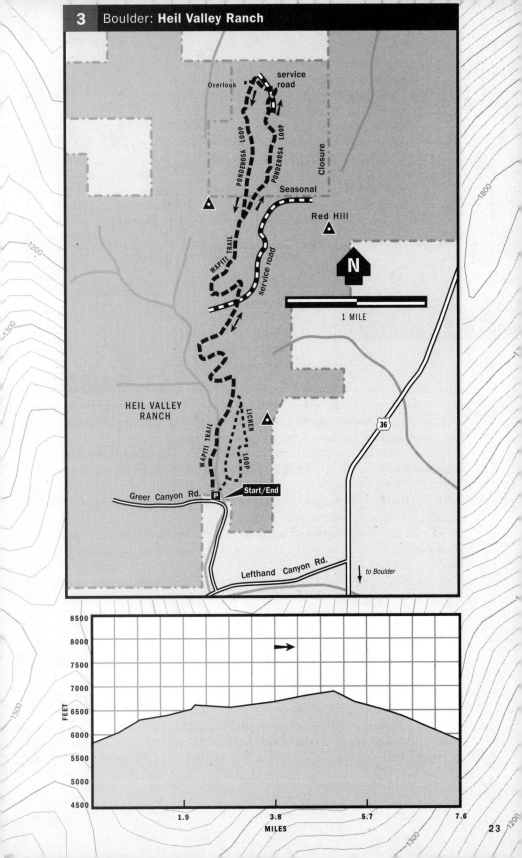

View of the valley from a higher point of the trail at Heil Valley Ranch

After another switchback, you eventually enter a lightly forested hillside. Ponderosa trees release a Christmastime pine smell on a hot day as the heat penetrates the needles. Pass through thin grass, yucca plants, and seasonal wildflowers. Cross the service road and keep going. Switch back around the remnants of an old, stone homestead building and follow the trail as it goes left.

After 2.5 miles, the Wapiti Trail intersects with the Ponderosa Loop. This is the intersection where the loop part of the balloon hike starts. Continue right, starting a counterclockwise circle, as the trail goes downhill slightly and crosses an open meadow. From here, look right to the expansive views of the Eastern Plains. The trail again travels through a sparse ponderosa forest.

Cross the service road and continue straight. In the distance are old mining relics. Heil Valley Ranch was an early homesteading and mining site. Today it's maintained by ranchers and farmers.

The trail crosses a hillside, meanders a little, then levels out as you begin to approach the top of the loop. Reach the outlook on the right and stop to take in the views west to Longs Peak and Mount Meeker; north to St. Vrain Canyon; and east to the Eastern Plains. Two benches at the overlook provide a nice respite; there are also some nice spots to spread a picnic blanket and have lunch.

Past the overlook, the trail becomes scattered with loose rocks as it climbs a gentle grade and remarkably turns to soft beachlike sand. Continue up the hill and the trail will level off, dropping into a flat, open meadow. Pass through a section of young trees in a small meadow. Evidence that workers have made great efforts to maintain the trail is clear here, where they have laid flat stones in the places prone to mud. Start descending as the trail heads back to the intersection of Ponderosa Loop and Wapiti Trail. Get back on the Wapiti Trail and retrace your steps to the trailhead.

# BOULDER:
# SOUTH BOULDER CREEK TRAIL

## ▶ IN BRIEF

This trail winds southward along a riparian corridor and is highlighted by self-guided interpretive displays. The area offers seasonal viewings of the bobolink, for which the first portion of the trail was named, and other ground nesting birds. Although an urban hike, this trail is a peaceful outing with plenty of wildlife, history, and beauty.

## ▶ DESCRIPTION

Leave the trailhead and travel south from Baseline Road. The first mile of the trail is soft-surfaced and runs parallel to a paved portion. No bikes are allowed on the soft surface, but hikers may wander back and forth between the two. The soft-surfaced path allows pedestrians to get a little closer to the banks of South Boulder Creek. The trail is well maintained and lined on the west with cottonwood trees and on the east with prairie grasses.

Pass large, old cottonwoods and lush undergrowth that hugs the creek. Travel along a split-rail fence and cross the paved path that has been running parallel to the soft-surface trail up until this point. Pass the East Boulder Community Center trail connection to the right as the trail becomes a narrow single track, but still very soft, smooth, and flat. The paved path splits and crosses a bridge that runs over the creek. Hikers continue straight on the soft-surfaced path.

The trail splits away from the creek just before reaching South Boulder Road. Continue

## ⓘ KEY AT-A-GLANCE INFORMATION

**LENGTH:** 6.68 miles

**CONFIGURATION:** Out-and-back

**DIFFICULTY:** Easy

**SCENERY:** Open meadow, urban, large creek, mountain views, cottonwoods, prairie grasses

**EXPOSURE:** Shady along creek

**TRAFFIC:** Heavy

**TRAIL SURFACE:** Dirt, some paved portions

**HIKING TIME:** 3 hours

**SEASON:** All year

**ACCESS:** Free; open sunrise to sunset

**MAPS:** USGS Louisville, Niwot

**FACILITIES:** Picnic table, grill

**SPECIAL COMMENTS:** This area is popular with people using wheelchairs, especially sport-equipped chairs. No restroom facilities. Bikes are allowed on the initial part of the trail that is paved (between Baseline Road and East Boulder Community Center). Dogs must be leashed, but are not allowed past South Boulder Road to Marshall Road. This makes for a short hike, so you may want to leave the pets at home. As with most Boulder trails, this trail is heavy with bike and pedestrian traffic and a few equestrians, as well.

## ▶ DIRECTIONS

From Denver, take I-25 north to US 36, to Foothills Parkway in Boulder. Turn right on Foothills Parkway off of US 36. Travel approximately 1 mile and turn right on Baseline Road. Take Baseline Road east until just before Cherryvale Road. The Bobolink trailhead is just west of the intersection of Baseline and Cherryvale Roads.

**Boulder: South Boulder Creek Trail**

**UTM Zone (WGS84)  13S**

**Easting  481700**

**Northing  4427520**

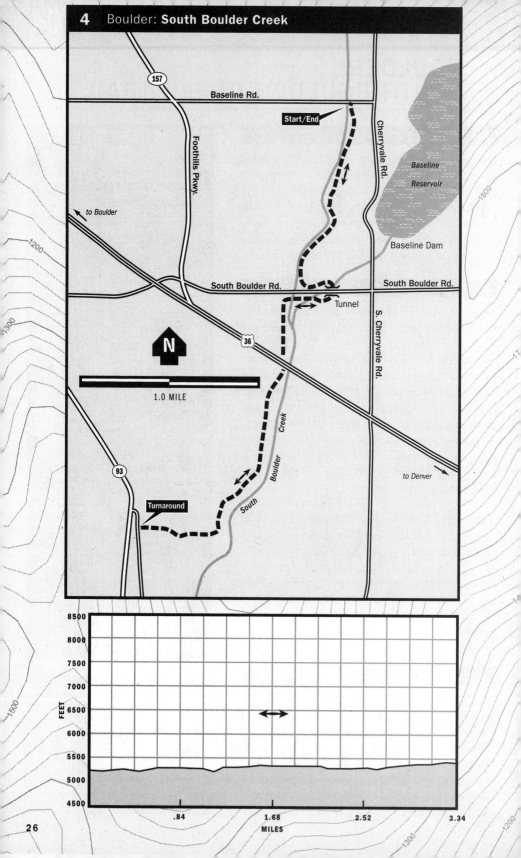

157

Baseline Rd.

Start/End

Cherryvale Rd.

Baseline
Reservoir

to Boulder

Baseline Dam

Foothills Pkwy.

South Boulder Rd.

South Boulder Rd.

Tunnel

N

36

S. Cherryvale Rd.

1.0 MILE

to Denver

93

South Boulder Creek

Turnaround

1200

1300

1500

1800

1300

1200

8500

8000

7500

7000

6500

FEET

6000

5500

5000

4500

.84          1.68          2.52          3.34

MILES

and cross a small concrete bridge, then turn left. You will now be going parallel with South Boulder Road. After just a few minutes' walk, there will be another concrete bridge, where you go right. The trail then passes through a tunnel under South Boulder Road.

On the other side of South Boulder Road, come to a gravel road and take a right. Take a left where the creek meets up with the trail again and go through a gate. Be sure to close all gates after you cross through them, because livestock roam the fields. Dogs are not allowed south of South Boulder Road because they tend to spook the grazing cows. Cattle are scattered throughout the perimeter of the trail, between South Boulder Road and CO 93, as are their cow patties. A posted sign also warns that the cattle may be aggressive. Ranching is still a part of this area.

Go through another gate, close it, and travel under US 36 via a covered, concrete tunnel. Pass through another gate and be sure to close it. The trail then opens up to a wide, open prairie with views of the Boulder mountains. The noise of US 36 and other roadways is prevalent, but not too distracting.

Continue straight all the way to the far end of the field. At the split-rail fence, take a right and go over the boardwalk, and through another gate. The prairie is wet, more meadowlike, and is home to deer, nesting birds, and fox. Hikers continuously travel along the creek, and the creek's shelter makes this urban trail feel secluded. The trail ends at CO 93, after passing through two more gates and crossing two more bridges. From here, retrace your steps back to the trailhead.

## ▶ NEARBY ATTRACTIONS

City of Boulder Open Space and Mountain Parks: **www.osmp.org**.

# BOULDER: WALDEN PONDS

## KEY AT-A-GLANCE INFORMATION

**LENGTH:** 2.5 miles

**CONFIGURATION:** Loop

**DIFFICULTY:** Easy

**SCENERY:** Prairie, ponds, wetland habitat

**EXPOSURE:** Partly shaded

**TRAFFIC:** Moderate

**TRAIL SURFACE:** Dirt, boardwalks

**HIKING TIME:** 45 minutes

**SEASON:** All year

**ACCESS:** Free; open sunrise to sunset

**MAPS:** USGS Niwot; Walden Ponds map available at trailhead

**FACILITIES:** Restrooms, picnic tables, shelters, ranger office

**SPECIAL COMMENTS:** Pick up a field checklist of birds at the trailhead. Fishing is allowed from the shore of the ponds with artificial bait, but wading and boats are prohibited. Leashed dogs are allowed, as are horses and bikes. Special, posted wildlife habitat areas are closed to the public. Many areas of this hike, including a special fishing pier, are wheelchair accessible. Don't let the county road maintenance facility with large piles of gravel and a wastewater treatment plant discourage you. Beyond this point, the shorelines of the ponds and the views of Indian Peaks are beautiful.

Boulder: Walden Ponds

UTM Zone (WGS84)   13T

Easting   484355

Northing   4432441

## IN BRIEF

The ponds—reclaimed gravel pits—now support a variety of wildlife, including waterfowl, songbirds, and mammals (beaver, deer, muskrats, and red fox). The hike around the ponds offers incredible views of the Indian Peaks. Interpretive nature signs along Cottonwood Marsh explain the history and geology of the area. This is a perfect family hike and a nice alternative for those needing accessible trails.

## DESCRIPTION

From the parking lot, go left on the trail. On the right you'll see boardwalks that cut through the marshes, which are thick with cattails and prairie grasses. This is the Cottonwood Marsh interpretive trail. If you like, you can take it now or at the end of the hike. The Walden Ponds are a haven for songbirds that can be heard throughout the trail.

After the boardwalk, continue on a gravel trail that parallels a service road. Leave the maintenance facility and gravel piles behind and enter a land of lush trees, healthy marshes, and boardwalks. Pass Duck Pond on the left and walk toward the ranger field station (open 8 a.m. to 4 p.m., Monday through Friday). The trail turns into a service road and goes past Island Lake and to the right of Bass Pond. Continue straight ahead on the well-marked trail, then bear left around the north side of Bass Pond. On the right is the Heatherwood Trail, which is a paved path offering residential neighborhood access.

## DIRECTIONS

From Denver, take I-25 north to US 36 to CO 7 (Arapahoe Avenue) in Boulder. Turn right on CO 7 and travel east for 5 miles to 75th Street. Turn left on 75th Street and travel 2 miles to the entrance of Walden Ponds Open Space. Turn left and park at the Cottonwood Marsh picnic area and trailhead.

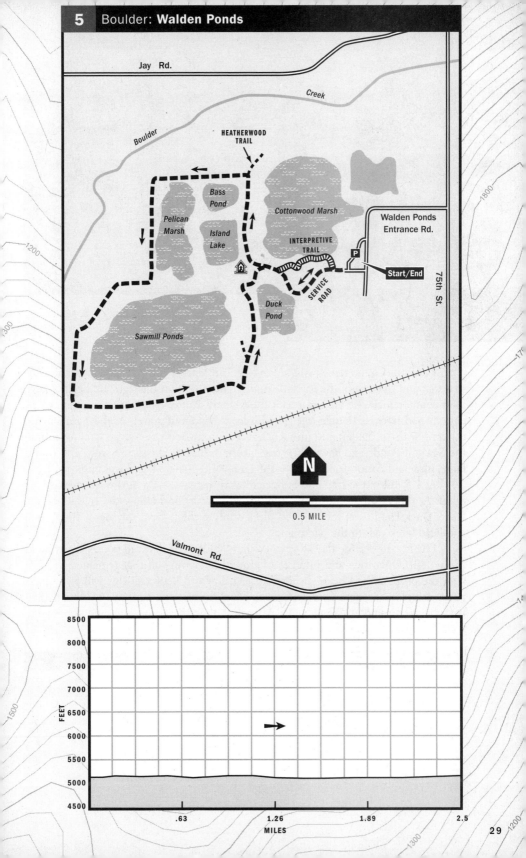

Jay Rd.

Boulder Creek

HEATHERWOOD
TRAIL

Bass
Pond

Pelican
Marsh

Island
Lake

Cottonwood Marsh

Walden Ponds
Entrance Rd.

INTERPRETIVE
TRAIL

P

Start/End

Duck
Pond

SERVICE
ROAD

75th St.

Sawmill Ponds

**N**

0.5 MILE

Valmont Rd.

Once a gravel pit, now a beautiful habitat; one of the many proud Walden Ponds offspring.

Continue counterclockwise around Pelican Marsh. Go left through a fence line to a sign and the first of the Sawmill Ponds. Take a right at the sign and begin a large loop counterclockwise around six of the Sawmill Ponds. The flat trail, sheltered by cottonwood trees, is double-tracked with loose sand and gravel. At the 1-mile mark, the trail bears to the left and into a stand of cottonwood trees. Keep circling around the Sawmill Ponds and savor the views of the Indian Peaks to the west. Look for a large, bleached cottonwood to the right—a favorite hangout for local birds of prey.

At 1.5 miles, the trail curves back toward the east and a bird-watching/viewing blind. At the viewing blind, take a left (going north) and follow the trail along the fence. Duck Pond is on the right, so flip around to the right at the top of Duck Pond and head back east to the parking lot.

Feel free to explore the 51 acres around Walden and Sawmill ponds at any point in the trail. Open pits and puddles of groundwater were all that remained in 1974 after the property had been stripped 15 feet down to bedrock. This will give hikers pause at the beauty that now exists. The effort to create an aesthetic wildlife habitat is visible all around and looks quite natural, though the destruction and subsequent reclamation are all at the hand of man.

## ▶ NEARBY ATTRACTIONS

Boulder County Open Space: **www.osmp.org**.

# CHAUTAUQUA PARK: FIRST FLATIRON

For the first-time visitor, as well as the native Boulderite, this is the perfect place to test your hiking mettle, with a serious elevation gain rewarded with a glimpse of the beautiful Chautauqua Park surroundings. Chautauqua Park lies on the southwestern edge of Boulder and is comprised of a park, cottages, auditorium, mountain park, and miles of mountain hiking trails.

> ## DESCRIPTION

To begin this hike, pass through the parking area and onto the paved Bluebell Canyon Road, which climbs to the left adjacent to the Chautauqua Ranger Cottage. Go directly to the trailhead and the opening of a fence that borders the Chautauqua Meadow. The Ranger Cottage is also the only place you will see a restroom for a while. The trailhead is about 100 yards from the parking lot, and as this hike starts on the Chautauqua Trail, you are on a smooth, dirt surface with a slight incline. This is a great time to enjoy flowers and prairie grasses, as well as magnificent views of the Flatirons. The road you see snaking far off to the right is Flagstaff Road.

The Colorado Chautauqua was founded in 1898 as a joint effort of the University of Texas,

> ## KEY AT-A-GLANCE INFORMATION

**LENGTH:** 4.7 miles

**CONFIGURATION:** Out-and-back, loop

**DIFFICULTY:** Difficult

**SCENERY:** Meadow, alpine, Flatirons (severe rock formations), views of Longs Peak and the Indian Peaks

**EXPOSURE:** Sunny in meadow portion year-round, shaded in alpine portion

**TRAFFIC:** Heavy

**TRAIL SURFACE:** Dirt, loose rocks, exposed tree roots

**HIKING TIME:** 3 hours

**SEASON:** All year

**ACCESS:** Free; open dawn to dusk

**MAPS:** At Ranger Station

**FACILITIES:** Restroom, water, food, entertainment, picnic area

**SPECIAL COMMENTS:** This trail is a local favorite, and heavily used, so there are many posted rules, one of which is that all waste products—human, dog, and otherwise—must be packed out with you.

> ## DIRECTIONS

From Denver take I-25 north to US 36 to the Baseline Road exit and take a left turn, going west. Continue past the intersection of Broadway and travel 1 mile to the entrance of Chautauqua Park, which is on the south side of the road. Pull directly into the large parking area at the trailhead, but if the lot is full (which it is most of the time), park along the south side of Baseline Road or along neighborhood streets. We hiked on a Thursday, and the trailhead parking lot and subsequent side streets were packed with cars.

Chautauqua Park: First Flatiron

UTM Zone (WGS84)   13S

Easting   475889

Northing   4427450

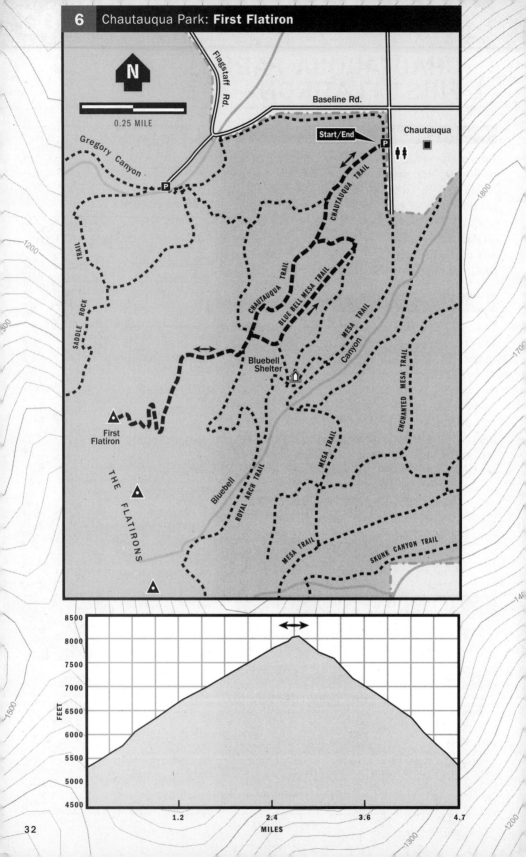

N

0.25 MILE

Flagstaff Rd.

Baseline Rd.

Start/End

Chautauqua

Gregory Canyon

CHAUTAUQUA TRAIL

SADDLE ROCK TRAIL

CHAUTAUQUA TRAIL

BLUE BELL MESA TRAIL

MESA TRAIL

Canyon

ENCHANTED MESA TRAIL

Bluebell
Shelter

First
Flatiron

THE FLATIRONS

Bluebell

ROYAL ARCH TRAIL

MESA TRAIL

MESA TRAIL

MESA TRAIL

SKUNK CANYON TRAIL

8500
8000
7500
7000
6500
6000
5500
5000
4500

FEET

1.2          2.4          3.6          4.7

MILES

the Gulf and Southern Railroad, and the City of Boulder. In 1978, the Colorado Chautauqua was added to the National Register of Historic Places and also designated as a City of Boulder Landmarked Historic District.

At the point where you start to get out of breath, that first trickle of sweat drops, and you pray for shade (the meadow portion has no shade), you'll reach the intersection of Chautauqua Trail, Ski Jump Trail, and Blue Bell Baird Trail. Continue straight at this intersection until you reach the intersection of Chautauqua Trail and Blue Bell Mesa Trail, and stay straight here as well, until you are welcomed by shade from ponderosa pines and large berry bushes that border the meadow.

A good place to stop and catch your breath after the slow-going, sharp, and steady incline from the trailhead is a small fenced-off area that is tucked off the main path just prior to a small wooden footbridge. Grab some gulps of breath here, because your battles with the switchbacks start soon.

Soon after tackling the wide switchbacks, reach an intersection with a sign explaining how to access the Ski Jump Trail on the right and Royal Arch, Bluebell Mesa Trail, and Bluebell Shelter Trail on the left. You are now standing at the base of the Third, Second, and First Flatirons at this point in the trail (going south to north). The Flatirons, colossal rock formations that jut up out of Chautauqua Park, are home to some of the best views of Boulder, Denver, the Colorado Plains, and even such famous mountain peaks as Long's Peak, Twin Peaks, and the Indian Peaks. Take the left turn and you will immediately spot a post without a sign at a fork in the trail. Turn right here at the fork onto the upper trail.

Up to this point the trail is a two-person-wide dirt and rock trail. After this turn onto the upper trail, the path thins, with a wide array of both large rocks and small loose ones.

Next, you encounter another fork where either direction leads to a second or third Flatiron technical climbing access and the Royal Arch Trail. Take a right turn here. From this point on, you will be treading on land that you will retrace on your descent.

You'll notice now that the low roar of distant traffic begins to diminish. In the heat of summer, an aroma of pine sap lingers in the air. As the narrow trail continues to climb to the top of the First Flatiron, tree roots and loose rocks jut up from the soil.

The trail opens up with a view of a huge rockslide that continues as high as the eye can see. These rocks and large boulders measure bigger than a bread box but not as large as a VW Beetle. The boulders were at one point part of a Flatiron peak and have come tumbling down. After a second turn on this switchback, the trail crosses the rockslide. Climb the staircased rocks, worn smooth by the passing of many boots.

The next fork in the trail leads right to the Flatironette, which is a technical climbing access point, and left toward the First and Second Flatirons. Continue to the left. At this point, emerge from the rockslide into an alpine terrain where the pine trees are thick and the trail is narrow. A footbridge and stairs to the right access technical climbing to the First Flatiron.

Now turn around, look down, and capture one of the first perfect views of Boulder that you will see on this hike. For those not familiar with Boulder, the University of Colorado is recognized by signature red-tile roofs; the Boulder reservoir sits straight in the distance; and downtown is to the north. Nestled within downtown Boulder is a popular pedestrian mall: Pearl Street. You can also view the trailhead below, many of the switchbacks, and Chautauqua Park. I hiked the trail with my husband on a beautiful 72-degree day, but this hike offers year-round access. Some of the best times to see the Flatirons are after they have been dusted by a fresh coat of powdery snow. The only wildlife we spotted up to this point were butterflies, but brochures on the area tout everything from striped skunks to the rarely seen mountain lion.

It may look like the trail has ended in a large pile of boulders, but continue straight up the Flatiron. Easily navigated footsteps and handholds are chiseled into the rocks at this point. However, I would not recommend this hike for toddlers, whether walking or being carried. Don't be surprised if hikers wielding everything from cell phones to 50 pounds of technical climbing equipment pass you on the way.

Continue up, up, up, and to the right. If you bear left, you will be guided to technical climbing access on the second flatiron, so bear to the right. Here, the hike is strenuous, with many switchbacks. By the time you have reached the false summit, you will have encountered around three dozen switchbacks.

Continuing straight, crest over a hill to a false summit between the First and Second Flatiron. To the left you can see the Third Flatiron jettisoning out of the mountain. Small mountain creatures such as chipmunks may be spotted through here. You can stop at this point and turn around to admire the view, but it is well worth it to continue on to the view from the true summit.

Pass a left-hand turn to Saddle Rock Trail, and continue to the right for our true summit. The mountain peaks that come into view are the long-promised Indian Peak range and Longs Peak. To reach the very top of the First Flatiron, you must have technical climbing skills and equipment. Lacking those, stop just short of the top of the First Flatiron here. This is your true summit, from which the National Center for Atmospheric Research is visible. On a clear day, Denver can be seen directly south. Turn around and head straight down the way that you just came.

Once you amble back down to the unmarked sign, hang a sharp right onto the Bluebell Trail. This is the opposite direction from which you came, yet loops back to the Chautauqua Trail and the trailhead. The trail widens and flattens, giving you a breather. At the next intersection, take a left down the Bluebell Mesa Trail, where you will meander through ponderosa pines on a much gentler downhill. The trail is heavily signed at this point, with directions to Bluebell Shelter Trail. Stay on the main Bluebell Trail by continuing to the left. At this point in the hike, the houses and the people walking around Boulder become clear. You will intersect with the start of the Bluebell Mesa Trail and the Chautauqua Trail; take a right to head down. Be sure to take a final look over your shoulder to the Flatirons to see where you've been.

## ▶ NEARBY ATTRACTIONS

Spend as much time as possible in the Chautauqua Park area while you are here. Rest in the large, shady park, which includes a playground. Try the Chautauqua dining hall, which is open seven days a week for breakfast, lunch, and dinner. There are 39 privately owned cottages at Chautauqua. The Chautauqua Association owns the community house, the preservation office, two lodges, and 60 cottages that are available for rent primarily to University of Colorado faculty and students. Maps for all Chautauqua buildings are available at the Ranger Station. For more information, City of Boulder Open Space and Mountain Parks: **www.osmp.org**.

# ELDORADO CANYON: ELDORADO SPRINGS TRAIL

## ▶ IN BRIEF

Eldorado Springs Trail is blessed with sunshine all year. Southern exposure makes this trail suitable for all seasons. Eldorado Canyon is world-famous for its rock climbing, and a multitude of climbers can be seen on the steep red rocks neighboring this trail. Occasionally, if the timing is right, you'll see trains traveling through the canyon. The trail can be a bit difficult, but is broken up by flat sections that give it a more moderate rating.

## ▶ DESCRIPTION

The trailhead is a short walk from the parking area. Cross the service road and begin the steep climb into North Draw. The switchbacks are well maintained, and steeper portions utilize man-made staircases. Trail workers have taken obvious pains with signs and barriers to discourage cutting switchbacks. The trail is a well-worn dirt path lined with yucca plants, and most of it is very sunny and exposed.

The man-made grade visible across the valley to the south is the railroad line that clings to the cliffs. SkiTrain and Amtrak use this line. At the top of the switchbacks, pass the technical climbing access signs to the Ricon Wall and others. You have great views to the north of technical climbing walls and Shirt Tail Peak.

The trail crosses a saddle, then travels into dense pine trees. Cross an old rockslide and continue up rock staircases. Here, the trail still

## ℹ KEY AT-A-GLANCE INFORMATION

**LENGTH:** 5.68 miles

**CONFIGURATION:** Out-and-back

**DIFFICULTY:** Moderate

**SCENERY:** Towering, sheer rock walls, views of railroad, pine trees, scattered forest, yucca

**EXPOSURE:** Sunny

**TRAFFIC:** Moderate

**TRAIL SURFACE:** Dirt, loose rocks

**HIKING TIME:** 4 hours

**SEASON:** All year

**ACCESS:** $5 or annual state park pass; open sunrise to sunset

**MAPS:** USGS Eldorado Springs

**FACILITIES:** Restrooms, picnic tables

**SPECIAL COMMENTS:** Horses and dogs on leash are OK. No mountain bikes. Although this area is teeming with technical climbers, they usually park in a different area (on the road) and don't use this trail to get to their climbs. For technical rock climbing, Eldorado Canyon offers more than 500 different routes. Enthusiasts from all over the world come to Eldorado Canyon to enjoy some of the best climbing available.

## ▶ DIRECTIONS

From Denver, take I-25 north to US 36 west, toward Boulder. Exit at Louisville-Superior and turn left at the light. Take the first right onto CO 170 to Eldorado Canyon. Continue 1 mile through the canyon to the visitor center. After paying the park fee, travel 0.5 miles to the end of the road, where there is parking and picnic tables.

**Eldorado Canyon: Eldorado Springs Trail**

**UTM Zone (WGS84)  13S**

**Easting   474939**

**Northing   4419936**

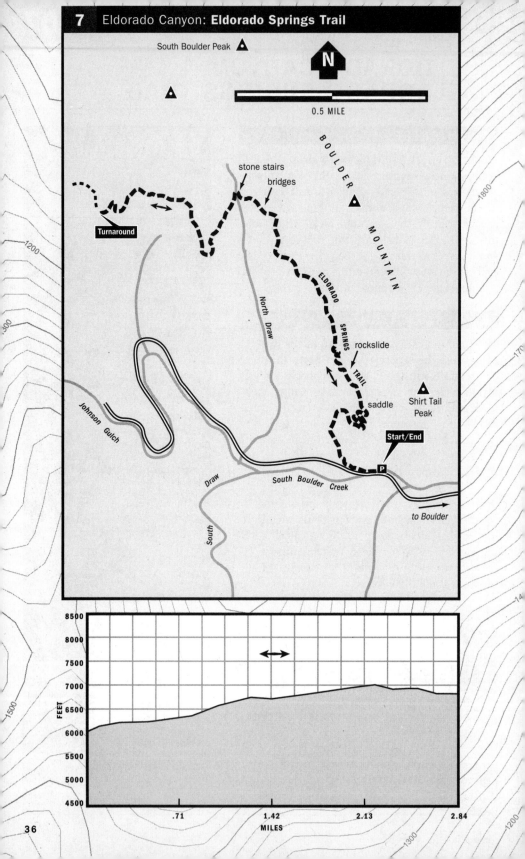

South Boulder Peak

N

0.5 MILE

stone stairs

bridges

Turnaround

BOULDER MOUNTAIN

ELDORADO SPRINGS TRAIL

rockslide

North Draw

saddle

Shirt Tail Peak

Johnson Gulch

Start/End

P

South Draw

South Boulder Creek

to Boulder

8500

8000

7500

7000

6500

6000

5500

5000

4500

FEET

.71    1.42    2.13    2.84

MILES

A train crossing, across the valley from the Eldorado Springs Trail. Hikers may hear the echo of the train whistle on railroad tracks cut into the mountain long ago.

provides views of the valley, the Indian Peaks, and the Continental Divide. Eldorado trail signs dot the trail, which is worn and packed down, making it easy to follow. Cacti, yucca, and wildflowers grow on this hillside. The trail levels out, ascends once more, then levels out again, with good views of the area's sun-worshipping rock formations.

Descend from here, cutting across another massive old rockslide. Continue through a hillside of lodgepole and ponderosa pines, as well as juniper and pinon. Colorful boulders provide cover for small springs. Travel past the boulders and rest, especially on hot days, since it is shaded and quite flat at this spot.

When we hiked, mountain lion tracks lined the trail for a few miles around this point, reminding us that it is always good to beware and be aware of your surroundings.

From here, the trail curves and crosses over a ridge and meanders through the same forest and boulders. Descend and cross a seasonal creek via tiny man-made bridges. Ascend more of the trail's characteristic switchbacks until the trees thin out. Here, you capture views of the plains to the left. Continue up the stone stairs. The rumbling sounds you may hear nearby are of the trains across the valley.

The trail opens into a modest meadow filled with yucca plants and ponderosa pines. The view is immense here and you can see all the way to downtown Denver. South Boulder Peak looms high above as the trail cuts across the meadow and then descends fairly quickly into Walker Ranch. There are views to the north of the Walker Ranch area and the back of Flagstaff Road. The trail continues to descend and hikers may continue on, but the Eldorado Springs Trail unofficially ends here. Return the way you came.

## ▶ NEARBY ATTRACTIONS

Walker Ranch Loop, Rattlesnake Gulch Trail, and Fowler Trail. For more information: **www.parks.state.co.us** and **www.osmp.org**.

# GREGORY CANYON:
# GREEN MOUNTAIN LOOP

## KEY AT-A-GLANCE INFORMATION

**LENGTH:** 4.7 miles

**CONFIGURATION:** Loop

**DIFFICULTY:** Difficult

**SCENERY:** Creek, pine trees, historic buildings, rock formations

**EXPOSURE:** Mostly southern and shaded

**TRAFFIC:** Heavy with dogs and humans

**TRAIL SURFACE:** Dirt, loose rocks

**HIKING TIME:** 4 hours

**SEASON:** May–November; watch for early or late snows; check on closures February through July for raptor and bat habitats

**ACCESS:** $3 for parking (correct change only); open sunrise to sunset

**FACILITIES:** Dog refuse bags provided. Restrooms, picnic table, and trash cans at trailhead and at summit.

**MAPS:** USGS Eldorado Springs, City of Boulder map available at trailhead

**SPECIAL COMMENTS:** Parking is based on a fee system; unless your vehicle is registered in Boulder County and you are a Boulder County resident, you must pay $3 a day to park, or an annual fee of $15. To avoid the parking fee, you can park at Chautauqua Park and walk to the trailhead. Parking fines start at $25.

## IN BRIEF

This is a crowded "Boulder trail," but it's also a true gem and an excellent workout. Green Mountain Loop is comprised of four unique trails: Gregory Canyon Trail, Ranger Trail, E.M. Greenman Trail, and Saddle Rock Trail.

## DESCRIPTION

Green Mountain Loop starts with the Gregory Canyon Trail, which begins from the right end of the Baird Park parking lot. Gregory Canyon Trail immediately intersects with Crown Rock Trail on the left. Head right, continuing on Gregory Canyon Trail toward a small creek, and then west along a ridge that crosses the creek and rises to the southwest. Watch for poison ivy along the trail, which is a former service road used for travel to gold mines near Central City. The trail is comprised of red dirt and loose rocks, and it ascends rather quickly in the beginning. We hiked in late fall and there were slick, wet leaves scattered on the trail. At this point, the well-maintained trail is only wide enough for one hiker at a time.

Cross an old wooden bridge that covers a small stream. As the terrain becomes more rugged and rocky, you face about 100 yards of semitechnical rock scrambling. No technical equipment is required, just steady footing.

The trail is now on a slight incline and continues uphill to more boulder fields. At a fork at

## DIRECTIONS

From Denver, take I-25 north to US 36 West. Exit west onto Baseline Road and take a left, going west to Chautauqua Park. Continue on Baseline, pass Chautauqua Park and the Flatirons, and turn left into the Gregory Canyon Trailhead and Baird Park parking lot before the road takes a sharp right onto Flagstaff Road.

**Gregory Canyon: Green Mountain Loop**

**UTM Zone (WGS84)  13S**

**Easting  475060**

**Northing  4427280**

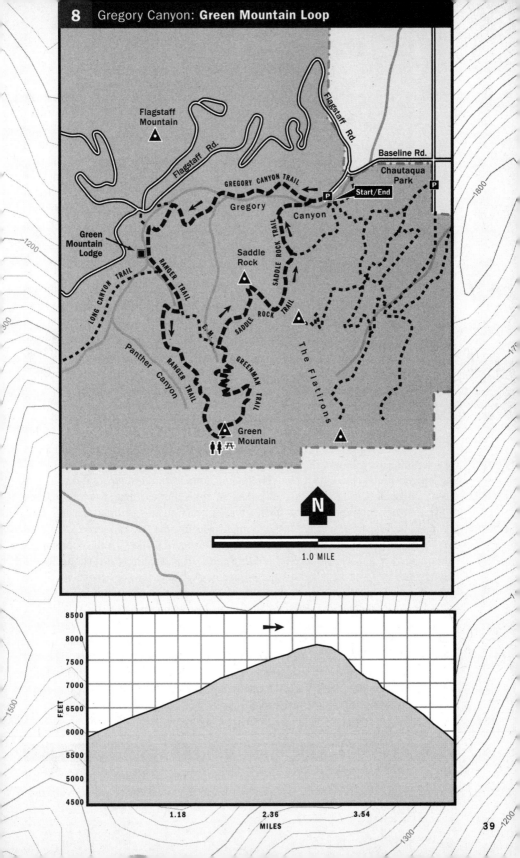

Flagstaff Mountain

Flagstaff Rd.

Flagstaff Rd.

Baseline Rd.

GREGORY CANYON TRAIL

Chautaqua Park

Gregory

Canyon

P

Start/End

P

Green
Mountain
Lodge

SADDLE ROCK TRAIL

LONG CANYON TRAIL

RANGER TRAIL

Saddle
Rock

SADDLE ROCK TRAIL

E.M.

Panther Canyon

RANGER TRAIL

GREENMAN TRAIL

The Flatirons

Green
Mountain

N

1.0 MILE

8500
8000
7500
7000
6500
6000
5500
5000
4500

FEET

1.18    2.36    3.54
MILES

Deserted Green Mountain Lodge sits as a welcome beacon and provides a nice photo opportunity along the early part of the Green Mountain Loop.

the top of the hill, continue on the main path to the left. The trail merges with a fire road and continues south to Green Mountain Lodge.

This historic yet deserted building holds ghosts of miners, such as John Gregory, as well as pioneers and ranchers. Named after John Gregory, the prospector who discovered the enormous Gregory lode behind Black Hawk, the Gregory Canyon Trail was originally built by settlers to provide wagon access to the gold fields near Black Hawk and Central City. According to historians, John Gregory paid two miners the equivalent of $1.50 a day each to remove $1,000 of gold every week from the lode.

At the intersection of Flagstaff Road, Gregory Canyon Trail, Long Canyon Trail, and Ranger Trail, turn left onto Ranger Trail. Ranger Trail begins on the east side of the lodge and passes through ponderosa pine and Douglas fir forest to intersect with E.M. Greenman Trail.

Stay on Ranger Trail as it intersects with various Green Mountain Trails coming in from the south. The last 0.8 miles of the Ranger Trail before the Green Mountain Summit features loose rocks, a long ascent, and plenty of switchbacks. If hiking anytime after the first snowfall (as early as the first of September), watch for ice that collects on this southern-facing ridge. We hiked in November and the last half-mile was snow-packed and icy.

You'll find restrooms and picnic tables at the summit of Green Mountain. A summit marker and hiking register are at the top of a large boulder. The Colorado Hiking Club has also installed a large bronze marker here that designates all of the major mountain peaks that can be seen from the summit. Some mountains are as far as Rocky Mountain National Park and others as close as the Indian Peaks Wilderness.

To start the descent, head back on E.M. Greenman Trail, opposite of the Ranger Trail. At the intersection of E.M. Greenman Trail and Saddle Rock Trail, take a right onto Saddle Rock Trail. Again, the downhill was steep and icy in early winter. The trail is much like the ascent, with switchbacks and steep rocks. To the west is the backside of the famous Boulder Flatiron rock formations and Chautauqua Park. Stay on Saddle Rock trail as it veers to the left in the loop's last half-mile. Saddle Rock Trail merges for a few yards with Gregory Canyon Trail, then ends back at the parking lot.

## ▶ NEARBY ATTRACTIONS

Boulder trails, including the Flagstaff Mountain Loops and Chautauqua Loops. For more information, City of Boulder, Open Space and Mountain Parks: **www.osmp.org**.

# INDIAN PEAKS WILDERNESS: DEVIL'S THUMB LAKE

## IN BRIEF

The hike to the Devil's Thumb Lake is one of the classic hikes into Indian Peaks Wilderness. It is also one of the most popular, and often crowded, area hikes. This trail takes you into beautiful scenery that includes alpine meadows, mountain lakes, and views of snowcapped mountains. The hike is long and often wet, but full of waterfalls in late spring and early summer. The trail crosses gently sloping terrain interspersed with steep stretches.

## DESCRIPTION

Cross the creek via the wood bridge and come to a kiosk and the Hessie Trailhead. Devil's Thumb Trail (#902) climbs steeply on an old road for 0.5 miles. The road is a very old, rough, four-wheel road that provides emergency forest service access. The Devil's Thumb Bypass turns right in 0.8 miles, just before the bridge. Either Devil's Thumb Trail or the Devil's Thumb Bypass takes hikers to the same destination, and the distance is the same. At the bridge, near a thundering waterfall and a neighboring snowdrift, take a right onto Devil's Thumb Bypass. The bypass trail crosses open meadows to the north of the creek. The main trail follows an old road along the south side of the creek, staying right past trail junctions with

## DIRECTIONS

From Denver, take I-25 north to US 36 into Boulder. Turn left on Canyon Boulevard (CO 119) and travel all the way to Nederland (approximately 45 minutes). Stay on CO 119 going south out of Nederland for 0.5 miles; turn right on CR 130, then follow signs to Eldora. Stay on CR 130 through Eldora and continue on dirt road. Bear left (staying on CR 130) at next fork and park here or drive 0.25 miles to Hessie Trailhead up the dirt road Note: Sometimes this road flows with runoff, since it is a cobblestone creek bed.

## KEY AT-A-GLANCE INFORMATION

**LENGTH:** 11 miles

**CONFIGURATION:** Out-and-back

**DIFFICULTY:** Difficult

**SCENERY:** Dense forest, alpine tundra, high mountain peaks

**EXPOSURE:** Alternating sun and shade, high-altitude sunshine

**TRAFFIC:** Heavy, especially on weekends

**TRAIL SURFACE:** Dirt, loose rocks, running water and wet areas, snowdrifts

**HIKING TIME:** 5.5 hours

**SEASON:** June–September (open all year)

**ACCESS:** Free, permits required for groups of more than 15 and for camping; limited parking; open sunrise to sunset.

**MAPS:** USGS East Portal and Nederland

**FACILITIES:** None

**SPECIAL COMMENTS:** Access to trailhead requires high-clearance vehicle and four-wheel drive. Those with passenger cars can park 0.25 miles before the trailhead, where parking is also limited. Parking regulations are strictly enforced. Dogs allowed, but must be leashed. Most of the trail is in Indian Peaks Wilderness and special regulations apply. No bicycles or other mechanical transportation, and special regulations apply for horses. In the off-season, hikers can drive only to the end of the town of Eldora, where they ski or snowshoe to the trailhead, then hike with the appropriate winter gear. Keep in mind that winter can stretch into June here.

**Indian Peaks Wilderness: Devil's Thumb Lake**

**UTM Zone (WGS84)   13S**

**Easting   448675**

**Northing   4422620**

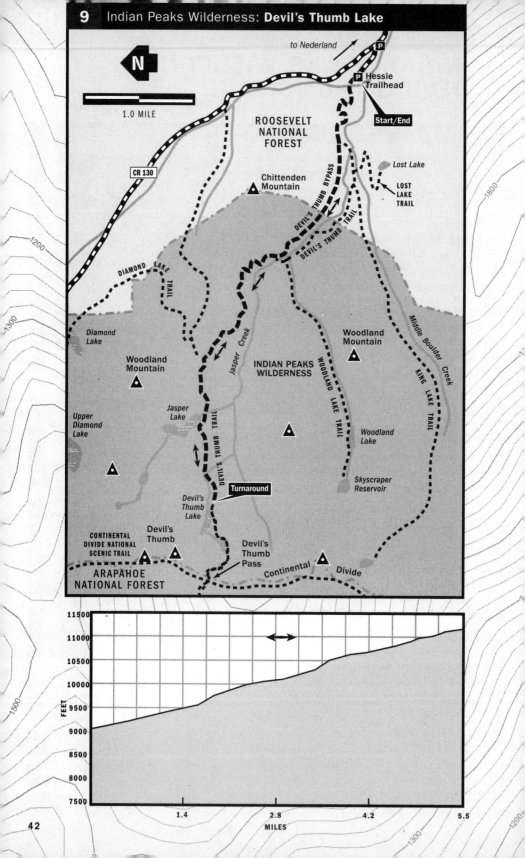

Lost Lake Trail, King Lake Trail, and Woodland Lake Trail. It is flooded most of the year and is best accessed in July.

The main trail bears to the right, goes uphill, and moves away from the creek a little bit. Social paths indicate that many hikers veer off of the main path to check out the waterfalls. The bypass trail is wet and has water running in places. As you continue to hike uphill, the trail opens into little meadows, with views of the Indian Peaks and the Continental Divide straight ahead. You now enter Indian Peaks Wilderness (marked with a sign) and travel a trail that is much easier to follow.

At the end of the meadows, the trail enters forest again. Continue gradually uphill through trees, and at the marked intersection, take a right back onto the main Devil's Thumb Trail. King Lake Trail and Woodland Lake Trail go left. The trail is now steep, ascending, and very rocky. The signs point out that this was once a mining road. Keep an eye out for when the mining road bears left uphill and the main trail goes to the right. You'll see a little sign that points hikers to the right. The trail is wider here and the sound of waterfalls reminds you that you're never far from the main creek.

Eventually the trail comes back and runs parallel to the same mining access road. Cross the road and stay on the trail with a stream to the right. We hiked in mid-June and snowbanks dominated the trail. Here it is steep, rocky, and the elevation climbs. You're encouraged to travel up and over the snowbanks in the trail even if they are rather large. Continue up the rock stairs on the other side of the creek.

Eventually, the trail joins up again with the old mining road. Don't be discouraged by the steepness of the trail—it levels out soon. Traverse the ridge, which is an old four-wheeling road that was cut into a shelf road. The shelf road continues across an old rockslide. At this point, you are in a big mountain basin surrounded by a cirque of high peaks.

Continue straight past the turnoff to Diamond Lake Trail and travel 0.6 miles to Jasper Lake, which is surrounded on three sides by trees and a steep ridgeline. Here you cross a spillway with a bridge traveling through shallow water. Often there's a social plank placed across the spillway 100 yards downstream. The trail continues another mile over a small ridge, north of a pond, and up a slope to Devil's Thumb Lake. It lies directly below the vertical wall of Devil's Thumb. Rest before you turn around and head back to the trailhead.

### ▶ NEARBY ATTRACTIONS

Hessie Trailhead is also the trailhead for the Continental Divide and Devil's Thumb Pass, and other Boulder Ranger District Trails (Lost Lake Trail #813, King Lake Trail #901, and Woodland Lake Trail #811). For more information, USDA Forest Service, Arapaho and Roosevelt National Forest, Pawnee National Grassland: **www.fs.fed.us** (reference Devil's Thumb Trail #902).

# INDIAN PEAKS WILDERNESS: GLACIER RIM TRAIL

## KEY AT-A-GLANCE INFORMATION

**LENGTH:** 12.2 miles

**CONFIGURATION:** Out-and-back

**DIFFICULTY:** Difficult

**SCENERY:** Alpine tundra and high mountain peaks; views toward Boulder

**EXPOSURE:** Shaded for first few miles and then exposed due to high altitude

**TRAFFIC:** Light

**TRAIL SURFACE:** Hard-packed dirt, extremely rocky

**HIKING TIME:** 6.5 hours

**SEASON:** June–September (open all year)

**ACCESS:** Free; open sunrise to sunset

**MAPS:** USGS Monarch Lake and Ward

**FACILITIES:** Restroom

**SPECIAL COMMENTS:** Dogs must be leashed. Most of the trail is in Indian Peaks Wilderness and special regulations apply. No bicycles or other mechanical transportation, and special regulations apply for horses. In the off-season, hikers can only drive to the gate where the road forks, ski or snowshoe to the trailhead, and then hike with the appropriate winter gear. Keep in mind that winter can stretch into June here. The trail is not well marked and is hard to follow in bad weather. The majority of this trail is above timberline and is extremely exposed to sun, wind, hailstorms and blizzards, even in midsummer. Please go equipped accordingly.

Indian Peaks Wilderness:
Glacier Rim Trail

UTM Zone (WGS84)   13T

Easting   451240

Northing   4428880

## ▶ IN BRIEF

Arapaho Glacier is the most southern glacier in the Rocky Mountains, and it is melting. This trail takes you to the glacier along a high and exposed route that earns its place among the longest and most difficult in this book. There is not much left of the glacier, which is surrounded by high mountain peaks and alpine tundra, but its destination is a reward and a good turnaround point. There is an alternate access to the glacier overlook, but this one is a better workout, is more scenic, and is less used.

## ▶ DESCRIPTION

The Glacier Rim Trail (#905) trailhead is well marked and is just after the one-way sign near the end of the road. Hike past the wilderness sign that marks the Indian Peaks Wilderness boundary and continue straight. Pass a barbed-wire fence to your right and a sign indicating City of Boulder Watershed. This area is the source for most of Boulder's drinking water and is heavily patrolled. Public access is prohibited.

The first several miles of this hike follow the watershed boundary, so please stay on the trail. The high elevation causes a shortness of breath. Even at the trailhead, this is evident in the short stature of the vegetation.

## ▶ DIRECTIONS

From Denver, take I-25 north to US 36 into Boulder. Turn left on Canyon Boulevard (CO 119) and travel all the way to Nederland (approximately 45 minutes). At the traffic circle, go north on CO 72 for 7.5 miles, until you see a sign for University of Colorado Mountain Research Station Turn left there on FR 298 (CR 116), go 1 mile, bear left on the same road and travel 4.5 miles until the end of the road. There are two trailheads next to each other: The first one is Glacier Rim Trail.

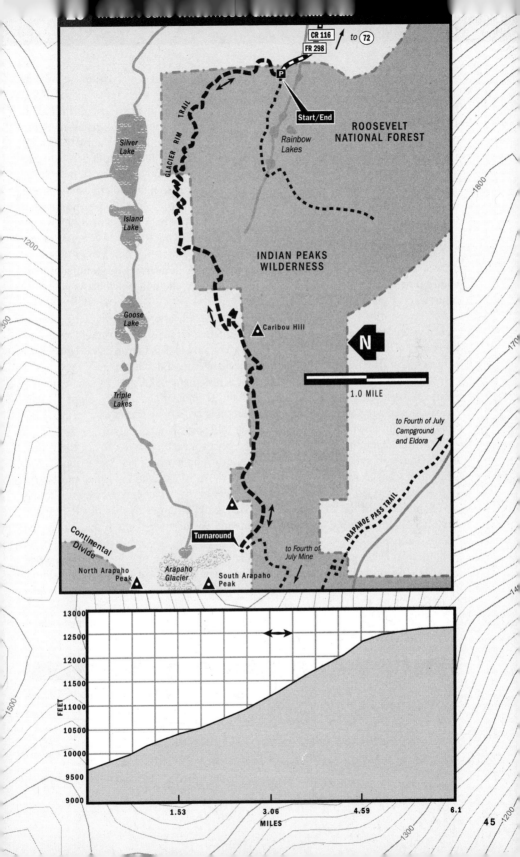

CR 116    to 72
FR 298

Start/End

ROOSEVELT
NATIONAL FOREST

Rainbow
Lakes

Silver
Lake

GLACIER RIM TRAIL

Island
Lake

INDIAN PEAKS
WILDERNESS

Goose
Lake

△ Caribou Hill

N

Triple
Lakes

1.0 MILE

to Fourth of July
Campground
and Eldora

△

Turnaround

ARAPAHOE PASS TRAIL

to Fourth of
July Mine

Continental
Divide

North Arapaho
Peak △

Arapaho
Glacier

△ South Arapaho
Peak

13000
12500
12000
11500
11000
10500
10000
9500
9000

FEET

1.53    3.06    4.59    6.1

MILES

Travel through occasional switchbacks as the trail gets steeper and climbs at each turn. The trees end abruptly and the rest of the hike is left very exposed. After reaching timberline, you're treated to incredible views into the heart of the Indian Peaks Wilderness. Glance over your right shoulder and look for Silver Lake. As the trail goes straight southwest, up Caribou Hill, it switches back to the right, around the north to the top. Across the valley are views of Niwot Ridge. From here you can see the University of Colorado Mountain Research Station.

Notice the tree line is higher across the valley due to the southern exposure and constant sunshine. A switchback high up on the northern slope will take you through jumbled rocks. The last switchback (for a while) puts you on a long southwest traverse.

Pass the top of Caribou Hill to the left and set your sights on the next ridge. The Corona Bowl of Eldora Ski Area will now be visible along with Barker Reservoir, as well as the town of Nederland off to the left. A new group of mountain peaks comes into view to the southwest and just as it does, the trail switchbacks going the other way, to the north.

Traverse the south slope and ascend. To the left are some of the long, narrow glacial valleys left from when the Rocky Mountains were created. Several hikes in this book are in that direction, including Devil's Thumb Lake and Heart Lake. James Peak is directly south. This traverse includes a welcome, mild descent.

After the downhill, continue due west across the next hillside. Pass an extremely weathered sign, right in the middle of the hillside, indicating 1 mile to Arapaho Glacier. The traverse remains level for a while, crossing an extremely rocky slope. Enjoy the level and slight downhill grade, because the trail starts climbing again.

At the beginning of the climb, glance over your left shoulder to see the Fourth of July Trailhead and, in a few moments, South Arapaho Peak and its pyramid shape straight in front. A trail on the left that goes down to Arapaho Pass Trail and Fourth of July Trail is in fact a steeper, faster way down in case of an emergency, but there is no telephone until the town of Eldora. That trail continues by way of the Arapaho Pass Trail as it goes west, over the Continental Divide toward the Grand Valley and Winter Park.

Reach the Arapaho Glacier overlook in the shadow of South Arapaho Peak. From this point, ambitious hikers can continue as the trail goes up the south side of the peak with a little scrambling required. Otherwise, turn around from here and head back the 6.1 miles to the car.

Note that hikers with two cars can leave one at Fourth of July trailhead above Eldora and do a shuttle hike.

## ▶ NEARBY ATTRACTIONS

Rainbow Lakes Trail #918, Arapaho Pass Trail #904, and other Indian Peaks Wilderness hikes: **www.fs.fed.us/r2/arnf.**

# INDIAN PEAKS WILDERNESS: MOUNT AUDUBON

## IN BRIEF

Hikers reach Mount Audubon by a strenuous march straight up to 13,000 feet from 10,000 feet. The hike's trailhead may be enough beautiful alpine scenery for some, but the higher panoramic alpine views and alpine lakes are quite rewarding. Those who take this challenge will be above tree line for most of the hike and exposed to alpine elements and tundra.

## DESCRIPTION

Start from the north corner of the parking lot at the Beaver Creek trailhead. The trail is well maintained and well marked, and it proceeds directly into a subalpine evergreen forest. Enjoy the gentle grade and the shade for a short time, since the trail will climb, become very steep, and eventually emerge from the trees, becoming totally exposed for the remainder of the hike

Views to the east stretch across the plains. You can also see Brainard Lake, Long Lake, Niwot Ridge, and the nearby Indian Peaks. Follow the trail as it traverses across the eastern slope.

At 1.3 miles, the Beaver Creek Trail goes right down to Coney Flats Road. Veer left on Mount Audubon Trail. Views to the north open up

## DIRECTIONS

Denver, take I-25 north to US 36 into Boulder. Turn left on Canyon Boulevard (CO 119) and travel all the way to Nederland (approximately 45 minutes). Go north on CO 72 to the small town of Ward. Look for the signs that indicate a left turn to Brainard Lake Recreation Area, and turn left onto CR 102. Go toward Brainard Lake; come to a gate where the $7 fee is collected. The road becomes one-way and travels counterclockwise around the lake. Follow the signs to the Mitchell Lake Area and turn right. Park at the Mitchell Lake Trailhead parking area.

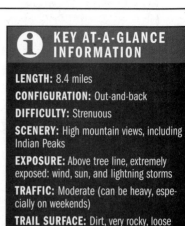

## KEY AT-A-GLANCE INFORMATION

**LENGTH:** 8.4 miles

**CONFIGURATION:** Out-and-back

**DIFFICULTY:** Strenuous

**SCENERY:** High mountain views, including Indian Peaks

**EXPOSURE:** Above tree line, extremely exposed: wind, sun, and lightning storms

**TRAFFIC:** Moderate (can be heavy, especially on weekends)

**TRAIL SURFACE:** Dirt, very rocky, loose trail

**HIKING TIME:** 4.5 hours

**SEASON:** June–September (open all year)

**ACCESS:** $7; open sunrise to sunset

**MAPS:** USGS Ward

**FACILITIES:** Emergency telephone, restrooms, picnic areas, campgrounds

**SPECIAL COMMENTS:** Indian Peaks Wilderness rules apply, including no bikes, no vehicles of any kind, camping limitations with permits required for any overnight visit, and dogs must be leashed. The last section of this hike is above timberline and is exposed to violent lightning. Time hikes for early morning with a minimum noon summit goal. Access in the off-season is limited to ski-in travel from CO 72. Hikers must park near the highway and ski or snowshoe in, then use snowshoes for the hike.

---

**Indian Peaks Wilderness: Mount Audubon**

**UTM Zone (WGS84)  13T**

**Easting  450510**

**Northing  4436930**

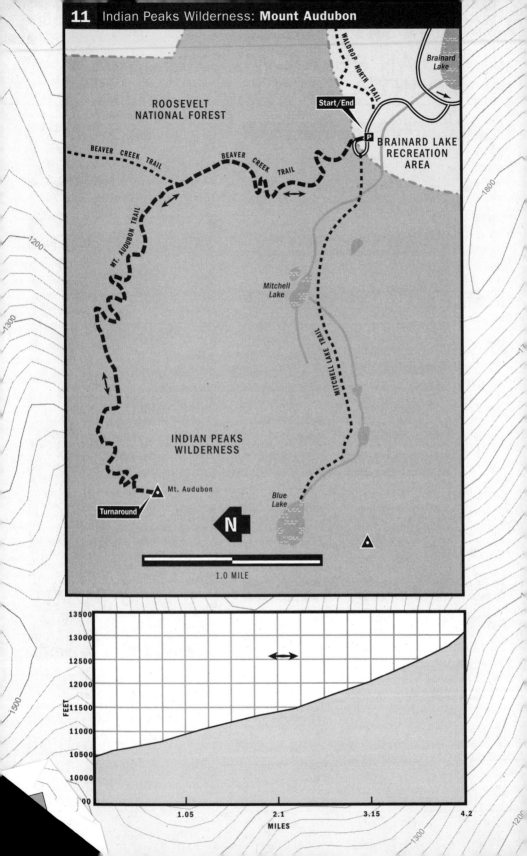

ROOSEVELT
NATIONAL FOREST

BEAVER CREEK TRAIL

BEAVER CREEK TRAIL

MT. AUDUBON TRAIL

WALDROP NORTH TRAIL

Brainard
Lake

Start/End

P

BRAINARD LAKE
RECREATION
AREA

Mitchell
Lake

MITCHELL LAKE TRAIL

INDIAN PEAKS
WILDERNESS

Mt. Audubon

Turnaround

Blue
Lake

N

1.0 MILE

13500
13000
12500
12000
11500
11000
10500
10000
00

FEET

1.05    2.1    3.15    4.2
MILES

A hiker and child-in-tow walk through the gnarled trees at timberline along the trail at Mount Audubon.

to Longs Peak and Mount Meeker. You'll face Mount Audubon at this point, and it tends to loom in the distance as the climb continues. The trees disappear as the trail cuts over a small stream and across an alpine meadow to a snowfield. Even into June and July, the trail will climb toward the snowfield, taking a sharp right and climbing through a boulder field to a flat ridge.

A direct headwind is normal for the remainder of the hike, and the real huffing and puffing begins after a few switchbacks. At 3.5 miles, the trail bears left up a steep and rocky portion before it eventually comes to a flat square spot in the tundra and disappears. Go left and scramble up the rock face.

Follow the cairns and take the main route to the summit. You'll think you can see the peak, but it is not visible and still requires approximately 20 minutes of steep scrambling from the bottom of the rock face. Stop and take a breath, since 13,000 feet has thin air. Keep scrambling up the rock face as it does finally level off, signaling the summit of Mount Audubon. Rest, enjoy the summit, and turn around to head back to the trailhead.

## ▶ NEARBY ATTRACTIONS

Beaver Creek Trail #911, Mitchell and Blue Lakes trails #912, and Pawnee Pass Trail: **www.fs.fed.us**.

# JAMES PEAK WILDERNESS: HEART LAKE

## KEY AT-A-GLANCE INFORMATION

**LENGTH:** 7.96 miles

**CONFIGURATION:** Out-and-back

**DIFFICULTY:** Difficult

**SCENERY:** Dense forest, alpine tundra, high mountain peaks

**EXPOSURE:** Shaded until tree line, high-altitude sunshine

**TRAFFIC:** Moderate

**TRAIL SURFACE:** Dirt, loose rocks, tree roots

**HIKING TIME:** 4.5 hours

**SEASON:** June–September (open all year)

**ACCESS:** Free; open sunrise to sunset

**MAPS:** USGS East Portal and Empire

**FACILITIES:** None

**SPECIAL COMMENTS:** The trailhead has recently been moved; hikers are no longer allowed to cross railroad property and use the bridge by Moffat Tunnel to cross the creek. The trailhead now leaves from the northwest corner of the parking lot and goes around the north side of the railroad facilities. Hikers must cross a creek multiple times and it is likely that your feet will get wet, so be sure to wear the appropriate foot gear. Dogs are allowed and recommended to be leashed, but it's not mandatory. The regulations are less strict than in other wilderness areas, but still prohibit bikes, strollers, or anything wheeled, except for aiding a disabled person. Horses and camping are allowed.

James Peaks Wilderness: Heart Lake

UTM Zone (WGS84)  13S

Easting  444985

Northing  4416955

## IN BRIEF

Several hikes in the book, such as Walker Ranch and South Boulder Creek, follow South Boulder Creek in lower elevations. This hike goes to Rogers Pass Lake and Heart Lake, the source of South Boulder Creek. The hike travels through cool, dense spruce and fir forest, leading up into a beautiful alpine basin ringed with high mountain peaks. Hikers frustrated with parking in nearby Indian Peaks Wilderness will have an easy time here. This trail is less crowded than its neighbors.

## DESCRIPTION

Follow the small signs in the northwest area of the parking lot pointing to the trail. Start out on South Boulder Creek Trail #900. The trail immediately enters aspen and pine forest that is lush in late summer and dotted with wildflowers. A five-minute walk takes you to a kiosk with trail information.

The trail immediately passes the railroad facilities at the east portal of the Moffat Tunnel. The big buildings primarily house ventilators. Don't be alarmed if the ventilator fans come on when you're walking by. At 6.2 miles, this is one

## DIRECTIONS

From Denver, take I-25 north to US 36 into Boulder. Turn left on Canyon Boulevard (CO 119) and travel all the way to Nederland (approximately 45 minutes). Stay on CO 119 going south out of Nederland for 5 miles into Rollinsville. Take a right onto CR 16 (Forest Road 149), go 7 miles to where CR 16 (FR 149) technically ends, but the road continues on. Go straight here and follow sign directions to East Portal. Be extremely careful of the two railroad crossings on the road. This is a heavily used railroad line, including simultaneous trains traveling in different directions. Some automobiles have to wait a long time while trains are being switched in this valley.

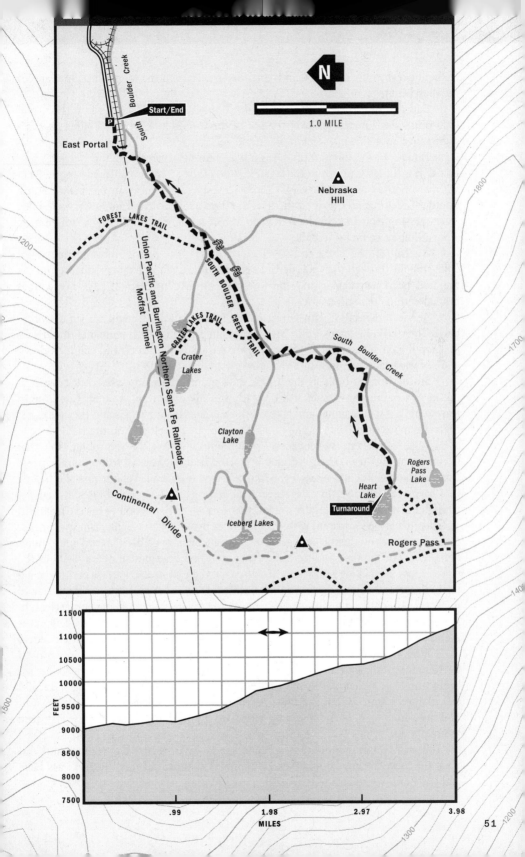

of the longest railroad tunnels in the United States, and the large ventilators are for the diesel fumes.

Railroad buffs may want to also take a drive up Rollins Pass. The original railroad route was constructed over the top of the Continental Divide. Rollins Pass is a right turn about 1.5 miles before the trailhead.

Parallel to the railroad tunnel is a water tunnel operated by the Denver Water Board that brings water from the western side of the Continental Divide to the Denver metropolitan area. Follow the trail as it curves right near an old cabin. South Boulder Creek rushes down on the left. You'll parallel this creek for most of the hike. After crossing Arapaho Creek on a wooden bridge, look up to the right and glimpse a beautiful, cascading waterfall.

A stroll on the paths to the left takes hikers into heavily forested campsites. Hike straight through the cool, dense evergreen forest along a very gradual uphill. As the trail becomes rockier and the forest becomes dense, you'll pass many trees draped with lichen and mosses.

At the intersection with Forest Lakes Trail, continue straight up via a switchback. The trail now opens up to high mountain meadows with remnants of old cabins. You'll gain substantial elevation above South Boulder Creek and can look down and see waterfalls that feed into the creek.

Sturdy bridges built in the 1990s have eliminated many wet creek crossings, but at this point, you should still be ready to walk on a very wet trail. Continue to travel uphill. An occasional trail goes off the left near the waterfalls and the creek, but there are more waterfalls coming up and you might as well stay on the trail.

Begin consistent switchbacks away from the creek. At this point, the trail becomes narrow, steep, and rocky, and is marked by an occasional red dot on the trees. Continue straight at the intersection with Crater Lakes Trail. Walk across the boards that have been laid to help navigate difficult sections. Due to snowdrifts and water in springtime, many trails meander around this area, so pay attention to the red dots and the trail. It's always apparent within a minute or two if you're on the main trail or not.

If you veer off the trail and get lost, just remember to go back toward South Boulder Creek. For the first 3 miles of this hike, the trail does not stray too far from the creek. Cross a small log bridge over a side creek, then immediately cross another small log bridge over the main South Boulder Creek. Continue hiking along the south side of the creek. After a short while, you switchback to the left, away from the creek. Here, in late spring or early summer, you'll encounter snowdrifts. The Forest Service requires everyone to hike through the snowdrifts and water so the trail is not further eroded.

After about 15 minutes, cross the next bridge and go through a site often used for camping. Walk across the wet area on the other side and continue. This is the last bridge, and the remainder of the trail is extremely wet. As hikers approach 11,000 feet, the trees start to thin and most people will have significant shortness of breath. The trees open up here and hikers are rewarded by stunning alpine scenery; Haystack Mountain and James Peak are to the left. Take a right at the fork to Heart Lake and the trail will continue uphill to the namesake lake. At Heart Lake, turn around and trace the route back to the trailhead. Going left will take hikers to Rogers Pass Lake and the Continental Divide.

# WALKER RANCH: MEYERS HOMESTEAD TRAIL

## ▶ IN BRIEF

Walker Ranch has two popular hikes, and Meyers Homestead Trail is definitely the laid-back sibling of the Walker Ranch Loop. This peaceful hike travels along a spacious fire road through aspens, meadows, and ponderosas. It even travels back in time, passing by an old homestead. A jogging stroller glides right along and gives Mom and Dad quite a workout, thanks to a gradual climb that gets the blood flowing.

## ▶ DESCRIPTION

Leave the parking area and head toward the trailhead, which is marked by a kiosk. The trail descends slowly and empties into an open meadow before descending again and emptying into a smaller meadow. To the left is the old Meyers Homestead and the trail's namesake. Colorado homesteaders staked their claim here in the late 1800s. This high-country valley would have looked much the same, yet would have been considered quite rugged since most Colorado settlements were not yet thriving.

A small stream follows along the left of the trail, which begins a gentle ascent. You may see deer that find shelter and forage in the willow and aspen trees that border the stream. A hill on the right is covered with large boulders, sparse ponderosa pines, and wildflowers. Cross a culvert and continue climbing. After 1 mile the trail reaches an intersection with an old fire road. Continue straight.

Follow the trail as it roller-coasters up and down the gully that has been carved by the stream.

## ▶ DIRECTIONS

From Denver, take I-25 north to US 36 to Baseline Road in Boulder, go left. Take Baseline Road west until it turns into Flagstaff Road. Travel 5.5 miles total from US 36 to Walker Ranch trailhead on the right.

## ⓘ KEY AT-A-GLANCE INFORMATION

**LENGTH:** 5 miles

**CONFIGURATION:** Out-and-back

**DIFFICULTY:** Moderate

**SCENERY:** Open meadow, old homestead, stream; scattered aspen trees, willow trees, and ponderosa pines

**EXPOSURE:** Partial shade, mostly exposed

**TRAFFIC:** Heavy

**TRAIL SURFACE:** Dirt, sandy

**HIKING TIME:** 2.5 hours

**SEASON:** All year

**ACCESS:** Free; open sunrise to sunset

**MAPS:** USGS Eldorado Springs

**FACILITIES:** Picnic area, restrooms

**SPECIAL COMMENTS:** Leash law for dogs is strictly enforced; tickets are issued for noncompliance. Boulder County Open Space provides loaner leashes at the trailhead. Self-serve fee stations are all the way up Flagstaff Road, but no fee is required at Walker Ranch. No motorized vehicles. Meyers Homestead Trail can be crowded with mountain bike traffic, but not as crowded as neighboring Walker Ranch Loop.

**Walker Ranch: Meyers Homestead Trail**

**UTM Zone (WGS84)  13S**

**Easting   471130**

**Northing  4422910**

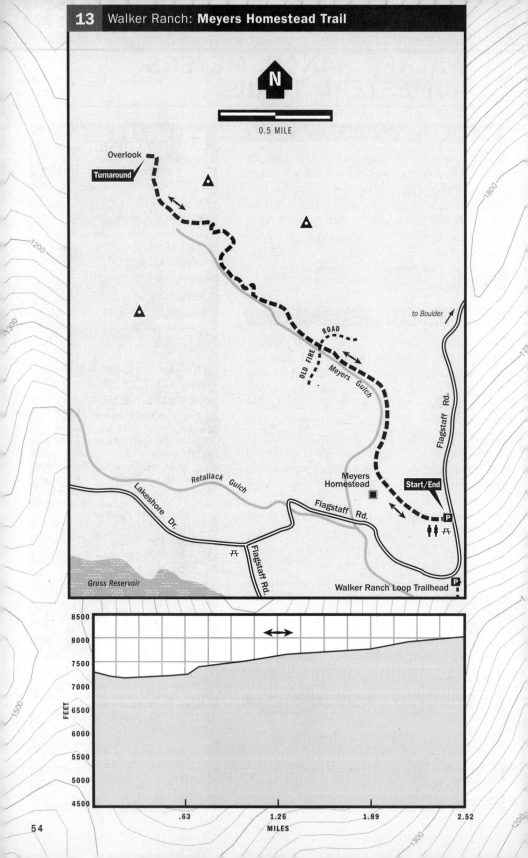

N

0.5 MILE

Overlook

Turnaround

to Boulder

OLD FIRE ROAD

Meyers Gulch

Flagstaff Rd.

Retallack Gulch

Lakeshore Dr.

Meyers Homestead

Start/End

Flagstaff Rd.

Flagstaff Rd.

Gross Reservoir

Walker Ranch Loop Trailhead

8500
8000
7500
7000
6500
6000
5500
5000
4500

FEET

.63   1.26   1.89   2.52

MILES

Trees bear the weight of a new snow along the Meyers Homestead Trail. The path has remarkably kept clear—just a little wet—and attests to the warmth of the earth.

Loose rocks and tree roots begin to appear on the trail, but it is still spacious and sandy. Smaller streams and tributaries meet up with the larger stream that follows the trail.

The trail becomes steeper and exposed. Pass a steep hillside and an aspen forest, then enter into a large meadow 2 miles into the hike. This broad, green meadow is filled with wildflowers and wild grasses. To the left is another small stream lined with aspens and willows. The trail climbs through the meadow and reaches a crest in the hill. From here, you can look north and east to Boulder.

Continue as the trail curves west into the rocks and trees. Reach a saddle that signifies the end of the trail. The overlook at trail's end points to views of Sugarloaf Mountain and the Indian Peaks and further to views of Longs Peak. Turn around here and retrace the route back to the trailhead.

## ▶ NEARBY ATTRACTIONS

All Walker Ranch Trails and Eldorado Canyon Trails: City of Boulder Open Space and Mountain Parks. Visit **www.osmp.org**.

# WALKER RANCH:
# WALKER RANCH LOOP

## KEY AT-A-GLANCE INFORMATION

**LENGTH:** 7.66 miles

**CONFIGURATION:** Loop

**DIFFICULTY:** Difficult

**SCENERY:** Meadows, aspen groves, ponderosa pines, Douglas firs, South Boulder Creek

**EXPOSURE:** Mostly shaded

**TRAFFIC:** Heavy

**TRAIL SURFACE:** Dirt, loose rocks, extremely rocky in places

**HIKING TIME:** 4.5 hours

**SEASON:** April–October

**ACCESS:** Free; open sunrise to sunset

**MAPS:** USGS Eldorado Springs; maps at trailhead

**FACILITIES:** Information kiosk, portable toilet

**SPECIAL COMMENTS:** Dogs must be leashed. Self-serve fee stations are along Flagstaff Road, but no fee is required at Walker Ranch. The loop can be done either way, but for this hike it is counterclockwise. No motorized vehicles. Walker Ranch is crowded with mountain bikes on the weekends and after work on weekdays.

Walker Ranch: Walker Ranch Loop

UTM Zone (WGS84)   13S

Easting   471180

Northing   4422180

## IN BRIEF

The spectacular drive up Flagstaff Road, popular with Boulder cyclists, is only a hint of the amazing views, plentiful wildflowers, and fishing at Walker Ranch. The loop takes hikers around the old homestead of James Walker and along South Boulder Creek.

## DESCRIPTION

From the trailhead, step over the gate and bear right onto Walker Ranch Loop Trail. It descends through 168 acres of recent wildfire burn area: The scorched ground is covered with small, green regrowth and charred pine trees stripped of all greenery. The smooth dirt trail traverses open hillside. Start a long decent. Follow an old road and pass several boulders on the right. Plenty of erosion-control berms assist steep staircase conditions.

Although this is a popular trail, deer appear all year. Other frequent spottings include mountain lions and bears. At the bottom of the hill, cross a small creek that flows during all seasons. Immediately after the creek, the trail levels out. Follow South Boulder Creek, which also seems to always have a healthy water flow. You'll find a picnic area next to the creek, sheltered by large trees.

Pass noticeable South Boulder Creek rapids and small waterfalls. The trail is in a small canyon here with a lot of condensed groups of boulders and a cliff. Take a left at the bridge that crosses the creek and pass a sign directing hikers to stay on Walker Ranch Loop Trail. Climb for 400 yards on a steep trail, then gradually ascend on hard-packed

## DIRECTIONS

From Denver, take I-25 north to US 36 to Baseline Road in Boulder. Take a left on Baseline Road, going west until it turns into Flagstaff Road. Travel 6 miles to the Walker Ranch trailhead on the left.

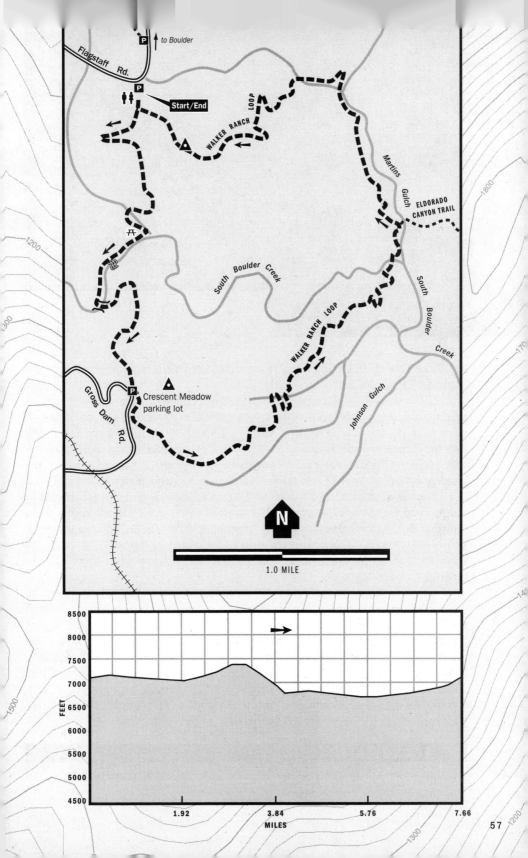

to Boulder

Flagstaff Rd.

Start/End

WALKER RANCH LOOP

Martins Gulch

ELDORADO CANYON TRAIL

South Boulder Creek

South Boulder Creek

WALKER RANCH LOOP

Johnson Gulch

Gross Dam Rd.

Crescent Meadow
parking lot

N

1.0 MILE

8500
8000
7500
7000
6500
6000
5500
5000
4500

FEET

1.92        3.84        5.76        7.66

MILES

Walker Ranch poses many challenges, but this crooked staircase makes a harrowing descent navigable.

dirt. After a steady 0.5-mile ascent, take a right. The trail is more forgiving here and levels out for a short time.

Continue to hike through the same mix of ponderosa pines and Douglas firs that are common on this trail. A few aspen groves help break up the mix. The trail starts to go up, up, and up again. It narrows, but is still hard-packed and easy to follow. You'll come to a dirt road that parallels the trail; continue on the trail. Pass Crescent Meadows Parking Lot off Gross Dam Road. Bear left at the little spur to the parking lot. Off to the right you can see Gross Dam and a great view of Indian Peaks.

The trail crosses open meadows with views to the east of the plains framed by Eldorado Springs State Park. Continue as the trail enters dense forest. Begin a slight downhill trek, which turns into a steep downhill quickly. The trail descends continuously for 1.5 miles down to South Boulder Creek. This long descent is broken up by a few flat stretches and eventually ends with a steep descent via a giant staircase made of rock and log steps.

Continue down the harrowing, man-made stairs, reach the creek, and begin to walk downstream. Climb a dozen stairs up over a rockslide. Drama is the only word for this portion of the hike, since South Boulder Creek runs wild with its roaring rapids and subsequent noise echoing through the canyon. Cross a large bridge and the trail will ascend and look more like a service road. Continue straight, passing a turnoff for Eldorado Canyon Trail on the right. Take a left onto the single-track trail and reenter the forest. The trail switchbacks and eventually emerges on an arid, shrub-filled ridge top. A short trail on the left leads to an overlook; the main trail goes right, along the ridge top. Follow this back to the parking area.

## ▶ NEARBY ATTRACTIONS

All Walker Ranch Trails and Eldorado Canyon Trails: City of Boulder Open Space and Mountain Parks. Visit **www.osmp.org.**

# DENVER
## *Including Foothills and Mountains*

# ALDERFER THREE SISTERS OPEN SPACE PARK: PONDEROSA SISTERS LOOP

## KEY AT-A-GLANCE INFORMATION

**LENGTH:** 3 miles

**CONFIGURATION:** Double loop

**DIFFICULTY:** Moderate

**SCENERY:** Open, marshy meadow; boulder fields, forest

**EXPOSURE:** Exposed in meadow, shady in other areas

**TRAFFIC:** Moderate

**TRAIL SURFACE:** Dirt, loose rocks

**HIKING TIME:** 1.75 hours

**SEASON:** All year

**ACCESS:** Free; open one hour before sunrise to one hour after sunset

**MAPS:** USGS Evergreen, Conifer

**FACILITIES:** Picnic table, restrooms

**SPECIAL COMMENTS:** Dogs must be leashed at all times. Collection of wildflowers or other natural resources is prohibited. Bears and mountain lions have been seen on this trail and users must report any sightings to Open Space Rangers or call Jefferson County Natural Resources at (303) 271-5993.

Alderfer Three Sisters Open Space Park: Ponderosa Sisters Loop

UTM Zone (WGS84)   13S

Easting   469150

Northing   4385750

## ▶ IN BRIEF

Alderfer Three Sisters Open Space Park boasts 770 acres of open land. Ever since Evergreen was settled, the four rock formations called the Three Sisters and The Brother have been landmarks, providing views of the Bear Creek Basin and Mount Evans. More than 10 miles of trail lead hikers around the Three Sisters and up to The Brother. The Ponderosa Sisters Loop is a great way to take a cursory look at this mountain park.

## ▶ DESCRIPTION

Head out of the parking lot and take a right onto Bluebird Meadow Trail as it curves eastward past an old barn by the trailhead. The trail travels through open meadow, which is grassy and marsh-like in early summer. Reach the Bluebird Meadow and Silver Fox trail crossing and turn left onto Silver Fox Trail.

Pass the Homestead Trail crossing, but continue straight on Silver Fox. As the trail curves east through the meadow, you see your first views of the Three Sisters. Pass another Homestead Trail crossing and continue straight on Silver Fox.

At the intersection of Ponderosa and Silver Fox trails, go left on Ponderosa Trail, leaving the meadow for ponderosa pine and woodland forest. Travel 0.2 miles to the intersection of Ponderosa and Sisters trails. Take a left on Sisters Trail (full of loose rocks, sand, and exposed tree roots). The next 1.3 miles are the most difficult of this hike.

## ▶ DIRECTIONS

From Denver, take I-70 west to Evergreen Parkway (CO 74). Go left, traveling south on CO 74 to Evergreen. Turn right onto CO 73, then turn right at the stoplight onto Buffalo Park Road. Take Buffalo Park Road 2.3 miles to the trailhead and parking lot on the right, just before reaching Le Masters Road.

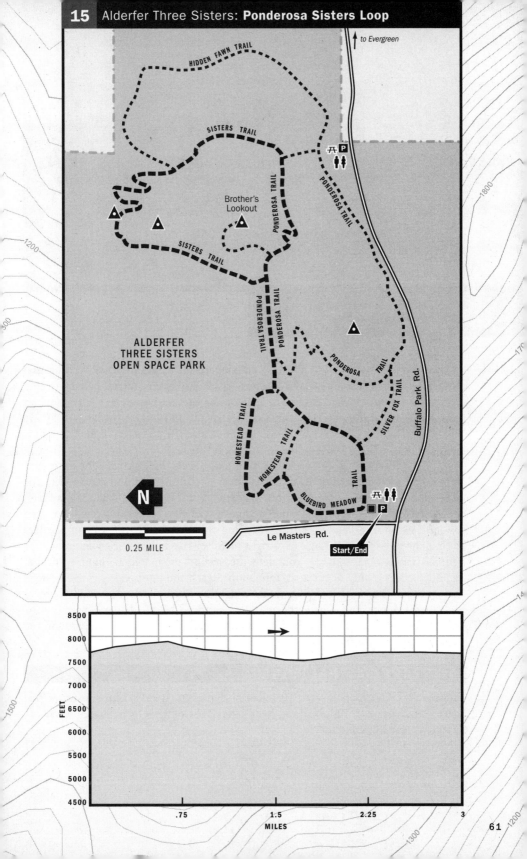

to Evergreen

HIDDEN FAWN TRAIL

SISTERS TRAIL

Brother's
Lookout

PONDEROSA TRAIL

PONDEROSA TRAIL

SISTERS TRAIL

ALDERFER
THREE SISTERS
OPEN SPACE PARK

PONDEROSA TRAIL

PONDEROSA TRAIL

PONDEROSA
TRAIL

Buffalo Park Rd.

SILVER FOX TRAIL

HOMESTEAD TRAIL

HOMESTEAD TRAIL

BLUEBIRD MEADOW TRAIL

**N**

0.25 MILE

Le Masters Rd.

**Start/End**

61

Looking out across the meadow to a rock formation at the Ponderosa Sisters Loop trailhead and parking lot

Cut straight across the hillside and prepare for a series of switchbacks that travel between the second and third sisters. Reach a saddle in the trail after the long ascent and look out toward Evergreen Lake on the left and Evergreen High School on the right. After cresting the hill, the hike is a steady and forgiving downhill. Sisters Trail intersects with Hidden Fawn Trail; continue straight on Sisters Trail. The trail is flanked by quaking aspen trees and low, thick brush.

At the intersection of Ponderosa Trail and Sisters Trail, go straight onto Ponderosa Trail and climb three distinct switchbacks. The Brother and a turnoff to the Brother's Lookout are to the right, but stay straight on Ponderosa Trail. Pass a familiar intersection with Sisters Trail and Ponderosa Trail after completing one loop, then continue straight on Ponderosa trail, retracing old trail. At the intersection of Silver Fox Trail and Homestead Trail, take a right on Silver Fox Trail and then an immediate right on Homestead Trail. To complete the second loop, follow Homestead Trail around the north side of the rock formation. Reach the intersection of Homestead Trail and Bluebird Meadow Trail and take a right on Bluebird Meadow Trail. Follow it back into the meadow, where the trail is comprised of wooden walkways in the wettest portions. Come out at the far end of the parking lot, or continue around the split-rail fence to the trailhead.

## ▶ NEARBY ATTRACTIONS

There are 14 hiking trails with 10 miles of hiking in Alderfer Three Sisters Open Space Park; for more information, visit Jefferson County Open Space, **www.co. jefferson.co.us/openspace.**

# BARR LAKE STATE PARK: LAKE PERIMETER TRAIL

The Lake Perimeter Trail at Barr Lake offers a rare opportunity to explore a major prairie reservoir in Colorado. The lake is lined with cottonwoods, marshes, and aquatic plants. Its southern half has been designated as a wildlife refuge to shelter animals and birds, including the 350 species of birds that have been spotted here.

▶ **DESCRIPTION**

Turn right out of the parking lot and the area around the Barr Lake Nature Center. The trail begins 100 yards from the lake, and it was muddy when we hiked in late fall. Cottonwood trees provide some shade in the morning and complete shade in the afternoon. Along with cottonwood trees, irrigation ditches line the trail, and two such ditches are found to the left and right of the trailhead. The trail starts counterclockwise from the nature center, and the mile markers are for those traveling the other direction on the Pioneer Trail to the wildlife observation station and gazebo on the lake.

You see houses at the beginning of the trail, but they disappear as prairie meadows and cottonwood trees take over all line of sight. Early in the trail, hikers may encounter horseback riders and mountain bikers. Continue to a parking area (for boat-ramp users) and a gate; cross the paved road and go through the gate on the other side. The dam comes into view across the lake. Continue around to the east. At the northeast corner of the

## KEY AT-A-GLANCE INFORMATION

**LENGTH:** 9.2 miles

**CONFIGURATION:** Loop

**DIFFICULTY:** Easy

**SCENERY:** Lake, prairie, cottonwoods, dam, and irrigation ditches

**EXPOSURE:** Shaded in cottonwoods, open and exposed in other areas

**TRAFFIC:** Mild

**TRAIL SURFACE:** Paved, dirt

**HIKING TIME:** 4.5 hours

**SEASON:** All year, muddy in shoulder seasons

**ACCESS:** $5 or Colorado State Park Pass, open one hour before dawn to one hour after dusk

**MAPS:** USGS Brighton and Mile High Lakes

**FACILITIES:** Pay phone, restrooms, nature center, ranger station; picnic areas with tables and grills

**SPECIAL COMMENTS:** Pets are not permitted because of their restriction in the wildlife refuge. No swimming or wading; boating is permitted. Collecting living or dead plants, wood, or animals (wildlife and insects) is prohibited. However, fishing and waterfowl hunting is permitted. Thorns line the trail, so sturdy shoes are recommended. Irrigation companies use the trail; hikers are asked to yield right of way to their personnel and equipment.

▶ **DIRECTIONS**

From Denver, take I-76 northeast to the Bromley Lane exit. Take a left, going east on Picadilly Road, then another left, going south to the park entrance. Follow the paved road from the ranger station to the nature center and the trailhead.

**Barr Lake State Park:
Lake Perimeter Trail**

**UTM Zone (WGS84)  13S**

**Easting  521280**

**Northing  4420610**

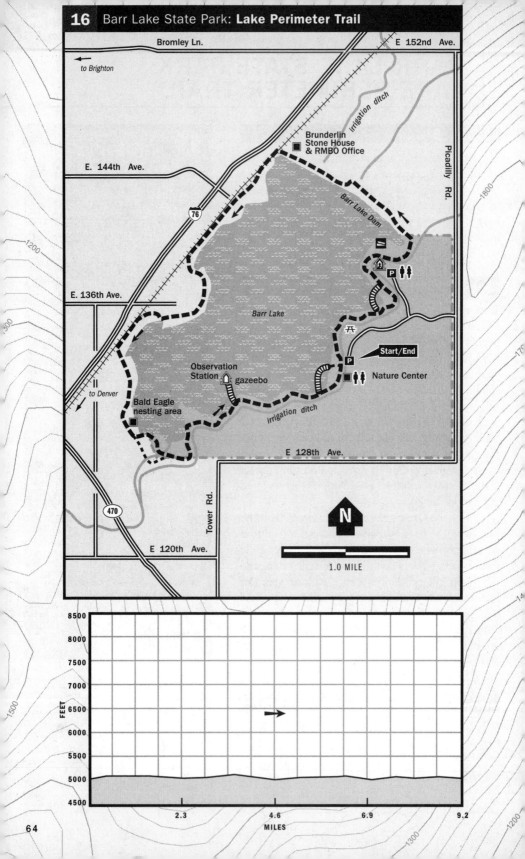

lake is a big sign that says the lake is 8.8 miles around. Go left here and follow the dirt road that travels to the back of the dam.

At this point, the grass-covered dam is to the left and elevated about 10 feet above the trail. On the right is an irrigated field, but no other signs of civilization are visible here.

Pass mile marker 7 and continue to pass these mile markers going backward. Due to the unique views and ease of the trail, they seem to go by rather quickly. Cross an irrigation ditch where the water exits the reservoir. Numbered blinds for bird hunting line the trail.

Continue left up the dam on the Barr Lake Crest Trail. The hill is steep for 100 yards, but it deposits hikers directly onto the top of the dam. The trails run parallel at this point, one on the top and the other on the bottom to the right. From here you see views of the mountains, including, most prominently, Longs Peak.

The upper and lower trails merge at the northwest part of the dam. Pass the Bruderlin Stone House and the Rocky Mountain Bird Observatory office. Veer left, continue along the lake, and travel alongside I-76 with its traffic noise. There is a gate and private property to the left and the trail veers to the right of that, with barbed wire on both sides. The western side of the lake is the Wildlife Refuge, which does not have as much traffic as the other side. The trail, which is double-track dirt with low grasses on either side, runs about 0.25 miles from the lake. Go through an opening in the fence, cross the road, and enter the gate on the other side. Continue on an old double track along train tracks to the right.

While the trail is flat, various thorns have collected and are quite dense here. Continue along the lake and take a left before the next gate. Bear left down a small hill toward the lake. Continue straight, behind a dozen homes, some with horses in back. The trail takes a sharp right after the last house.

There are quite a few marshes along the trail and to the right is a cattle pasture and a bald eagle nesting area. Warning signs advise all trail users to stay out.

Take a left at an intersection of the trail and the main road; do not go straight on the main road. The trail is now a well-maintained gravel walking path. This area of the reservoir is a little more active, with more bald eagles and more signs of human life. Cross the bridge over a large irrigation ditch and continue as the trail rejoins a service road. Go left; pass the gazebo and boardwalk on the lake used for wildlife viewing. Pass another observation area and head back to the parking lot.

### ▶ NEARBY ATTRACTIONS

The Gazebo Trail (or Pioneer Trail) is a shorter (3 miles) trail at Barr Lake. For more information: **www.parks.state.co.us.**

# BEAR CREEK LAKE PARK: BEAR CREEK TRAIL

 **KEY AT·A·GLANCE INFORMATION**

**LENGTH:** 4.42 miles

**CONFIGURATION:** Balloon

**DIFFICULTY:** Easy

**SCENERY:** Bear Creek, Bear Creek Reservoir, plains, riparian ecosystem

**EXPOSURE:** Mostly shaded

**TRAFFIC:** Heavy in spots

**TRAIL SURFACE:** Hard-packed dirt, paved in portions

**HIKING TIME:** 2 hours

**SEASON:** All year

**ACCESS:** Free; May–Labor Day, 6 a.m–10 p.m.; April and October, 7 a.m.–8 p.m.; November–March, 8 a.m.–6 p.m.

**MAPS:** USGS Morrison

**FACILITIES:** Visitor center, marina, 50 picnic sites, restrooms, 4 reservable park shelters, 50 campsites

**SPECIAL COMMENTS:** This trail starts outside the Bear Creek Lake Park, but if hikers choose to start inside the park, there are entrance fees. A general daily pass is $4 and an annual pass is $40. Dogs must be leashed. Dogs may not swim in the creeks or lakes within the park.

Bear Creek Lake Park: Bear Creek Trail

UTM Zone (WGS84)   13S

Easting   484330

Northing   4389040

## IN BRIEF

The 2,500 acres of prime real estate that make up Bear Creek Lake Park have all the makings of an urban hideaway. Located in Lakewood, just southwest of Denver, Bear Creek Lake Park sits at the base of the foothills. Its grassy dam catches the waters of both Bear and Turkey creeks. Bear Creek Trail follows Bear Creek and winds through giant cottonwoods and across arid prairie without any telltale urban signs. Remote sounds from nearby roads are the only hint that civilization is close by.

## DESCRIPTION

Leave the parking area and cross Morrison Road to the start of the Bear Creek Trail, which is concrete here and perpendicular to Morrison Road. Immediately take a left, start through the canopied river basin, and walk parallel to Bear Creek. Walk through the entrance of Bear Creek Lake Park and pass the ranger station. Since you parked outside the park and foot traffic is not regulated, you don't have to pay.

Follow the entrance road until it intersects with a trail right before Skunk Hollow. Go left and begin to head toward Bear Creek Reservoir. There is no sign here, but the trail is obvious.

Reach the intersection of Owl Trail and Visitors Center Trail and take a left onto Owl Trail. Pass the Owl Trail marking posts with the owl silhouettes and numbers.

Travel along the river and stay on the south bank, even though bridges cross Bear Creek via side trails. A horse trail, the Fitness Loop, and the Owl Trail all converge at a crossroads. Continue straight and pass a trail that goes up over the ridge.

## DIRECTIONS

From Denver, take C 470 south to the Morrison Road/CO 8 exit. Park across from the Conoco Break Place just after exiting C 470.

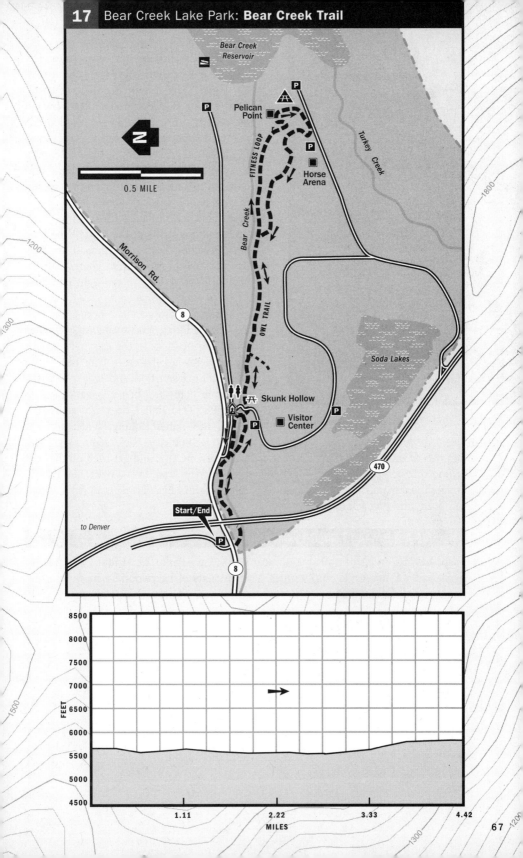

Bear Creek
Reservoir

P

Pelican
Point

P

Horse
Arena

FITNESS LOOP

Bear Creek

Turkey Creek

N

0.5 MILE

Morrison Rd.

8

OWL TRAIL

Soda Lakes

Skunk Hollow

Visitor
Center

P

470

Start/End

to Denver

P

8

1200

1300

1500

1800

1300

1200

**FEET**

8500
8000
7500
7000
6500
6000
5500
5000
4500

1.11          2.22          3.33          4.42

**MILES**

A swollen Bear Creek, evidence of the namesake that flows along part of the Bear Creek Trail.

Bear Creek Reservoir comes into view as trail begins to veer away from the roar of Bear Creek. The terrain is still river basin, but the trail is wider and flanked by tall grasses. The dirt is less compact and loosens up into a sandlike consistency. Travel up a hill, leaving the river completely, and enter a semiarid landscape. Go around a bend and come out to a newly constructed picnic shelter with deluxe beach volleyball and horseshoes. This area, called Pelican Point, is the 2-mile mark and sits at the base of the Bear Creek Reservoir Dam and its small overflow lake. The trail passes Pelican Point and then makes a large U-turn to the right and continues, passing a horse arena.

After you cross a small bridge, the trail parallels road for a short while. At 2.85 miles and an obvious fork in the trail, take a right turn back toward the creek bed. Follow the pedestrian-marked trail and take a left. Hit the 3-mile point and begin to backtrack on the familiar Owl Trail. Go straight across the road to the Skunk Hollow Picnic area. Do not turn right and go back to the ranger station. Go through the parking lot, pass a covered picnic site, and get back on the trail behind the picnic grills. Reach the concrete Bear Creek Trail, take a right, and cross a bridge. Immediately take a left, head back to the start of Bear Creek Trail, cross Morrison Road, and go back to the car.

## ▶ NEARBY ATTRACTIONS

There are 15.7 miles of trails within Bear Creek Lake Park. The Mount Carbon Loop is the park's longest hike at 6.9 miles. Visit the City of Lakewood for more information: **www.lakewood.org.**

# DEER CREEK OPEN SPACE PARK:
## MEADOWLARK PLYMOUTH CREEK LOOP

## ▶ IN BRIEF

Deer Creek Canyon has a good mix and 12.2 miles of multiuse trails, but the Hiker Only options are what really attract pedestrians. This is a popular location, close to Denver with access all year, and it can be quite crowded with mountain bikes. No bikes are allowed on the Meadowlark Trail, where hikers can enjoy a gradual climb, sunny exposure, southern views of Denver, and views of the Dear Creek valley.

## ▶ DESCRIPTION

Leave the abundant facilities at the trailhead and go right. Take an immediate left onto Meadowlark Trail and follow the Hiker Only signs. Pass through Rattlesnake Gulch and its sage scrub and prairie grasses as the trail begins to climb at a steady 10 percent grade. Look east and northeast at new luxury homes and a Lockheed Martin campus.

Travel through two switchbacks and the trail opens to views west, up Deer Creek Canyon. Looking west, it is eerie to think that Colorado's most famous cannibal, Alfred Packard, lived and worked his last years in this area.

The trail has ascended for 1 mile and now roller-coasters up and down with plenty of flat sections in between. The trail is cut into the hillside and comes close to the edge many times, so steady footing is required.

Continue onto the backside of the scrubby hillside and the trail again reaches the east-facing

## ℹ KEY AT-A-GLANCE INFORMATION

**LENGTH:** 2.5 miles

**CONFIGURATION:** Loop

**DIFFICULTY:** Moderate

**SCENERY:** Foothills, meadows, scrubby hillside, forest, stream; views of Denver and Deer Creek Valley

**EXPOSURE:** Exposed on Meadowlark Trail and last portion of Plymouth Creek; lush sections on rest of Plymouth Creek

**TRAFFIC:** Heavy

**TRAIL SURFACE:** Smooth and hard-packed dirt; loose rocks

**HIKING TIME:** 1.5 hours

**SEASON:** All year

**ACCESS:** Free; open sunrise to sunset

**MAPS:** USGS Indian Hills

**FACILITIES:** Restrooms (handicap accessible), covered picnic tables, pay phone, drinking water

**SPECIAL COMMENTS:** Dogs permitted, but must be leashed. Dog refuse pick-up bags provided at trailhead. This Jefferson County trail is Hiker Only on Meadowlark Trail portion.

## ▶ DIRECTIONS

From Denver, take C-470 south 6.7 miles to Kipling Parkway, exit south. Go right on West Ute Avenue and turn right again on Deer Creek Canyon Road. Follow Deer Creek Canyon Road west 2.7 miles to Grizzly Road. Turn left on Grizzly Road and follow it 0.4 miles to the park entrance on the right.

**Deer Creek Open Space Park:**
**Meadowlark Plymouth Creek Loop**

**UTM Zone (WGS84)   13S**

**Easting   486840**

**Northing   4376880**

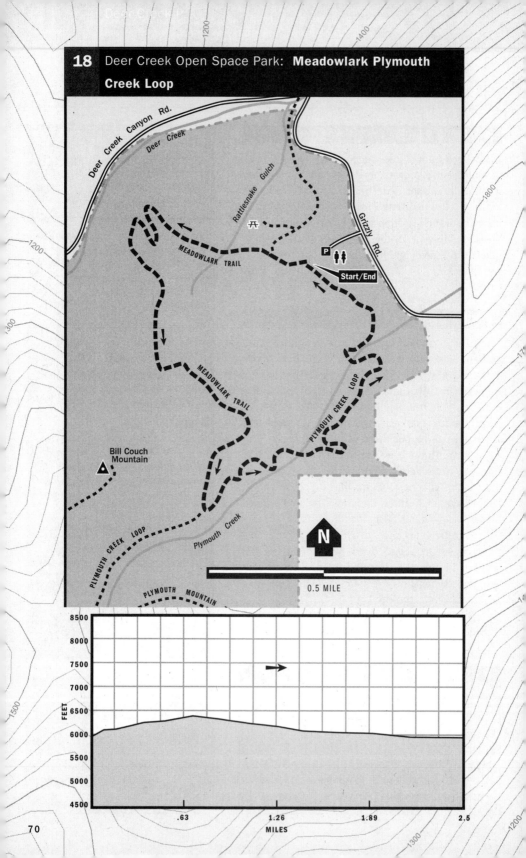

**18** Deer Creek Open Space Park: **Meadowlark Plymouth Creek Loop**

Deer Creek Canyon Rd.

Deer Creek

Rattlesnake Gulch

Grizzly Rd.

P

Start/End

MEADOWLARK TRAIL

MEADOWLARK TRAIL

Bill Couch
Mountain

PLYMOUTH CREEK LOOP

PLYMOUTH CREEK LOOP

Plymouth Creek

PLYMOUTH MOUNTAIN

N

0.5 MILE

slopes. There, it crosses the southeast face of the mountainside with views of the southern plains, downtown Denver, and the hogback.

Traverse two ravines and descend to a bridge in a lush, pine-shaded valley. At the intersections of Meadowlark Trail and Plymouth Creek Loop, take a left and begin a steady descent. The trail is wide and steep with loose rocks as it follows Plymouth Creek. Although mountain bikers are permitted here, they must travel up this steep, technical section and prove no space challenge to hikers.

The trail skirts the south side of the ravine as you cross through three switchbacks and head northeast. The trail travels up and down along the edge of hillside, eventually leading back to the southern side of the trailhead.

## ▶ NEARBY ATTRACTIONS

South Valley Park, 6.9 miles of trails (Swallow Trail is Hiker Only): **www.co. jefferson.co.us/openspace.**

# DENVER: WASHINGTON PARK

## KEY AT-A-GLANCE INFORMATION

**LENGTH:** 2 miles

**CONFIGURATION:** Loop

**DIFFICULTY:** Easy

**SCENERY:** Urban park with mature trees, lakes

**EXPOSURE:** Mostly shaded

**TRAFFIC:** Heavy

**TRAIL SURFACE:** Dirt, concrete, grass, and asphalt

**HIKING TIME:** 45 minutes

**SEASON:** All year

**ACCESS:** Free; open 6 a.m.–11 p.m.

**MAPS:** USGS Englewood

**FACILITIES:** Restrooms, picnic facilities, tennis courts, basketball courts, recreation center, pay phone, playgrounds, lawn-bowling park, boating, fitness course, fishing, soccer field, boathouse pavilion, youth fishing pond, flower gardens, and croquet park

**SPECIAL COMMENTS:** Dogs must be leashed and you must pick up all waste. Be aware of your urban surroundings and watch out for vehicle traffic. Be aware of other dogs. Pit bulls are not allowed in the Denver city limits. Washington Park is host to many public events, so check a Denver newspaper or Web site before heading out, which will save the headache of hiking during a crowded festival.

Denver: Washington Park

UTM Zone (WGS84)   13S

Easting   502650

Northing   4394210

## IN BRIEF

Washington Park, known as Wash Park to locals, is an urban haven for fitness enthusiasts. Along with its proximity in the South Denver Park District, it is home to amazing facilities, National Historic Landmark park buildings, and an easy hike. Take in this hike on an early weekend morning and then treat yourself to a stroll through the beautiful neighborhoods that surround Wash Park.

## DESCRIPTION

Leave your parking space and find a spot on the Wash Park trail just before Kentucky Avenue. Once you've oriented yourself, travel north along the crushed-granite path that outlines Wash Park. You may also travel along the shoulder of the asphalt road that follows along the Wash Park trail. The trail is well maintained and surrounded by manicured grass. Continue to walk through the large cottonwood and maple trees and pass the maintenance facility at 820 South Humble Street. Pass older park buildings to the left and coveted Wash Park bungalow homes to the right. An old wagon with big red wheels sits along the trail, hinting at Denver's pioneer beginnings. Stay on the path around the park as it alternates between asphalt and crushed gravel.

Pass the Washington Park recreation building on the left and soon start a counterclockwise

## DIRECTIONS

From Denver, take I-25 south to the South University Boulevard exit and go left, traveling north through the Washington Park neighborhood. Turn left (west) on Mississippi Avenue. Turn right on Franklin Street, which is the east boundary of Washington Park, and park in this vicinity. The starting point is 2 blocks north, near Kentucky Avenue, which is perpendicular to South Franklin Street.

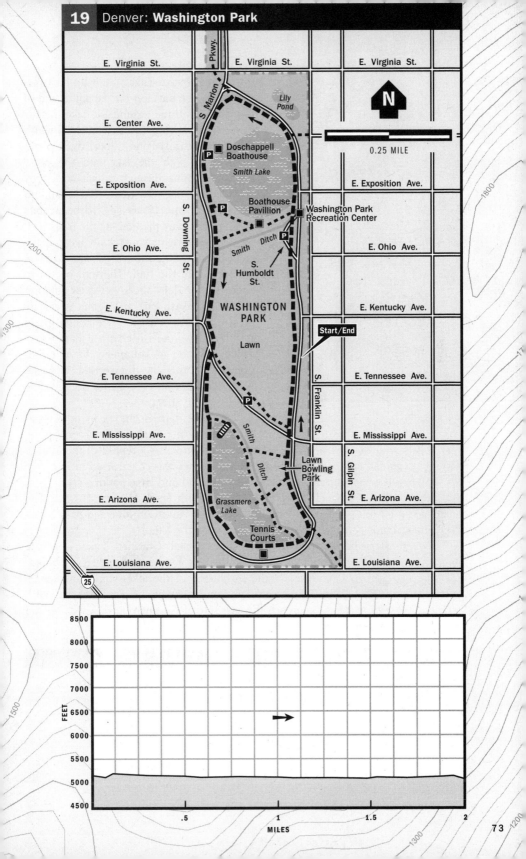

E. Virginia St.

E. Virginia St.

E. Virginia St.

S Marion Pkwy.

Lily Pond

**N**

0.25 MILE

E. Center Ave.

Doschappell Boathouse

Smith Lake

E. Exposition Ave.

E. Exposition Ave.

S. Downing St.

Boathouse Pavilion

Washington Park Recreation Center

E. Ohio Ave.

Smith Ditch

E. Ohio Ave.

S. Humboldt St.

**WASHINGTON PARK**

E. Kentucky Ave.

E. Kentucky Ave.

Lawn

Start/End

E. Tennessee Ave.

E. Tennessee Ave.

S. Franklin St.

E. Mississippi Ave.

E. Mississippi Ave.

Smith Ditch

Lawn Bowling Park

S. Gilpin St.

E. Arizona Ave.

Grassmere Lake

E. Arizona Ave.

Tennis Courts

E. Louisiana Ave.

E. Louisiana Ave.

25

FEET

8500
8000
7500
7000
6500
6000
5500
5000
4500

.5          1          1.5          2
**MILES**

Weekend warriors, busy along the ponds, grass, and trails in Washington Park.

trip around Smith Lake. You'll find a large, old boathouse pavilion on the south end of the lake. Continue around the lake. Across the street from the northeast side is a youth fishing pond (Lily Pond). Local duck populations call both the lake and the pond home. Continue through a shaded canopy provided by large pine trees. Hikers can find old stone picnic tables and barbecue pits here, or most any place along the trail.

On the right, you pass a large apartment building and a memorial statue that is set back from the trail. The trail begins to curve to the left once you pass another entrance to Wash Park at Virginia Street. Its surface is more consistently dirt and gravel as hikers pass the Doschappell Bathhouse, which is home to Volunteers for Outdoor Colorado. Pass the intersection and the Wash Park entrance of Exposition Avenue and Downing Street.

On the right is one of 54 flower gardens within the park's 165 acres. Spring color begins with iris and peonies. Near the large garden is a replica of the Martha Washington garden at Mt. Vernon, Virginia. The replica was constructed in 1926.

Follow the bend as it curves left to a playground and large parking area. Cross over a small irrigation canal that is part of the Smith Ditch Historic District. The canal packs a lot of history as it flows through Wash Park. Continue and pass horseshoe courts, tennis courts, and basketball courts on the left.

Soon the trail begins to border a larger city lake: Grasmere Lake. Continue along its perimeter in a counterclockwise motion. On your immediate left is a boardwalk that extends over the lake. At the south end of the lake, you'll find tennis courts, the Wash Park Tennis Club, bathrooms, and a pay phone. Pass over the Smith Ditch one more time as you approach the east side of Grasmere Lake. Cross Mississippi Avenue and venture back to the car or into the park.

## ▶ NEARBY ATTRACTIONS

Denver parks, shopping, restaurants and attractions: **www.denvergov.org**
Washington Park Recreation Center: (303) 698-4962.

# ELK MEADOW OPEN SPACE PARK: SLEEPY S LOOP

## ▶ IN BRIEF

As the name suggests, Elk Meadow's trail system is home to elk and deer. Hiking the Sleepy S Loop almost guarantees deer sightings. Perhaps it's the secluded pine forest or the meadow and mountain views that attracts the deer and sometimes the elk. Either way, it's a beautiful place to call home and a beautiful place for a moderate hike.

## ▶ DESCRIPTION

Start in the parking lot and go right onto Meadow View Trail as it climbs gently to the northeast. The wide, dirt trail is well maintained and flanked on both sides by erosion-control railway ties. Pass a picnic table directly to the right. A staircase to the left leads to a hidden picnic area.

Keep moving on Meadow View Trail and pass a restroom on the left. These facilities are a small hike from the trailhead.

The trail ascends and starts a roller coaster before leveling out. After 0.3 miles, take a right on the Sleepy S Trail as it intersects with Meadow View Trail. Start a gradual descent and pass covered picnic tables and benches scattered about.

The trail takes a large curve to the left and continues to descend before it levels out a little and begins to climb again. Pass through shady ponderosa pine trees. Once the trail reaches the grassland and the views, you will see the intersection of Sleepy S Trail and Elk Ridge Trail. Take a left onto Elk Ridge Trail, which ascends gradually into ponderosa pine tree stands, switchbacks a few times, and continues to climb. Continue up, up, up at a steady pace for 0.5 miles.

## ▶ DIRECTIONS

From Denver, take I-70 west to Evergreen Parkway (CO 74). Go left, traveling south on CO 74 to Stagecoach Boulevard. Turn right and travel 1.25 miles to the south parking lot.

## ⓘ KEY AT-A-GLANCE INFORMATION

**LENGTH:** 2.5 miles

**CONFIGURATION:** Balloon

**DIFFICULTY:** Moderate

**SCENERY:** Forest, boulder field, mountain view

**EXPOSURE:** Partly shaded

**TRAFFIC:** Moderate

**TRAIL SURFACE:** Dirt, loose rocks

**HIKING TIME:** 1.5 hours

**SEASON:** All year

**ACCESS:** Free; open one hour before sunrise to one hour after sunset

**MAPS:** USGS Evergreen

**FACILITIES:** Picnic table, restrooms

**SPECIAL COMMENTS:** Dogs must be leashed at all times. Across Stagecoach Boulevard, you'll find an off-leash dog park with a 0.3-mile hiking trail. Collection of wildflowers or other natural resources is prohibited. Bears and mountain lions have been spotted on this trail and users must report any sightings to Open Space Rangers or call Jefferson County Natural Resources at (303) 271-5993.

Elk Meadow Open Space Park:
Sleepy S Loop

UTM Zone (WGS84)   13S

Easting   468570

Northing   4389240

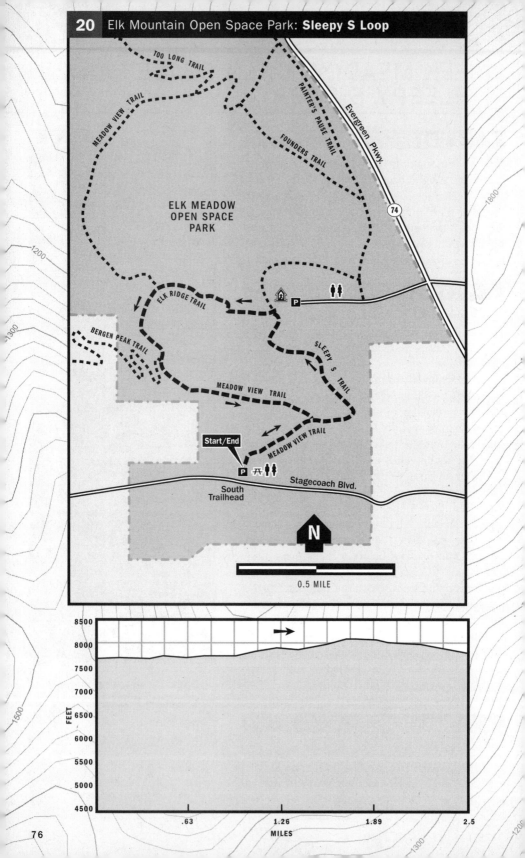

TOO LONG TRAIL

MEADOW VIEW TRAIL

PAINTER'S PAUSE TRAIL

Evergreen Pkwy.

FOUNDERS TRAIL

74

ELK MEADOW
OPEN SPACE
PARK

ELK RIDGE TRAIL

BERGEN PEAK TRAIL

SLEEPY S TRAIL

MEADOW VIEW TRAIL

MEADOW VIEW TRAIL

**Start/End**

Stagecoach Blvd.

South
Trailhead

**N**

0.5 MILE

8500
8000
7500
7000
6500
6000
5500
5000
4500

FEET

.63    1.26    1.89    2.5
MILES

Equestrians share the road along the Sleepy S Loop.

Reach the intersection of Meadow View Trail and Elk Ridge Trail. Go left onto Meadow View Trail and immediately pass the Bergen Peak Trail trailhead. The trail descends, sometimes steeply, through the tall, widely spaced ponderosa pine trees. Reach the intersection of Meadow View Trail and Sleepy S Trail and take a right, heading back to the trailhead.

## ▶ NEARBY ATTRACTIONS

There are seven hiking trails with 13 miles of hiking in Elk Meadow Open Space Park. For more information, visit Jefferson County Open Space: **www.co.jefferson.co.us/ openspace.**

# EVERGREEN: EVERGREEN LAKE

## KEY AT-A-GLANCE INFORMATION

**LENGTH:** 1.28 miles

**CONFIGURATION:** Loop

**DIFFICULTY:** Easy

**SCENERY:** Mountain lake

**EXPOSURE:** Partly shaded

**TRAFFIC:** Moderate

**TRAIL SURFACE:** Dirt, paved, bridges

**HIKING TIME:** 1 hour

**SEASON:** All year

**ACCESS:** Free; open 5 a.m.–11 p.m.

**MAPS:** USGS Evergreen

**FACILITIES:** Lake house, boat rentals, ice-skate rental, restrooms, picnic tables, grills

**SPECIAL COMMENTS:** The beautiful log lake house is open to the public and available to rent for special events. Call (303) 512-9300 or (303) 674-0532 for facility information, or visit **www.evergreenlake-house.com**. The fishing pier is handicap-accessible. Ice-skating season lasts from mid-December to mid-March, weather permitting. Summer activities include non-motorized boating and outdoor concerts. The southwest side of Evergreen Lake on Upper Bear Creek Road is an Evergreen Golf Public Course; call the pro shop for more information: (303) 674-6351.

Evergreen: Evergreen Lake

UTM Zone (WGS84)   13S

Easting   471550

Northing   4386680

## IN BRIEF

Evergreen Lake reflects the beauty of this mountain town: a sparkling creek, pine trees, sunshine, and a calm, serene demeanor. A small dam with cascading water sits at the opposite end of the lake house. The hike around Evergreen Lake is a splendid respite from the Denver bustle.

## DESCRIPTION

Head toward the lake house, which is visible from the entrance. At the lake house, take a left to a boardwalk that covers a large, marshy area. This is the start of the Evergreen Lake Trail clockwise around the lake. Continue on the boardwalk and go over the bridge that crosses Bear Creek as the creek enters Evergreen Lake.

Cross another feeder bridge and take a sharp right before the road. Walk on the trail which travels along the road on the left and the lake on the right. Reach the dam and you can see downtown Evergreen in the distance. Walk down the stairs to the spillway, just below the dam. A high-altitude garden is planted here. Cross a long bridge that spans Bear Creek, walk in front of the dam's waterfall, and head up the stairs on the left. Now the lake is on your right and the mountainside and mountain residences are on your left. To the left are staircases built into the rocks that lead to a lake lookout.

Stay on the lower portion of the trail and do not head up to the road. Get on a wooden boardwalk as it crisscrosses in and out over the lake. Cross another bridge and come around to the

## DIRECTIONS

From Denver, take I-70 west to Evergreen Parkway (CO 74). Go left, traveling south on CO 74 to Evergreen. Turn right on Upper Bear Creek Road and take it around to the entrance of Evergreen Lake.

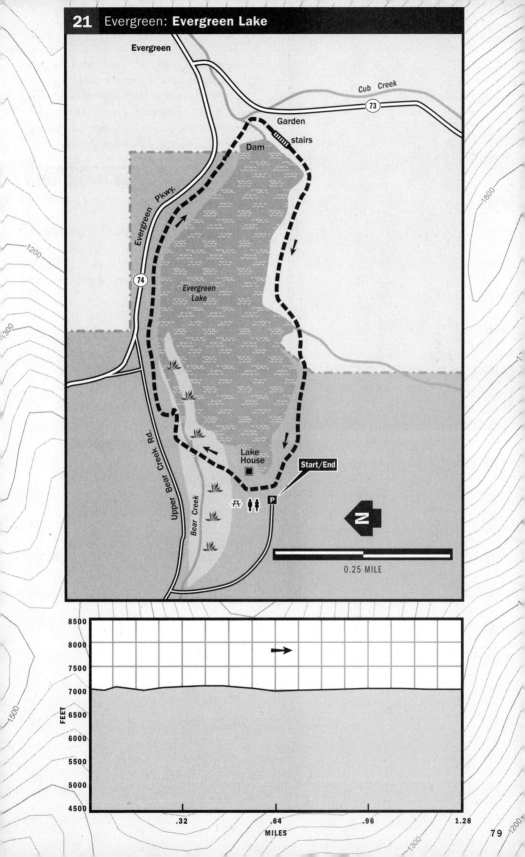

Evergreen

Cub Creek

73

Garden
stairs

Dam

Evergreen Pkwy.

74

Evergreen
Lake

Upper Bear Creek Rd.

Bear Creek

Lake
House

Start/End

P

N

0.25 MILE

Evergreen Lake is seen from all angles on this hike. The magic of the mountain water only leaves the view for a short while.

Evergreen Meadow side. Switchback as the trail ascends onto an upper portion of the trail. On this hillside, you'll overlook the lake and the old ice-skating shelter. Do not go to the shelter. Instead, go right and head back to the lake house and the end of the trail.

## ▶ NEARBY ATTRACTIONS

Denver Mountain Parks manages many of Evergreen's parks. See their Web site for more information: **www.denvergov.org.**

Most of Evergreen's Open Space parks and hiking trails are managed by Jefferson County Open Space: **www.co.jefferson.co. us/openspace.**

# GOLDEN GATE CANYON STATE PARK: MOUNTAIN LION TRAIL

## IN BRIEF

Seldom visited, Golden Gate Canyon State Park is just outside of Golden and 25 miles west of Denver. The park offers a few large loop trails, and rangers at the visitor center recommend this one. Mountain Lion Trail is a rugged mountain trail with great views that offers hikers plenty of solitude.

## DESCRIPTION

Head east out of the parking lot and get onto the Mountain Lion Trail. The single-track trail immediately starts an uphill climb. A stream flows downward on the left. Hikers are transported from the start to the feel of the backcountry. The trail is hard-packed, rocky, and only wide enough for a single hiker.

The trail cuts across a hillside and makes a large, arched switchback. Trails in this park are named after animals and have an accompanying symbol on signage. The Mountain Lion Trail's symbol is a mountain lion paw print.

Cross a gully with a seasonal stream and continue across the hillside. The area is lightly wooded with tall evergreen trees. Views of evergreen trees extend to the surrounding hillsides.

## DIRECTIONS

From Denver take I-70 west to CO 58 traveling toward Golden. Turn right off of CO 58 onto CO 93 and after 2 miles turn left on Golden Gate Canyon Road at the Golden Gate Canyon State Park sign. The road winds 13 miles to the visitor center. Stop here to buy your $5 park pass for the day. Take a right out of the visitor center parking lot and continue on Ralston Creek Road, which actually leaves the state park for 1 mile before reentering. Continue 3 miles; pass a number of trailheads until you see the Nott Creek sign. Turn left here and drive to the Mountain Lion Trailhead parking lot.

## KEY AT-A-GLANCE INFORMATION

**LENGTH:** 6.36 miles

**CONFIGURATION:** Loop

**DIFFICULTY:** Difficult

**SCENERY:** Green mountain meadows, lush aspen groves, pine-covered hills, fresh water creeks, views of Denver

**EXPOSURE:** Mostly shaded

**TRAFFIC:** Mild

**TRAIL SURFACE:** Hard-packed dirt, loose rocks

**HIKING TIME:** 4 hours

**SEASON:** May–October

**ACCESS:** $5 for the day or a buy a yearly Colorado State Parks Pass; open sunrise to sunset

**MAPS:** USGS Ralston Buttes; maps at visitor center

**FACILITIES:** Outhouse; no facilities at this trailhead, but plenty of restrooms, picnic spots, and campsites in the park

**SPECIAL COMMENTS:** Hikers must cross a creek multiple times. Your feet will probably get wet so wear appropriate footgear. This is a multiple-use trail for hikers, bikers, and equestrians. Leashed dogs are permitted. Fishing is allowed in any stream or pond except for the visitor center show pond. Weddings for 40 guests or fewer are allowed at Panorama Point Scenic Overlook and picnic area (on the opposite side of the park from Mountain Lion Trail). For scheduling information, call the park office at (303) 582-3707.

---

**Golden Gate Canyon State Park: Mountain Lion Trail**

**UTM Zone (WGS84)** 13S

**Easting** 469210

**Northing** 4411010

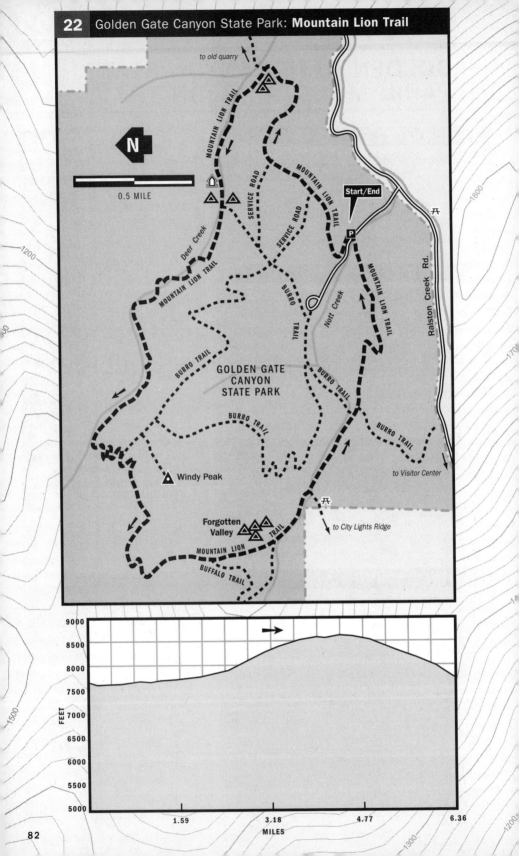

A snow-covered bridge in a winter
wonderland on Mountain Lion Trail

Come to an intersection with a double-track service road and take a right. Continue across an open hillside. A service road veers to the left, but the Mountain Lion Trail continues straight. It is very well marked, and an intersection such as this one is signed with the mountain lion paw.

The trail descends slightly into ponderosa pines. Continue down into the valley, where you can hear the sounds of gurgling Deer Creek. Here the trail becomes dense with mature pine trees. When you cross Deer Creek by traversing a wooden footbridge, look for mining gear and a large, old mining boiler in the water. Take a left after the bridge and head toward Windy Peak. To the right is a former quarry. The trail here is a narrow, rocky single track that parallels the creek.

Cross Deer Creek again and enter a rocky area that leads away from the creek. Here you'll find a well-marked backpacking campsite. It is a premier campsite and worth making a mental note for your next trip to Golden Gate Canyon. More of these campsites come into view, and each one is reached by crossing a private little bridge that straddles the creek. Take the trail across Deer Creek on another small wooden footbridge. A smaller side trail goes to a sleeping shelter.

Here, the rocky, wooded trail begins to ascend. Continue straight at the intersection of Burro Trail and Mountain Lion Trail and follow the signs to Windy Peak. The trail is still narrow, flanked by thick brush, pine trees, and willow trees. For the next half-mile, continue in this heavy growth along the creek. Follow a number of bridges that crisscross over the water for 2 miles. The terrain opens up a bit and becomes less overgrown. The trail is still near Deer Creek in the bottom of a gully. As it continues its gradual ascent, the hillside becomes rocky, with views of boulder fields.

Enter a lodgepole pine forest and follow a couple of long, steep switchbacks, going left just before an old barbed-wire fence. The trail continues across the hillside, ascending steep switchbacks. Pass another intersection with Burro Trail that cuts off to Windy Peak. Hike to the top of a ridge, go over, and drop down to a severe descent. Descend an extremely steep hill before the trail levels out and cuts across a hill overlooking an early settlement that's now called Forgotten Valley. The trail switchbacks and descends quickly, going to the bottom of this valley and joining up with Nott Creek. It is easy hiking from here, down an old abandoned service road. The trail quickly turns back into a single track with small rocks and gravel and ascends for five minutes.

Continue straight past the intersection with the Buffalo Trail, which turns right to Rifleman Phillips Group Campground. Pass an intersection to City Lights Ridge. Merge with the Burro Trail and jog to the left on Mountain Lion Trail to go back to the Nott Creek Trailhead.

The trail levels out and goes across the top of a ridge before the trail drops down. As you approach Ralston Creek Road, take a sharp left and descend toward the access road to the parking lot. The trail parallels the access road and comes out in the far corner of the parking lot where you started.

### ▶ NEARBY ATTRACTIONS

Try the 11 additional trails in Golden Gate Canyon State Park. See the Colorado State Parks Web site for more information: **www.parks.state.co.us.**

# LAKEWOOD: GREEN MOUNTAIN TRAIL

## ▶ IN BRIEF

The slopes and summit of Green Mountain are in Lakewood's second-largest park—William Frederick Hayden Park—covering 2,400 acres of open space. The steep terrain here includes a challenging system of trails and great views of the city. Some locals come every day to run the trail featured here. One time up the slope and hikers will either love it or regret it.

## ▶ DESCRIPTION

Start in the parking lot, where you can see Green Mountain, and head right. Go straight up the steep hillside. After a half-mile of exertion, reach a fork in the trail and go left to continue the ascent. Proceed up and across the hillside and travel through open meadow and seasonal wildflowers.

At the intersection of Green Mountain Trail and Hayden Trail, continue straight on Green Mountain Trail. As you catch your breath, glance at views of Metro Denver, including downtown Denver and the southwest Denver area. Bordered only by short brush, the trail is well maintained, considering its exposure and heavy use.

At the 1-mile point, the trail begins to level out and ascend gradually. Pass a large radio tower on the right. You see mountain views to the left and Denver over your shoulder to the right. Turn left at the tower and travel on a path wide enough for two hikers to walk side by side.

Reach another intersection of Green Mountain Trail and Hayden Trail at 1.33 miles, and take a sharp left. Red Rocks and Dinosaur Ridge are

## ⓘ KEY AT-A-GLANCE INFORMATION

**LENGTH:** 3.3 miles

**CONFIGURATION:** Loop

**DIFFICULTY:** Difficult

**SCENERY:** Open fields, views of Metro Denver

**EXPOSURE:** No shade

**TRAFFIC:** Heavy

**TRAIL SURFACE:** Dirt, loose rocks

**HIKING TIME:** 2.5 hours

**SEASON:** All year

**ACCESS:** Free; open 5 a.m.–10 p.m.

**MAPS:** USGS Morrison

**FACILITIES:** Restrooms

**SPECIAL COMMENTS:** Dogs are allowed, but must be leashed at all times. Mountain bikers and equestrians use this trail, so be cautious.

Lakewood: Green Mountain Trail

UTM Zone (WGS84)   13S

Easting   486940

Northing   4393150

## ▶ DIRECTIONS

From Denver, take I-70 west to C-470 south. Exit at West Alameda Parkway (CO 26) and turn left onto West Alameda Parkway. Green Mountain Trail's trailhead is on the left at West Florida Drive.

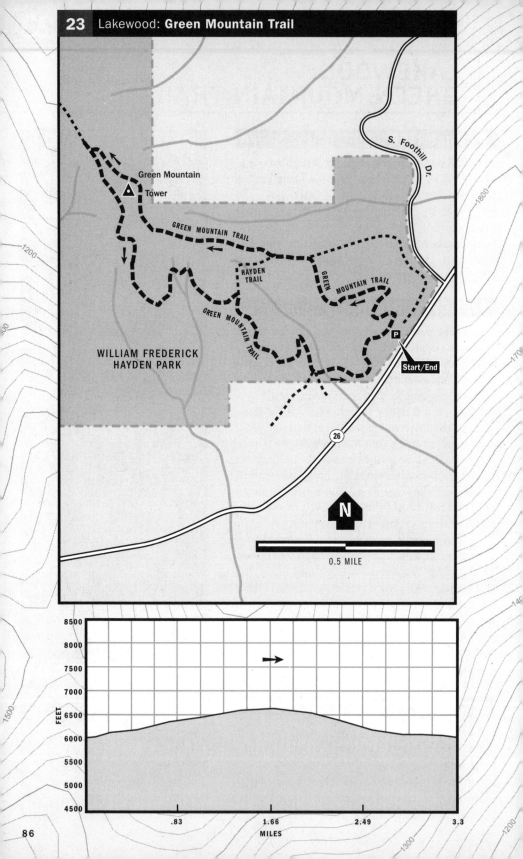

S. Foothill Dr.

Green Mountain
△ Tower

GREEN MOUNTAIN TRAIL

HAYDEN
TRAIL

GREEN
MOUNTAIN TRAIL

GREEN MOUNTAIN TRAIL

**WILLIAM FREDERICK
HAYDEN PARK**

P

Start/End

26

**N**

0.5 MILE

visible to the right. The trail begins a slight descent, cutting into the hillside with gradual switchbacks. As it continues to descend and come around to the western side of the mountain, the trail opens up to views of the hogback. Any roaring engines are the sounds from cars and the nearby Bandemere Speedway. Green Mountain Trail intersects again with Hayden Trail; stay right on Green Mountain Trail. Continue down the trail, reach a T, and turn left, staying on Green Mountain Trail. At 2.86 miles, the trail empties into a small gully. There is a small, cruel spurt of uphill and then the trail heads back down to the trailhead, coming out on the opposite side of the parking lot from where you started.

## ▶ NEARBY ATTRACTIONS

North Dinosaur Open Space Park, Rooney Hogback Open Space Park, and Loveland Tail Open Space Park; for more information, City of Lakewood: **www. lakewood.org.**

Matthews Winters Open Space Park; for more information, Jefferson County Open Space: **www.openspace.co.jefferson.co.us.**

# MEYER RANCH OPEN SPACE PARK: LODGEPOLE LOOP

## KEY AT-A-GLANCE INFORMATION

**LENGTH:** 2 miles

**CONFIGURATION:** Balloon

**DIFFICULTY:** Easy

**SCENERY:** Heavily forested with lodgepole pine trees

**EXPOSURE:** Shaded

**TRAFFIC:** Moderate

**TRAIL SURFACE:** Smooth and hard-packed dirt

**HIKING TIME:** 1 hour

**SEASON:** All year

**ACCESS:** Free; open sunrise to sunset

**MAPS:** USGS Conifer

**FACILITIES:** Restrooms, picnic facilities

**SPECIAL COMMENTS:** Dogs permitted, must be leashed. No hunting or overnight camping. The Meyer family still owns and resides in the historic Victorian home adjacent to the park on the north side of US 285. Please respect their privacy.

Meyer Ranch Open Space Park: Lodgepole Loop

UTM Zone (WGS84)   13S

Easting   476650

Northing   4377180

## IN BRIEF

Meyer Ranch is a wonderful family, novice hiking area with easy trails and plentiful picnic sites. The Lodgepole Loop is true to its nomenclature, as the pines dominate the route. Add-on trails render this an ideal spot for hardy and adventurous hikers. The all-year access plus moderate crowds make this a well-rounded area desirable to all.

## DESCRIPTION

Depart the parking lot and travel a short way to the trailhead kiosk. Walk through the meadow, toward the bathroom, located far from the trailhead. Leave the service road–like trail, turn right, and head to the left side of the Owl's Perch Trail. Pass the first of many picnic-table sites on the right and travel along a well-maintained, single-track hiking path. Owl's Perch Trail loops around the picnic area, but both the left and right access lead to Lodgepole Loop.

At the intersection of Owl's Perch Trail and Lodgepole Loop, take a right. Travel along until the trail forks at a service road and a hiking path. Take a right onto the hiking path and follow the arrows that mark the trail, which drops right into a meadow and passes a bench. The path travels through a few switchbacks as it goes into thick forest. Pass the spur for Sunny Aspen Trail on the right. This trail eventually meets up with Ski Run Trail. A portion of what is now Meyer Ranch was used in the early 1940s as a ski hill. Remnants are still visible in the upper end of the park, now a forested aspen grove.

## DIRECTIONS

From Denver, take C-470 south for 6 miles to US 285. Follow US 285 west for 11.5 miles until it intersects with South Turkey Creek Road. Turn right at signs for Meyer Ranch Open Space and follow road under the highway to the parking lot.

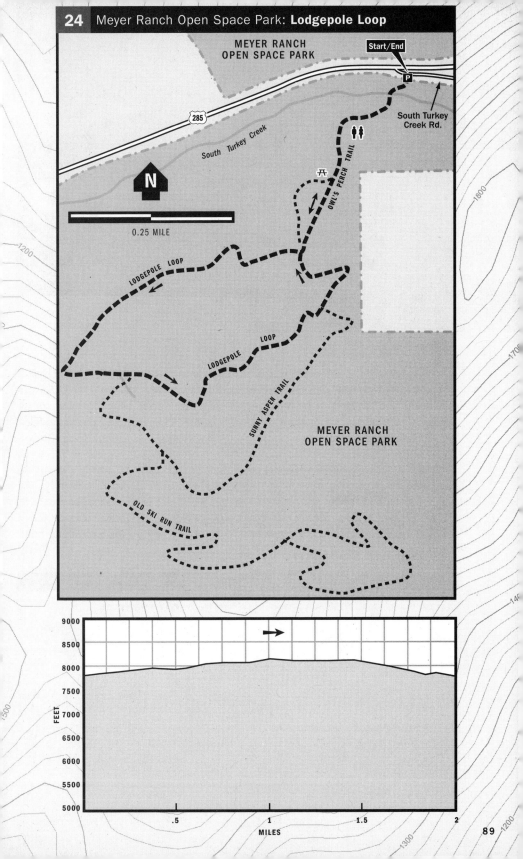

MEYER RANCH
OPEN SPACE PARK

Start/End

P

South Turkey Creek Rd.

285

South Turkey Creek

N

0.25 MILE

OWL'S PERCH TRAIL

LODGEPOLE LOOP

LODGEPOLE LOOP

SUNNY ASPEN TRAIL

MEYER RANCH
OPEN SPACE PARK

OLD SKI RUN TRAIL

9000
8500
8000
7500
7000
6500
6000
5500
5000

FEET

.5          1          1.5          2

MILES

Mountain bikers leave the trailhead at
Meyer Ranch Open Space.

The Lodgepole Loop continues through dense forest, with cool patches of shade, and crosses through a small, open meadow area. If you encounter a circus animal, do not be alarmed. Legend has it that the ranch served as winter quarters for animals of the P.T. Barnum Circus in the late 1880s. (When the Meyers remodeled the ranch house in 1995, they found a board with the inscription "Circus Town, 1889.")

Pass a second spur for Sunny Aspen Trail on the right. Continue straight on Lodgepole Loop and dip down, crossing shaded stairs over a small, wet gully. The trail is a roller coaster, going up and down, but never at a large descent or ascent. A few gentle switchbacks through the lodgepoles lead down to familiar territory. Back at the Owl's Perch Trail, take a right (or left) and head back to the bathrooms, trailhead, and parking lot.

## ▶ NEARBY ATTRACTIONS

Other Jefferson County Open Space hikes: **www.co.jefferson.co.us**.

# MOUNT EVANS WILDERNESS: HELL'S HOLE TRAIL

## ▶ IN BRIEF

Don't let the name of this hike deter. Hell's Hole is a difficult hike, but its challenge is rewarded. This trail travels through the woods to a high alpine basin in the Mount Evans Wilderness. When it ends at Hell's Hole, the path opens to a meadow where alpine willows grow in the shadow of Gray Wolf Mountain and Mount Evans. The only hell of the day will be found in the busy passing lanes of I-70 on the way there.

## ▶ DESCRIPTION

Hell's Hole Trail #53 starts by traveling through the Chicago Creek picnic area, surrounded by pine trees. The trail is not well defined at first, so walk uphill, stay to the left going toward the creek, and then enter an aspen grove. Here, the trail is easier to find and travels along West Chicago Creek for about a mile.

Around five minutes into the hike, a self-issuing permit station seems to come out of nowhere. Registration is mandatory; there are no fees or quotas, but the forest service tracks how many people use this trail and what they do here, so just fill out the form, deposit the white slip below, and keep the tag.

Follow the trail through several large groves of aspen trees, and cross the small creek two times. These aspen trees are bent way over to the left and look like a big gust of wind once came through here and tried to blow them all down.

The trail alternates between steep, rocky

### ℹ KEY AT-A-GLANCE INFORMATION

**LENGTH:** 9.32 miles

**CONFIGURATION:** Out-and-back

**DIFFICULTY:** Difficult

**SCENERY:** Dense forest that opens to views of high mountain peaks

**EXPOSURE:** Mostly shaded

**TRAFFIC:** Moderate

**TRAIL SURFACE:** Hard-packed dirt, rocky

**HIKING TIME:** 4.5 hours

**SEASON:** June–October

**ACCESS:** Free

**MAPS:** USGS Georgetown

**FACILITIES:** Restrooms and picnic areas

**SPECIAL COMMENTS:** Although access is free, users must obtain a wilderness usage permit at the trailhead. Dogs are allowed, but must be leashed. Bicycles and any motorized vehicle are not permitted.

## ▶ DIRECTIONS

From Denver, take I-70 west to Idaho Springs (exit 240). Go left, traveling south on CO 103, which is also Mount Evans Road. Go 6.5 miles and take a right at the sign for Chicago Creek Campground. Go 3 miles on West Chicago Creek Road. The trailhead is at the end of the road.

**Mount Evans Wilderness: Hell's Hole Trail**

**UTM Zone (WGS84)  13S**

**Easting  443648**

**Northing  4392349**

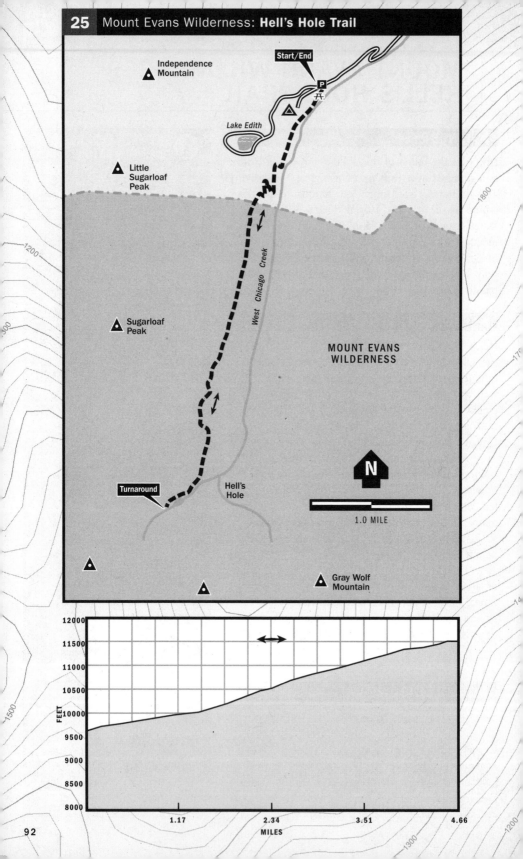

Start/End

Independence
Mountain

Lake Edith

Little
Sugarloaf
Peak

West Chicago Creek

MOUNT EVANS
WILDERNESS

Sugarloaf
Peak

N

Turnaround

Hell's
Hole

1.0 MILE

Gray Wolf
Mountain

The gnarled trunks of the bristle-cone pine at timberline and the Hell's Hole turnaround

sections and smooth, level sections for most of the hike. After a half hour, you officially enter Mount Evans Wilderness. Views open up a little toward the left as the trees begin to transition from aspens to evergreens, which thin with elevation. There are views in all directions. The tall mountain that you have been able to see for most of this hike is Mount Evans. The last mile of the trail is a gentle grade at tree line that ends at a valley with small ponds and oddly shaped, big trees with bushy tops called bristlecone pine. Mount Evans is still off to the left and the dominant mountain. Gray Wolf Mountain sits to the right and is closer to this trail. Once you arrive at the base of Gray Wolf Mountain, the trail ends at the meadow area called Hell's Hole. From here, turn around and head back the way you came.

## ▶ NEARBY ATTRACTIONS

Mount Evans Wilderness hikes: **www.fs.fed.us/r2/arnf** (reference Clear Creek Ranger District).

# MOUNT EVANS WILDERNESS: MOUNT BIERSTADT

## KEY AT-A-GLANCE INFORMATION

**LENGTH:** 7.4 miles

**CONFIGURATION:** Out-and-back

**DIFFICULTY:** Difficult

**SCENERY:** Alpine tundra and high mountain peaks

**EXPOSURE:** Heavily exposed due to high altitude

**TRAFFIC:** Heavy

**TRAIL SURFACE:** Hard-packed dirt, extremely rocky, large talus

**HIKING TIME:** 4 hours

**SEASON:** June–October

**ACCESS:** Free; open sunrise to sunset

**MAPS:** USGS Evans and Georgetown

**FACILITIES:** None

**SPECIAL COMMENTS:** Although access is free, users must obtain a wilderness usage permit at the trailhead. Dogs must be leashed. Bicycles and any motorized vehicles are not permitted.

Mount Evans Wilderness:
Mount Bierstadt

UTM Zone (WGS84)   13S

Easting   439060

Northing   4382960

## ▶ IN BRIEF

Mount Bierstadt and Mount Evans are two of the closest fourteeners to Denver. (A fourteener is any mountain peak above 14,000 feet.) Mount Bierstadt is easy to find and fairly easy to navigate. The trail is steep in places. A 3-mile summit reached from the Guanella Pass approach is a great way to start an addiction to the Colorado Fourteeners.

## ▶ DESCRIPTION

Set out on Mount Bierstadt Trail #711 and deposit the required wilderness usage permit in the drop box. The hike starts above tree line and takes you through the largest willow bog in Colorado. A boardwalk has been built so hikers can keep their feet dry from the bog that dominates the first 1.5 miles of the hike and protects the alpine willows. The boardwalk has made rather difficult terrain manageable, otherwise, the trail is well-defined, with stable, packed dirt and some rocks.

The first 1.5 miles are also a steady descent from the trailhead; passing Deadmans Lake on the left and continuing to the Scott Gomer Creek crossing.

At the fork in the trail, veer right on the more heavily used trail. Here is a good place to

## ▶ DIRECTIONS

From Denver, take I-70 west to Georgetown (exit 228). Go down the exit ramp, turn left under I-70, then turn right at Argentine Street and follow the signs leading to Guanella Pass. Stay left at a fork in the road and at Rose Street turn right. Go through the next stop sign; the road turns to the left and becomes Guanella Pass Road. Take this road 10 miles to the Mount Evans Wilderness. The road becomes dirt, but is passable by most passenger cars. The trailhead is on the east side of the road.

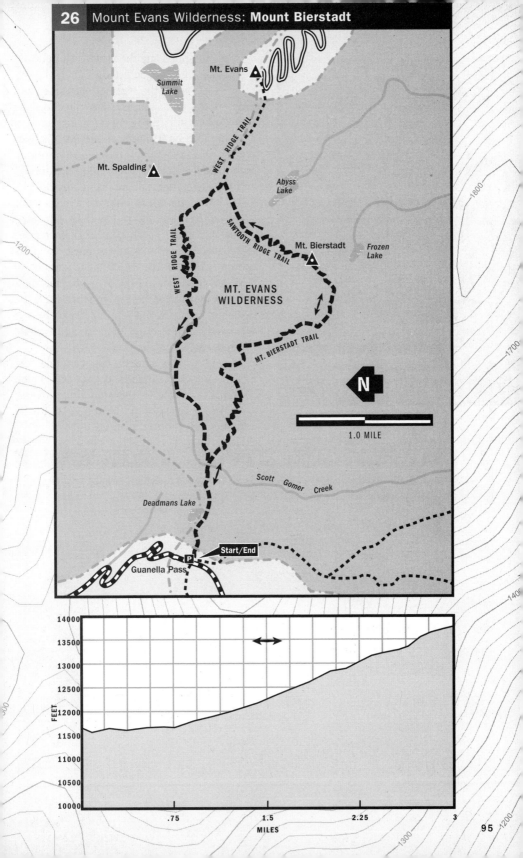

A boardwalk at the beginning of the hike up Mount Bierstadt.

stop and appreciate the view of Mount Bierstadt and the Sawtooth Ridge. Once the willows fade away, the trail becomes steep and continues in a southeastern direction. As the trail winds up the west-facing slope of Mount Bierstadt, keep an eye out for marmots or pikas. At 13,760 feet, turn northeast and hike along the ridge. Most landmarks along this entire trail are marked by cairns.

The summit is only 0.25 miles away right after where the willow trees fade away from the trail. The terrain is characterized by larger talus, and hikers must scramble over a few. At the 14,060-foot summit of Mount Bierstadt, relish the panoramic view. To the northwest, two more fourteeners are visible: Grays Peak (14,270 feet) and Torreys Peak (14,267 feet). To the east, you can see Abyss Lake.

From the summit you can take the Sawtooth Ridge Option (see page 97), which connects hikers to the summit of Mount Evans. Or turn around from here and head back 3 miles to the trailhead.

## ▶ NEARBY ATTRACTIONS

Mount Evans Wilderness hikes: **www.fs.fed.us/r2/arnf** (reference Clear Creek Ranger District).

# MOUNT EVANS WILDERNESS: MOUNT EVANS

## ▶ IN BRIEF

There are approximately 12 different ways to reach this fourteener summit. The Sawtooth option allows hikers to summit two fourteeners in one day—both Mount Bierstadt and Mount Evans. Generally, summit Mount Bierstadt first and then Mount Evans since the peaks are 1.5 miles apart. The West Ridge option is a good out-and-back hike on the less popular side of Mount Evans. Most tourists access Mount Evans from Echo Lake or Mount Evans Road on the east and northeast side.

## ▶ DESCRIPTION

**SAWTOOTH OPTION:**

Hike to the summit of Mount Bierstadt (see page 94) and head north toward the Sawtooth Ridge. The trail along the Sawtooth is not as harrowing as it may appear. Lightning storms are more frequent after noon, so assess the weather, the time, and your physical condition at this point.

Begin descending to the north on the east side of the Sawtooth Ridge. Pass through talus and be prepared to do some light scrambling. Follow the cairns as they direct hikers to a point below a significant saddle. From here, regain elevation as you approach the saddle. Cross over the saddle to the west side of the Sawtooth Ridge.

## ▶ DIRECTIONS

From Denver, take I-70 west to Georgetown (exit 228). Go down the exit ramp, turn left under I-70, then turn right at Argentine Street and follow the signs leading to Guanella Pass. Stay left at a fork in the road, and at Rose Street turn right. Go through the next stop sign; the road turns to the left and becomes Guanella Pass Road. Take this road 10 miles to the Mount Evans Wilderness. The road becomes dirt, but is passable by most passenger cars. The trailhead is on the east side of the road.

## ⓘ KEY AT-A-GLANCE INFORMATION

**LENGTH:** Sawtooth option, 1.5 miles one-way (add on to Bierstadt summit); West Ridge option, 9 miles

**CONFIGURATION:** Sawtooth—balloon; West Ridge—out-and-back

**DIFFICULTY:** Difficult

**SCENERY:** Alpine tundra and high mountain peaks

**EXPOSURE:** Heavily exposed due to high altitude

**TRAFFIC:** Heavy

**TRAIL SURFACE:** Hard-packed dirt, extremely rocky, large talus

**HIKING TIME:** 4.5 hours

**SEASON:** June–October

**ACCESS:** Free; open sunrise to sunset

**MAPS:** USGS Evans and Georgetown

**FACILITIES:** None

**SPECIAL COMMENTS:** Sawtooth option: Mount Bierstadt summit to Mount Evans summit via Sawtooth Ridge is 1.5 miles one-way, plus the 3 miles one-way to Mount Bierstadt's summit; West Ridge option: Uses the Guanella Pass trailhead, same trailhead as Mount Bierstadt, but reaches the summit via a different, 9-mile route.

Although access is free, users must obtain a wilderness usage permit at the trailhead. Dogs are allowed but must be leashed. Bicycles and any motorized vehicle are not permitted.

---

**Mount Evans Wilderness: Mount Evans**

**UTM Zone (WGS84)   13S**

**Easting   439060**

**Northing   4382960**

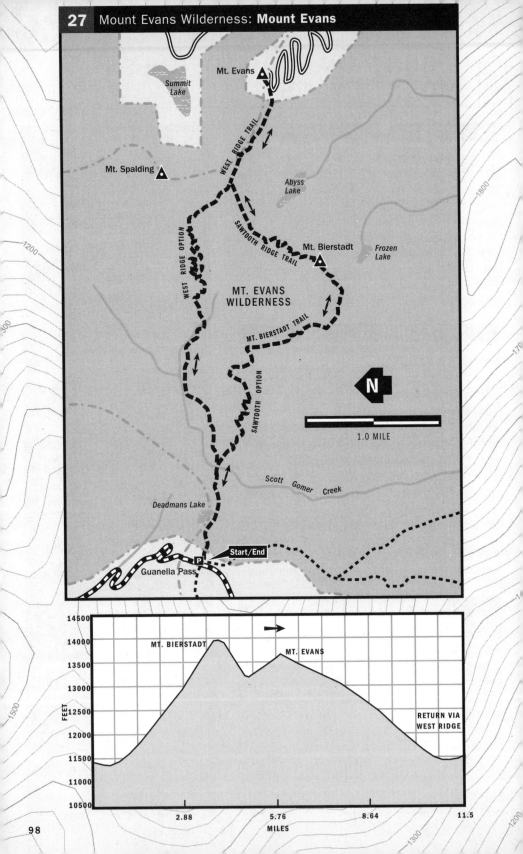

Mt. Evans

Summit
Lake

Mt. Spalding

Abyss
Lake

WEST RIDGE TRAIL

SAWTOOTH RIDGE TRAIL

Mt. Bierstadt

Frozen
Lake

WEST RIDGE OPTION

MT. EVANS
WILDERNESS

MT. BIERSTADT TRAIL

SAWTOOTH OPTION

**N**

**1.0 MILE**

Scott  Gomer  Creek

Deadmans Lake

**Start/End**

P

Guanella Pass

MT. BIERSTADT

MT. EVANS

RETURN VIA
WEST RIDGE

FEET

14500
14000
13500
13000
12500
12000
11500
11000
10500

2.88          5.76          8.64          11.5
MILES

Continue to follow the cairns along a wide ledge and across a gully of smaller, loose rock. You will now encounter a ledge that ascends diagonally across a cliff band. The ledge is exposed, so take your time and mind your footing.

Just beyond the Sawtooth is a gentle slope comprised of tundra and sporadic boulders. Follow this slope to the east as you prepare for the last segment of scrambling up the west ridge of Mount Evans. At 14,264 feet, you have accomplished a difficult task. Two fourteeners in one day! Be prepared to see people who have walked the few hundred feet up from the parking lot. Yes, there is a parking lot, observatory, and paved road that lead all the way up to Mount Evans on this side. Retrace your steps or hike down Mount Evans as detailed in the West Ridge option below.

## WEST RIDGE OPTION:

Set out on Mount Bierstadt Trail #711 and deposit the required wilderness usage permit in the drop box. The hike starts above tree line and takes you through the largest willow bog in Colorado. A boardwalk has been built so hikers can keep their feet dry from the bog that dominates the first 1.5 miles of the hike and protects the alpine willows. The boardwalk has made rather difficult terrain manageable, otherwise, the trail is well-defined, with stable, packed dirt and some rocks.

The first 1.5 miles are also a steady descent from the trailhead; passing Deadmans Lake on the left and continuing to the Scott Gomer Creek crossing.

At the fork in the trail, go left. (Mount Bierstadt hikers go right).

Pass the cliff walls that extend 1 mile north of Sawtooth and come to the open tundra of Mount Spalding. Cross to the south side of Spalding's ridge, pass Spalding's summit, and reach the west end of Mount Evans at 13,900 feet. Scramble approximately 1 mile to Mount Evans' summit. Most of this traverse is on solid talus rock. After reaching the summit, turn around and head back the way you came to the trailhead.

## ▶ NEARBY ATTRACTIONS

Mount Evans Wilderness hikes: **www.fs.fed.us/r2/arnf** (reference Clear Creek Ranger District).

# MOUNT FALCON PARK: CASTLE AND PARMALEE TRAIL LOOP

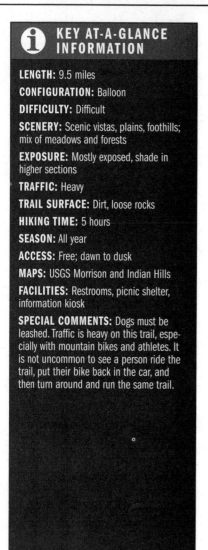

## KEY AT-A-GLANCE INFORMATION

**LENGTH:** 9.5 miles

**CONFIGURATION:** Balloon

**DIFFICULTY:** Difficult

**SCENERY:** Scenic vistas, plains, foothills; mix of meadows and forests

**EXPOSURE:** Mostly exposed, shade in higher sections

**TRAFFIC:** Heavy

**TRAIL SURFACE:** Dirt, loose rocks

**HIKING TIME:** 5 hours

**SEASON:** All year

**ACCESS:** Free; dawn to dusk

**MAPS:** USGS Morrison and Indian Hills

**FACILITIES:** Restrooms, picnic shelter, information kiosk

**SPECIAL COMMENTS:** Dogs must be leashed. Traffic is heavy on this trail, especially with mountain bikes and athletes. It is not uncommon to see a person ride the trail, put their bike back in the car, and then turn around and run the same trail.

Mount Falcon Park:
Castle and Parmalee Trail Loop

UTM Zone (WGS84)   13S

Easting   483070

Northing   4388340

## IN BRIEF

Mount Falcon Open Space Park is an easily accessible hike from Denver that includes a blood-pumping climb through open meadows, ponderosa pine trees, and seasonal wildflowers. This trail covers most of the 11.1 miles of trails in Mount Falcon. Castle Trail leads from the plains to the foothills on a narrow road that once carried Stanley Steamer automobiles.

## DESCRIPTION

From the trailhead, take the well-marked Castle Trail. The view is dominated by Red RocksOpen Space and the Red Rocks amphitheater across the valley. Glance back for a view of downtown Denver. Quickly come to the intersection where Turkey Trot Trail, a hiker-only path, goes off to the right. Stay on Castle Trail, bearing left. Wind up the hillside going through yucca, oak trees, sage, and non-native thistle, considered an invasive species and quite a nuisance here. At many points, the ascent levels out and it feels as though you've reached the top of the hill. Pass the point in the trail where the Turkey Trot Trail reemerges and still you have quite a ways to go up the hill.

The cars in the trailhead parking lot become mere specks. On a clear day, the views expand many miles to the east over the Colorado prairie. The white dots, farther past downtown Denver, are the white tentlike spires of Denver International

## DIRECTIONS

From Denver, take I-70 west to the Morrison/Golden exit and CO 26. Take a left, traveling west on CO 26 for 4 miles to the town to Morrison. Go right into downtown Morrison on Main Street. Go left at CO 8 at the end of Morrison town and travel 1.6 miles to Forest Avenue. Turn right on Forest Avenue and follow the signs for Mount Falcon Open Space.

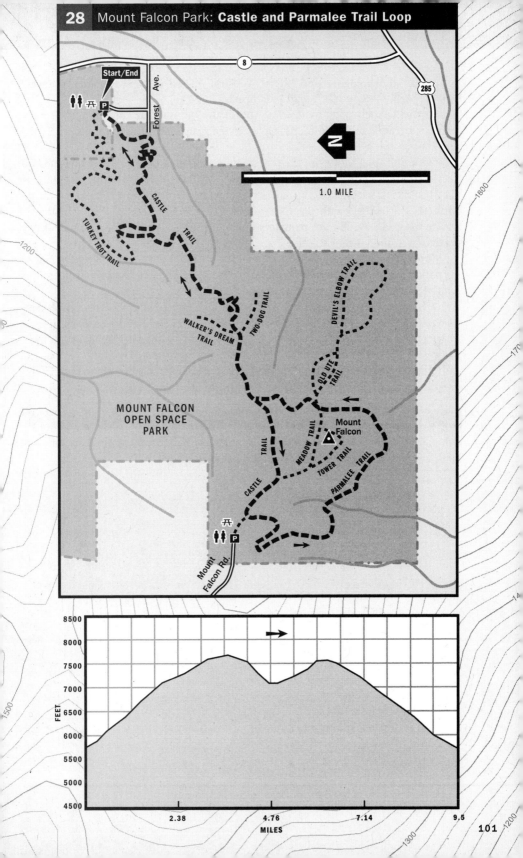

Start/End

Forest Ave.

8

285

N

1.0 MILE

1800

CASTLE TRAIL

TURKEY TROT TRAIL

1200

DEVIL'S ELBOW TRAIL

OLD UTE TRAIL

1700

WALKER'S DREAM TRAIL

TWO-DOG TRAIL

MOUNT FALCON OPEN SPACE PARK

Mount Falcon

MEADOW TRAIL

TOWER TRAIL

CASTLE TRAIL

PARMALEE TRAIL

Mount Falcon Rd.

1500

FEET

8500
8000
7500
7000
6500
6000
5500
5000
4500

2.38        4.76        7.14        9.5

MILES

1300

1200

Airport. Climbing higher and higher, you are rewarded by seasonal wildflowers, including columbines and Indian paintbrush.

A picnic shelter marks the true top of the hill and the intersection with the Walker's Dream Trail. Continue straight on the main Castle Trail and pass the Two-Dog Trail on the left.

From this point forward, the trail is wider, smoother, and easier to navigate. The trees also offer more shade. Travel another 0.5 miles and continue straight past the intersection with Meadow Trail. After another 0.4 miles, take a right where the Meadow Trail merges with the Castle Trail. You are on a smooth, well-maintained service road. On the left are remnants of a 1989 forest fire along with signs of new vegetation in the form of wildflowers.

Arrive at the opposite trailhead for Mount Falcon Park on the western side of the park. Near the restroom, take a left onto Parmalee Trail and travel on this trail for 2 miles.

The trail immediately descends through lush forest and gives you a nice break from sun on a hot day. The trail levels and gradually ascends across an open hillside. Turn right onto Meadow Trail, passing Mount Falcon on the left. Merge again in 0.3 miles with the Castle Trail and end the small balloon portion of the hike. Take a right and proceed down the long hill, back the way you came, all the way to the parking lot.

### ▶ NEARBY ATTRACTIONS

Other Jefferson County area hikes, including nearby Lair O' The Bear Park and Matthews Winters Park: **www.jeffco.us/openspace.**

# RED ROCKS: TRADING POST TRAIL

## ▶ IN BRIEF

Red Rocks Park is a well-known venue for Colorado's best outdoor concerts. The natural rock that jettisons out of the hillside is flaming red and attracts music lovers in the summer and outdoor enthusiasts all year. The Trading Post Trail offers an opportunity to pass through spectacular rock formations and catch a peek at the amphitheater.

## ▶ DESCRIPTION

The trail starts at the Trading Post Store traveling along the road on the northern side of the store; the trail leaves this roadside quickly. Take the northernmost entrance to the Trading Post Trail, which is on the right side of the Trading Post. The Red Rocks Pueblo, now commonly known as the Trading Post, is a registered Denver Landmark. You immediately pass the rocks that line the southern side of the amphitheater. The trail runs along Ship Rock Road and past the upper south parking lot.

Enter low-lying brush as the trail begins a slight descent. It is extremely crowded on weekends and mostly crowded any other time. The red-dirt path is wide enough for one person. Expect to kick up plenty of red dust if conditions are dry.

To the left are moderate-sized versions of the red rocks rocketing out toward the trail. Pass these formations and descend several sets of man-made stairs. The trail is well marked with signs that say "trail," with an arrow.

Cross a wooden bridge with a small stream that runs underneath, flanked by rocks. Cross

## ▶ KEY AT-A-GLANCE INFORMATION

**LENGTH:** 1.46 miles

**CONFIGURATION:** Loop

**DIFFICULTY:** Easy

**SCENERY:** Smooth, red stones; large rock walls; small trees and brush

**EXPOSURE:** Virtually no shade

**TRAFFIC:** Heavy

**TRAIL SURFACE:** Dirt

**HIKING TIME:** 1.5 hours

**SEASON:** All year

**ACCESS:** Free; open 5 a.m. to 30 minutes after sunset

**MAPS:** USGS Morrison

**FACILITIES:** Store, restrooms, restaurant, amphitheater, picnic shelter

**SPECIAL COMMENTS:** In the event of a live performance, visitors to the park will be instructed as to when the park will close. Most concerts are in the evenings. Dogs are permitted, but must be on a six-foot leash. Do not climb or rappel off the red rocks; you'll face a $999 fine or 180 days in jail. No horses or bikes are allowed.

## ▶ DIRECTIONS

From Denver take I-70 west to the Morrison exit and CO 26. Go left, traveling south on CO 26 to Red Rocks Park. Take the first park entrance on the right, West Alameda Parkway. Turn left on Trading Post Road and park at the Trading Post Store.

**Red Rocks: Trading Post Trail**

**UTM Zone (WGS84)    13S**

**Easting    482660**

**Northing    4390260**

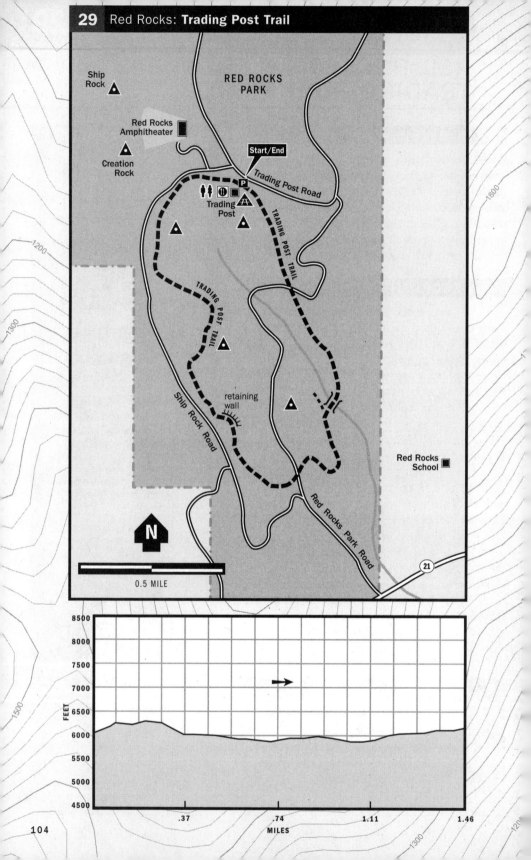

Ship Rock

RED ROCKS PARK

Red Rocks Amphitheater

Creation Rock

Start/End

Trading Post Road

TRADING POST TRAIL

Trading Post

TRADING POST TRAIL

Ship Rock Road

retaining wall

Red Rocks School

Red Rocks Park Road

21

N

0.5 MILE

8500
8000
7500
7000
6500
6000
5500
5000
4500

FEET

.37        .74        1.11        1.46
MILES

another man-made bridge over a dry stream bed. The trail widens for a moment and hikers can walk side by side. You're again bordered on the left by large, red boulder formations. In the distance is a view of southwest suburban Denver.

You may spot an occasional deer, as well as finches, blue jays, and magpies. Most noteworthy are sightings of mountain blue birds and the American kestrel. Wild plum, chokecherry trees, and evening primrose grow in this prairie-to-mountain transition zone. The trees you see include mahogany, sumac, cottonwoods, and ponderosa pine.

The trail turns into disintegrated asphalt that was once the main road. Stay on the asphalt portion of trail; do not veer to the left, where trail erosion has occurred. You will still be walking along smooth curvatures of the red rock formations. The trail continues to descend at a more gradual pace, where stairs are not needed. An open meadow appears on the left, and drought-resistant plants such as yucca mark the trail. Keep in mind that running a counterclockwise version of this trail means that hikers have fewer uphill climbs and more downhill walks.

Red Rocks is famous for its rock formations. Remember to just look up and don't touch.

Pass a man-made retaining wall on the left. This a good place to stop and look at the views. The trail turns to the left and starts another descent, heading directly to a long, red wall of rock. Keep winding down, down, down.

Cross another man-made bridge with a little creek running underneath. At the bottom of the hill, cross Red Rocks Park Road and watch for traffic. The trail widens and loose, red dirt borders miniature wildflowers, grass, and shrubbery.

On the left, pass a sign marked "Danger rattlesnake area—closed." To the right you'll see an area that has been fenced off for restoration. Further to the right is an elementary school. At a fork in the road, take a right toward the bridge and pass an old incinerator on the left. Cross a man-made bridge that is high over a creek. The trail begins to ascend gradually. As it does, a hillside of brush and yucca appears on the right. To the left is a little drop-off. Take the man-made stairs and cross Red Rocks Park Road again. After crossing the road, climb another set of man-made stairs. The trail continues to travel alongside a drastic drop-off and posted "Danger drop-off" signs mean what they say. Scramble across a long section of flat, red rock. Continue to the right and stay on the trail, even when you see a turnoff to the left. The Trading Post will be straight ahead. Take a right to get off the trail and you're free to explore some more.

## ▶ NEARBY ATTRACTIONS

Dakota Ridge Trail, Red Rocks Trail: **www.denvergov.org**.
Matthews/Winters Park, Dinosaur Ridge: **www.co.jefferson.co.us.**

# ROCKY MOUNTAIN ARSENAL NATIONAL WILDLIFE REFUGE: LAKES LOOP

 **KEY AT-A-GLANCE INFORMATION**

**LENGTH:** 1.7 miles

**CONFIGURATION:** Loop

**DIFFICULTY:** Easy

**SCENERY:** Barren prairie, some grasses; lakes and cottonwood trees

**EXPOSURE:** Full exposure; some shade in cottonwood trees

**TRAFFIC:** Moderate

**TRAIL SURFACE:** Smooth, hard-packed dirt; asphalt

**HIKING TIME:** 1 hour

**SEASON:** All year; some closures April 15–Oct. 15

**ACCESS:** Free; refuge trails open weekends only, excluding holidays, 8 a.m.–4:30 p.m

**MAPS:** USGS Montbello

**FACILITIES:** Restrooms, picnic facilities; visitor center with interpretive nature displays and activities

**SPECIAL COMMENTS:** Dogs, horses, and bikes are not allowed in the refuge. Assistance dogs are welcome for those needing help. It is illegal to keep any eagle feathers found here. A two-hour trolley wildlife viewing tour is available every Saturday and Sunday. Reservations are required; call the visitor center at (303) 289-0930. The refuge has special emergency response procedures since it is in tornado territory. A trail system map provided at the visitor center spells out these procedures.

Rocky Mountain Arsenal National Wildlife Refuge: Lakes Loop

UTM Zone (WGS84)   13S

Easting   511800

Northing   4407660

## IN BRIEF

This hike is unique, beautiful, and odd. This former Army arsenal and chemical munitions facility gives some visitors an eerie feeling because it is barren and deserted. Weapons were produced here during WWII, and then the land was leased to commercial pesticide companies. It is the largest contiguous open space in the Denver metropolitan area and the site is currently undergoing a major environmental restoration program. There is absolutely no sign of such activity on this short and sweet hike around two beautiful lakes, even through (over) one of the two lakes. But the whisper of ghosts may quicken your stride.

## DESCRIPTION

Leave the visitor center and travel south 0.1 mile until the trail merges with Prairie Trail. Take an immediate left, then continue until the trail splits around Lake Mary. Lined on both sides by railroad ties, the dirt trail is dusty in dry summer. At the Lake Mary fork, turn right onto the Lake Mary Trail and travel counterclockwise around the lake.

The trail is heavily exposed at first, but near the lake, you enter a nice respite in a cluster of cottonwood trees. Continue the counterclockwise trip around Lake Mary and ignore the many spurs and trail intersections that take hikers away from the lake.

At the intersection of Lake Mary Trail and Prairie Trail on the southwest side of Lake Mary, take a right onto Prairie Trial. The trails here are

## DIRECTIONS

From Denver, take I-70 east to the Havana Street exit. Go left, traveling north, cross over 56th Avenue, and enter the refuge. All visitors enter by passing a deserted military-guard station. Pass through and continue to the visitor center for mandatory check-in.

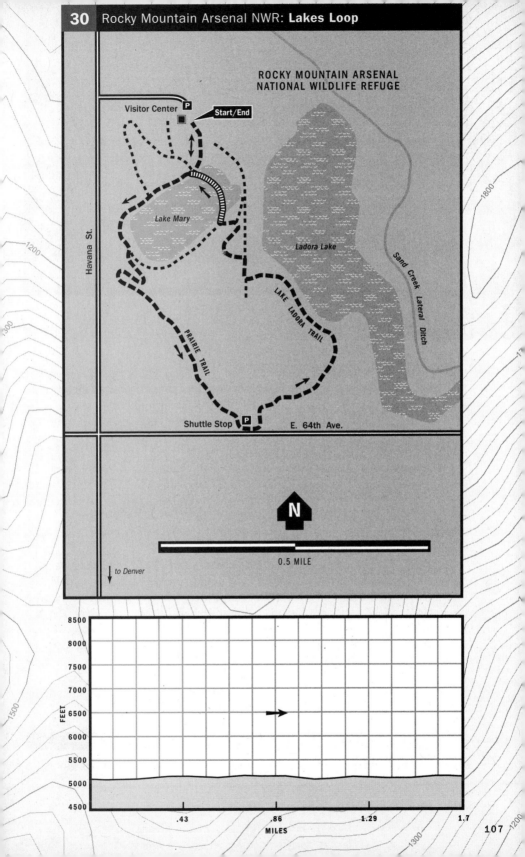

ROCKY MOUNTAIN ARSENAL
NATIONAL WILDLIFE REFUGE

Visitor Center

Start/End

Lake Mary

Ladora Lake

Sand Creek Lateral Ditch

LAKE LADORA TRAIL

PRAIRIE TRAIL

Havana St.

Shuttle Stop

E. 64th Ave.

N

0.5 MILE

to Denver

1800

1200

1300

1500

FEET

8500
8000
7500
7000
6500
6000
5500
5000
4500

.43          .86          1.29          1.7
MILES

The Lakes Loop offers hikers the opportunity to cross Mary Lake on a boardwalk.

well marked, and Prairie Trail is no exception. Here, the trail is again exposed, dry prairie land. You quickly come to a switchback built into a berm. After climbing up and over it, travel along a ridge, and walk through knee-high prairie grasses.

At the intersection of Prairie Trail and 6th Avenue, take a left turn onto 6th Avenue. Follow it for a short distance and then turn left into the shuttle-stop parking area, where there is a restroom and trailhead kiosk.

Go around the kiosk and enter the Lake Ladora Trail. This trail has nesting closures from October 15 to April 15, so be sure to check at the visitor center or call ahead. Pass a fork in the trail as the path approaches Lake Ladora. Take a left turn here and begin to travel clockwise around Lake Ladora. Pass beneath lakeside native cottonwood trees. These trees are used by many birds in the refuge, from cavity nesting flickers to prey-seeking hawks.

Lake Ladora is a man-made reservoir that provides habitat for many wildlife species that could not have lived here when it was an arsenal. Again, the trail departs from the lake and merges with a service road, where you turn right. Cross the road diagonally and take a left onto the trail that leads hikers back to Lake Mary. The trail is crushed rock mixed with asphalt and it splits again, almost immediately, to take you on Lake Mary Trail either direction. Take a left, pass a bull-frog sign, and take an almost immediate right on the portion of the trail that crosses directly over Lake Mary. Stroll along the floating boardwalk as it moves and gurgles with every step. After crossing the bridge that spans Lake Mary, take a right at a familiar intersection and follow the trail back around to the left to the visitor center.

## ▶ NEARBY ATTRACTIONS

Other Rocky Mountain Arsenal hikes: **www.rockymountainarsenal.fws.gov**.

# WESTMINSTER: COLORADO HILLS TRAIL

## ▶ IN BRIEF

Those who like quiet solitude will enjoy the lake at Mower Reservoir. Walk one-way for 1.5 miles through Westminster's Colorado Hills Open Space to reach this beautiful 11-acre pond. In the early summer, wildflowers bloom from the trailhead all the way to the lake. Most people come to this Open Space to give the dogs some exercise, and barely venture past the irrigation ditch. If you bring your pet and want to explore the trail, dogs must be leashed outside of the dog park.

## ▶ DESCRIPTION

Leave the parking area and go through the fence to the right of the trail kiosk. Note any posted rattlesnake warnings since this trail is rumored to be full of them. The first portion is a 20-acre off-leash, fenced dog park. The wide trail is mostly dirt and small, loose rocks.

Walk westward toward the power line and mountain views. Ahead is a bench and a small shelter; pass them on the right. Come to an irrigation ditch and a small pond and take a left across the bridge that spans the canal. After the bridge, take a right and continue to head through the grassy hills at a slight incline as the trail narrows. On the right, the canal and pond are still visible. To the left are power lines and an arid yucca field. In the mornings, songbirds call out across the meadow.

## ▶ DIRECTIONS

From Denver, take I-25 north to CO 36, exit at Church Ranch Road, and go left. When you cross CO 121, Church Ranch Road turns into West 100th Avenue. The road curves sharply to the right onto Simms Street. Look for 106th Avenue on the right and turn into the trailhead parking lot on the left.

## ⓘ KEY AT-A-GLANCE INFORMATION

**LENGTH:** 4.4 miles

**CONFIGURATION:** Reverse balloon

**DIFFICULTY:** Easy

**SCENERY:** Pond ringed with cottonwood trees, tall grasses, irrigation ditch, views of mountains

**EXPOSURE:** No shade

**TRAFFIC:** Heavy in dog park, mild otherwise

**TRAIL SURFACE:** Dirt

**HIKING TIME:** 1.5 hours

**SEASON:** All year

**ACCESS:** Free; sunrise to sunset

**MAPS:** USGS Louisville

**FACILITIES:** Kiosk

**SPECIAL COMMENTS:** There are no facilities at this trailhead. The first portion of the hike is a 20-acre, off-leash dog park. Off-leash parks are hard to find, so dog lovers wanting to give Rover some wild time come in droves. It is very crowded before 9 a.m. and after 5 p.m. on weekdays and all day on weekends.

For information on hiking trails at Standley Lake and other Westminster lakes and open space, contact the City of Westminster: **www.ci.westminster.co.us**.

The future Rocky Flats National Wildlife Refuge will be managed by the US Fish and Wildlife Service: **www.fws.gov**.

Westminster: Colorado Hills Trail

UTM Zone (WGS84)   13S

Easting   488897

Northing   4415222

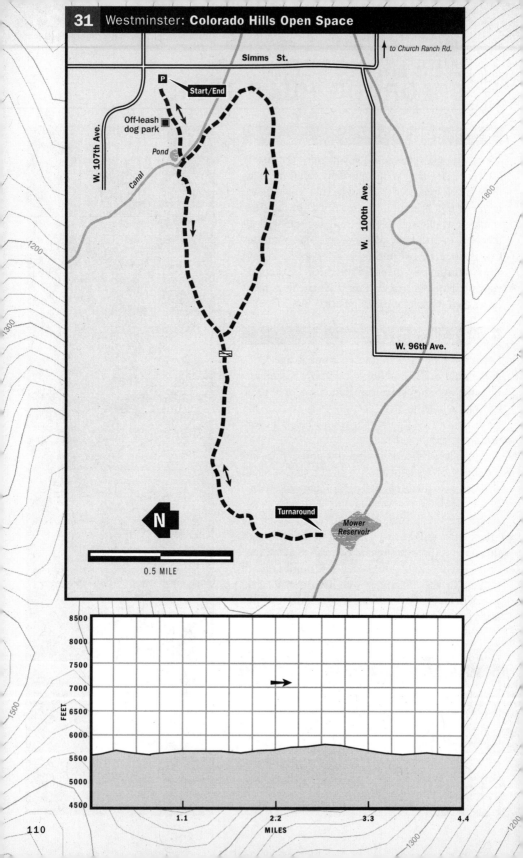

Simms St.

to Church Ranch Rd.

P

Start/End

Off-leash dog park

W. 107th Ave.

Pond

Canal

W. 100th Ave.

W. 96th Ave.

N

0.5 MILE

Turnaround

Mower Reservoir

FEET

8500
8000
7500
7000
6500
6000
5500
5000
4500

1.1     2.2     3.3     4.4
MILES

The author's dog, Bailey, carries her own weight with her doggy pack and enjoys the Colorado Hills Trail. She is, of course, off her leash legally.

The dirt path meanders, then widens into a dirt road. Curve a little to the left and begin to see unobstructed views of the Boulder Flatirons and all of its neighboring mountain peaks.

Any plane traffic that may rumble overhead is from the small planes that fly in and out of Jefferson County Airport, which is directly behind your right shoulder. Look over your left shoulder at views of Standley Lake, Denver Metro area's second largest lake after Barr Lake.

Come to a trail crossing and take a right at the sign that points to Mower Reservoir. The trail descends a little at this point. Prairie-dog mounds line the trail and constant prairie dog chatter fills the air.

Beyond Colorado Hills, to the west of Mower Reservoir, is the future Rocky Mountain Flats National Wildlife Refuge, which you can see from here. This 6,250-acre wildlife refuge will replace the controversial nuclear disposal plant and its buffer land after the cleanup is completed.

Go through a gate, pass an old, barbed-wire fence, and continue. Mower Reservoir comes into view on the left. Reach the crest of the hill and begin to descend toward the pond. Once at the lake, catch-and-release fishing is allowed and bait fishing is prohibited. Take a respite and watch waterfowl or sit in the shade of the cottonwood trees.

Trace back to where you came from, go back through the gate, and at the top of the hill, go right to make a loop back to the trailhead. This is where a Mower Reservoir directional sign is posted and where we originally turned right to get to the lake.

The trail makes a wide arc around to the right and circles back to the left. The landscape is still grass and shrubby meadow, and larger views of Standley Lake are to the right. Houses come into view as the trail goes to the left. Crest a hill and spot the dog park on the right. Take the trail down the hillside as it reconnects at the familiar canal and pond. Go right and back to the trailhead. Deposit any extra water into the dog dishes provided for furry companions at the trailhead.

# WHITE RANCH PARK: BELCHER HILL

White Ranch Park: Belcher Hill

UTM Zone (WGS84)  13S

Easting  478760

Northing  4405240

## IN BRIEF

Belcher Hill is a small part of the 19.7 miles of trails that make up White Ranch Park. It is a long, rocky, and very steep trail with great views.

## DESCRIPTION

Pass by the trailhead kiosk to the White Ranch Park Jefferson County Open Space sign and gate. Go through the gate and close it behind you. The trail at this point is arid and narrow, with room for only one hiker to pass at a time. Rocks and dirt are evenly spaced, yet the ground is hard-packed.

White Ranch Park was first settled in 1865 by immigrants James and Mary Bond after their son was killed under their wagon wheel en route to California. In 1913, Paul and Anna Lee White purchased part of the land and operated a cattle ranch until 1969. Anna Lee White gave the land to Jefferson County Open Space and dedicated White Ranch Park to the memory of Paul White in 1975.

You face an elevation gain of 1,800 feet on this trail; don't let its beginning fool you. Mountain-biking bloggers comment that this trail is "one of the best for quad and lung burners" or "long, busting climbs that will make you want to puke!"

On your right is a part of the hogback that dominates the Front Range. To the left are new

## DIRECTIONS

From Denver, take I-70 west and travel 3.5 miles to CO 58. Exit CO 58, going west toward Golden/Central City. Travel 5.4 miles on CO 58 then turn right onto CO 93. Take CO 93 north past Golden Gate Canyon Road, then travel 1.8 miles and take a left turn off of CO 93 onto West 56th Avenue (Pine Ridge Road) and continue about 1 mile until you see the trailhead parking lot on the right. CO 93 is a dangerous road; be cautious. Speed, blind spots, and wind play heavily in the accidents on CO 93.

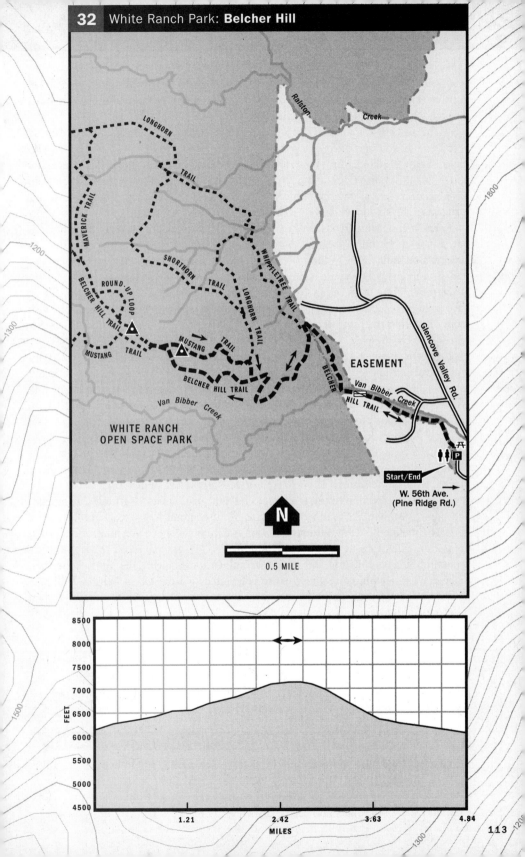

LONGHORN TRAIL

MAVERICK TRAIL

SHORTHORN TRAIL

ROUND-UP LOOP

BELCHER HILL TRAIL

MUSTANG TRAIL

MUSTANG TRAIL

LONGHORN TRAIL

WHIPPLETREE TRAIL

BELCHER HILL TRAIL

Ralston Creek

EASEMENT

BELCHER HILL TRAIL

Van Bibber Creek

Van Bibber Creek

Glencove Valley Rd.

WHITE RANCH
OPEN SPACE PARK

Start/End

W. 56th Ave.
(Pine Ridge Rd.)

**N**

0.5 MILE

8500
8000
7500
7000
6500
6000
5500
5000
4500

FEET

1.21        2.42        3.63        4.84
MILES

estates under construction. Cross an asphalt road and get right back on the trail. Do not turn and cross the cattle guard on the left. When you come to another gate, pass through, close the gate, and continue.

The trail crosses a footbridge and then curves to the left. Terrain changes quickly here because you enter a creek bed with trees, loose sand, exposed tree roots, and rocks. Large boulders skirt the trail. When I hiked with my husband, Bruce, we dodged a lot of horse poop and a few frogs. In the early fall, the height of skunk cabbage has been said to determine the severity of winter in the Rocky Mountains. If this is the case, the six-foot cabbage we saw called for a long winter with deep snow drifts.

The incline starts next, marked by a large fallen tree with an arm that protrudes out, almost a beacon to the trail. Since you are going up, the creek bed continues to fall down on your right. To the left is a wall of dirt covered by overgrown bushes. The trail is well maintained and characteristic of many of the Jefferson County Open Space trails: Volunteers tirelessly add erosion barriers such as landscaping logs that have been pushed into the sides of the trail. Barbed wire on the right side of the trail reminds us that the first part of the Belcher Hill trail is part of an easement before it enters true Open Space.

Pass or pause at a bench to your left and then take the roundabout to the right. Foot travel can take either the stairs or the flat slats of wood designed for mountain bikes. Wind downward, cross a bridge over a creek, and then continue up and around the foothills. The trail at this point is red dirt, starts a steady uphill climb, and is wide enough for hikers to walk side by side.

The scenery here is comprised of custom-built estate homes. A large lake also comes into view. This is Ralston Reservoir, along with the Ralston Buttes. Bears and mountain lions have been spotted on this trail but we only encountered chipmunks, black flies, and the sounds of crickets, airplanes, squirrels, and birds.

At the intersection of the Longhorn Trail and the Belcher Hill Trail, stay straight and do not go right. Views of Golden, Table Mountain, and Denver begin to peek out here. The incline is steady, although it does eventually relent. Exposure can be brutal on a sunny day without sunscreen. Continue up, up, up, until you reach the intersection of Belcher Hill Trail and Mustang Trail. In the shaded forest area of the trail, a bench awaits if you need a rest. Since you've reached the top of Belcher Hill, take a right on the Mustang Trail and continue on a plateau that takes you through open meadow. As the trail starts its descent, a natural staircase is carved into the trail by tree roots and by man-made trail-erosion-prevention landscaping. This part of the loop is steep and full of large, loose rocks.

At the intersection of Longhorn Trail and Mustang Trail, turn right. Come out of the trees and begin a more gradual downhill, where you will soon encounter the intersection of Longhorn and Belcher Hill Trail. Continue down, turn left on Belcher Hill Trail and back onto trail that you have already covered.

## ▶ NEARBY ATTRACTIONS

Belcher Hill hopefully will encourage you to grab a trail map and explore the other trails in this 4,391-acre Open Space Park. For further information, visit Jefferson County Open Space: **www.co.jefferson.co.us/openspace.** Golden is home to the Colorado School of Mines and the Coors Brewery.

# NORTH OF DENVER
## Including Fort Collins and Rocky Mountain National Park

# BUTTON ROCK PRESERVE: SLEEPY LION TRAIL

## KEY AT-A-GLANCE INFORMATION

**LENGTH**: 5.5 miles

**CONFIGURATION**: Balloon

**DIFFICULTY**: Moderate

**SCENERY**: River, forest, meadow, waterfalls, dam, lake

**EXPOSURE**: Exposed along river and lake, shaded in forest

**TRAFFIC**: Moderate, but heavy in summer with climbers and anglers

**TRAIL SURFACE**: Hard-packed dirt, loose rocks

**HIKING TIME:** 3.5 hours

**SEASON:** All year

**ACCESS:** Free; open sunrise to sunset

**MAPS:** USGS Lyons

**FACILITIES:** Restrooms

**SPECIAL COMMENTS:** No bikes, dogs, horses, or swimming allowed. Wheelchair access to river views and wheelchair-accessible restroom.

Button Rock Preserve: Sleepy Lion Trail

UTM Zone (WGS84)  13T

Easting  470930

Northing  4452960

## IN BRIEF

Along the river and through the woods to a beautiful lake you go. This is an exceptional hike that pleases all the senses, from the thundering sound of water pouring from the dam, to the sparkling ripples of the lake, to the musky smell of shavings from the tree-thinning demonstration area. The variety of scenery, moderate pace, and longer length of this hike reward participants with a memorable outing.

## DESCRIPTION

The trail begins at a white, metal fence that crosses a wide, dirt service road and allows only walk-in access. The trail is smooth, with a slight grade. Pass handicap-accessible viewing areas along the North Saint Vrain River (a popular spot for fly-fishing) and then the City of Longmont Reservoir. Several rock walls that line the spillway are popular with rock climbers; appropriate gear is required for this activity.

Pass signs to Button Rock Dam and turn left onto Sleepy Lion Trail. The trail, which is covered in loose rocks and shaded with dense pines, narrows and steepens. Begin to climb as if on a gym stair-stepping machine and watch for the hillside to the left, since the steady ascent has produced quite a drop-off. This area has been appropriately

## DIRECTIONS

From Denver, take I-25 north to CO 66. Travel west through Longmont on CO 66 and then through Lyons. Take a right of off CO 66 at the dead-end stoplight in Lyons and go west on CO 36 3.8 miles toward Estes Park. Look for Shelly's Cottage on the left. Turn left there onto a dirt road labeled CR 80. Travel 2.8 miles to the trailhead, which is marked by a white metal fence that creates a dead-end in the road and marks the beginning of the trail.

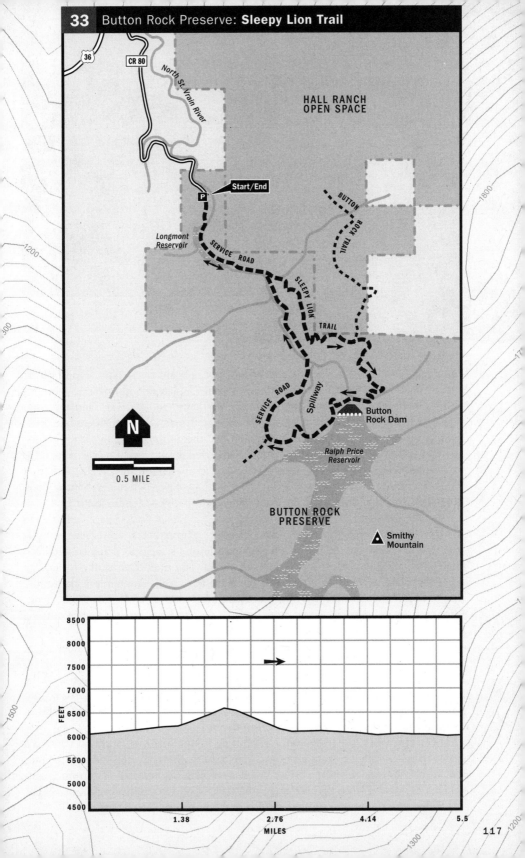

The cool waters of the Ralph Price Reservoir as seen after passing by the top of Button Rock Dam.

nicknamed Deadman Gulch. The roar of the river is heard along the trail and quiets as the trail climbs. Continue until the trail reaches a plateau and opens to a beautiful meadow, complete with a view of Rocky Mountain National Park and the comfortable sounds of a babbling brook, a light breeze through dried grass, and crickets. From here, ascend another hill and watch for the universal hiking signs (block human with hiking stick and legs in stride) scattered around to guide the way.

As they say, what goes up must go down, and at a significantly rocky portion of the trail, it begins to descend. Flecks of mica, moss-covered boulders, and a cool, wet, vanilla smell coming from the dense pines and junipers dominate the trail.

At the intersection of Sleepy Lion Trail and Hall Ranch Open Space, continue to the right. (We are still in Button Rock Preserve.) The reservoir is in view, but pay attention to the directional arrows on the signs. At first it looks as if you should head straight for the water, but trust the signs that take you uphill through the rocks. The trail goes to the right, passing an iron gate on the left. Oddly enough, this part of the trail now contains smatterings of asphalt. The trail ascends and crosses live creeks teeming with water bugs. Aspen trees line the way and are beautiful when turning golden in early fall.

At the base of the Ralph Price Reservoir is the steep wall of Button Rock Dam, where a large amount of water shoots out of a culvert and into the river. Pass this on the right, turn toward the dam, and start up the "bonus trail" to the right side of the dam wall. It takes hikers straight to the top of the dam wall and to the reservoir. Continue on the service road that winds around the right side of the lake. The water in the reservoir ranges from 60 to 100 feet in depth.

During the 1950s, Longmont was shifting from a highly agricultural town to a more technologically oriented economy. Mayor Ralph Price decided to build the Button Rock Dam over the North Saint Vrain River, just 7 miles upstream from Lyons. When a flood swept through the town, the dam saved Longmont from disaster. The flood filled the reservoir overnight instead of taking the projected years to fill.

When the service road forks, take a right. Continue past the ranger residence and through the tree-thinning demonstration area. A sign reads, "Learn how to Chip, Pile, Lop and Scatter." Turn right at the intersection of Ralph Price Reservoir and Ralph Price Reservoir North Shore Line. Pass a restroom on the right and turn left to continue down the service road. Pass the original turnoff for Sleepy Lion Trail and another restroom, and head back to the parking area.

## ▶ NEARBY ATTRACTIONS

The Golden Ponds Natural Open Space boasts 94 acres of nature walkways, bike-ways, ponds, and open space perfect for picnics, fishing, and wildlife observation. The park is located at Third Avenue and Hover Road in Longmont.

For more information, City of Longmont: **www.ci.longmont.co.us.**

# CATHY FROMME PRAIRIE: FOSSIL CREEK TRAIL

## KEY AT-A-GLANCE INFORMATION

**LENGTH:** 4.8 miles

**CONFIGURATION:** Out-and-back

**DIFFICULTY:** Easy

**SCENERY:** Meadow, views of Horsetooth Rock

**EXPOSURE:** Very exposed

**TRAFFIC:** Moderate

**TRAIL SURFACE:** Concrete

**HIKING TIME:** 2.5 hours

**SEASON:** All year

**ACCESS:** Free; open 5 a.m.–11 p.m.

**MAPS:** USGS Fort Collins

**FACILITIES:** Kiosk; restroom located just before Taft Hill Road

**SPECIAL COMMENTS:** Beware of the snakes sunning themselves on the concrete, especially the Western rattlesnake. Rangers ask that hikers refrain from reaching into burrows along the trail, since rattlesnakes and black widow spiders live there. Stay on the trail and keep pets leashed. The rattlesnakes and birds of prey would much rather eat the abundant prairie dogs.

Cathy Fromme Prairie:

Fossil Creek Trail

UTM Zone (WGS84)    13T

Easting    491870

Northing    4484340

## IN BRIEF

Cathy Fromme Prairie Natural Area, tagged as the jewel of the high plains, is an excellent and rare example of how the Colorado Front Range looked before it was settled. The rolling terrain, wetlands, and grasslands support a variety of plants and animals. The late Cathy Fromme was a local advocate for citizen involvement and environmental protection. She served on the Fort Collins City Council in 1991 and 1992.

## DESCRIPTION

After leaving the parking area, turn right onto Fossil Creek Trail. Walk along the paved trail, adjacent to tall prairie grasses and weeds. Pass through an open gate and head left, down into the prairie. Pass an intersection of the trail from a residential area on the right. Continue left and travel through native shortgrass species that include buffalo grass, blue grama, little bluestem, side-oats grama, and needle-and-thread. Short information displays along the trail discuss various aspects of the prairie. Replicated animal tracks are also pressed into the pavement at regular intervals.

Pass a spur off the trail that leads to a memorial plaque and bench. You see an abundance of signs that warn of rattlesnakes, which tend to draw your attention to the ground. Instead, all eyes should be on the views of Horsetooth Rock ahead. To the right is a new residential area and to the left is the prairie.

The trail, which started at a slight descent,

## DIRECTIONS

From Denver, take I-25 north to the Harmony Road exit in Fort Collins. Travel west on Harmony Road through Fort Collins; cross over College Avenue, and continue to Shields Street. Turn left and travel about 1 mile, where a parking sign directs you to the trailhead on the right.

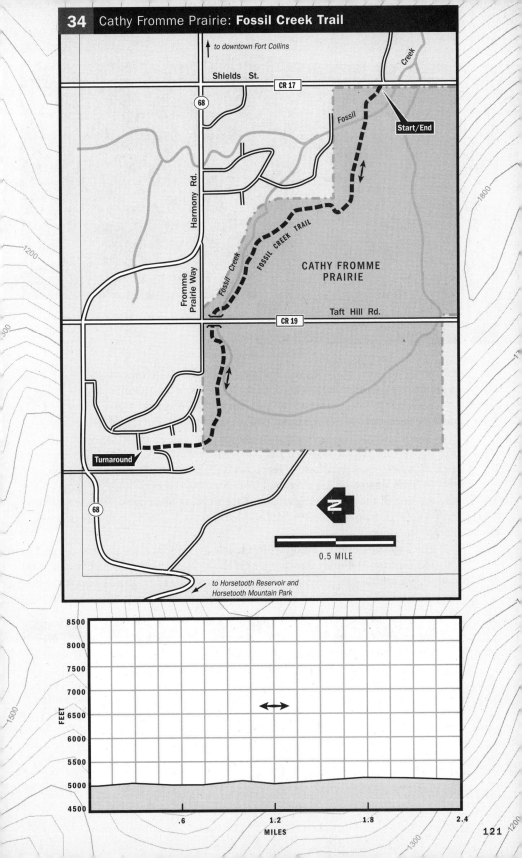

to downtown Fort Collins

Shields St.

CR 17

68

Fossil

Creek

Start/End

Fossil

Harmony Rd.

Fossil Creek

FOSSIL CREEK TRAIL

Fromme Prairie Way

CATHY FROMME
PRAIRIE

Taft Hill Rd.

CR 19

Turnaround

68

N

0.5 MILE

to Horsetooth Reservoir and
Horsetooth Mountain Park

8500
8000
7500
7000
6500
6000
5500
5000
4500

FEET

.6          1.2          1.8          2.4
MILES

Signs, warning hikers of rattlesnakes that frequent the area, line the edge of the Fossil Creek Trail.

now travels at a very slight ascent. It appears as if the entire trail will be rolling back and forth. Pass another spur that looks as if it leads to a residential area. When you pass a small rest area, continue toward Taft Hill Road. Cross over a bridge and the trail's namesake, Fossil Creek. Travel past another spur in the trail that goes to a restroom. Right after the spur for the restroom, go through an underpass with Taft Hill Road above you. Pass a sign that declares: "Great Raptor Watching." Birds of prey perch on trees, poles, benches, or fence posts: Red tail hawks and golden eagles are just two birds sighted on my afternoon hike. An observation building just beyond the opposite side of the trailhead is a good place to bring binoculars and identify these birds. There are also interactive displays that discuss the relationship between raptors and their prey.

The Larimer County Landfill is to the left, but it's far enough away to prevent a distraction from the hike. Pass a spur on the right that goes through a neighborhood. Pass a private property sign and a gate. Cross over a bridge and stop at the end of the concrete. This is the end of the trail and our turnaround point.

## ▶ NEARBY ATTRACTIONS

Other Fort Collins natural areas: **www.fcgov.com/parks/trails.php**. Horsetooth Mountain Park and Lory State Park are nearby: **www.coloradoparks.org**.

# FORT COLLINS: POUDRE RIVER TRAIL

## ▶ IN BRIEF

The Poudre River Trail began as a joint venture between the City of Fort Collins, the City of Greeley, and the town of Windsor. The trail extends 19 miles one-way from Greeley to Fort Collins along the beautiful Cache La Poudre River, named by early French trappers, and meaning ."the hiding place of powder." The Poudre River Trail offers an exciting recreational opportunity for walkers, hikers, joggers, bikers, and in-line skaters. Educational, historical, and wildlife hot spots are plentiful along this dynamic urban trail, which alternates between concrete surfaces and soft dirt.

## ▶ DESCRIPTION

From the parking lot, turn left onto the Poudre River Trail. The concrete trail is well maintained and flat at the trailhead. Travel under the Prospect Road bridge. This is a heavy industrial area with office parks that hikers quickly leave behind.

The trail moves from an urban atmosphere to wetlands as it coasts along the Cache La Poudre River, known for its accessibility and heavy recreational use upstream (rafting, kayaking, fishing, and camping). The office buildings begin to disappear as soon as the trail intersects Spring Creek Trail and passes Cattail Chorus on the left. These swamplike ponds are lush with wetland vegetation and wildlife and are characteristic of the small

## ▶ DIRECTIONS

Trailhead: From Denver, take I-25 north to Prospect Road in Fort Collins. Turn left, driving west on Prospect Road, then turn left on Sharp Point Drive. Make an immediate left into the first trailhead parking lot.

To leave a vehicle at the trail's end: Continue on Prospect Road to Taft Hill Road. Turn right and travel to the trailhead parking lot on the right.

## ℹ KEY AT-A-GLANCE INFORMATION

**LENGTH:** 6.94 miles

**CONFIGURATION:** One-way

**DIFFICULTY:** Easy

**SCENERY:** River and wetlands, cottonwood trees lining the Poudre River

**EXPOSURE:** Tree covering near river, transitions to exposed flatland

**TRAFFIC:** Moderate, can be heavy with bike traffic on weekends and in the afternoon

**TRAIL SURFACE:** Concrete and asphalt with a center line down the trail

**HIKING TIME:** 4 hours

**SEASON:** All year, but trail not maintained during winter months

**ACCESS:** Free; open dawn to dusk

**MAPS:** USGS Fort Collins, City of Fort Collins trail map available along trail

**FACILITIES:** Restrooms, water fountains, benches, and interpretive signs along trail

**SPECIAL COMMENTS:** Poudre River Trail is mapped one-way and it is recommended that hikers shuttle from the trailhead to the end of the trail (park one car at the trailhead and another at the end of the trail). If time allows, this trail can be completed as an out-and-back trail of nearly 15 miles. It is often under construction as improvements and additions are made. Check the City of Fort Collins Web site (www.fcgov.com) or trail site (www.poudretrail.org) for current closures.

Fort Collins: Poudre River Trail

UTM Zone (WGS84)   13T

Easting   497553

Northing   4490180

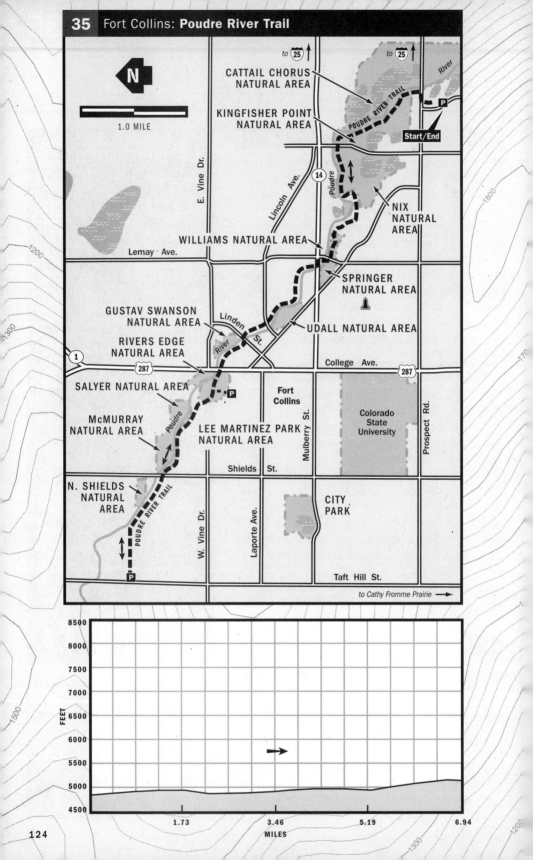

**N**

1.0 MILE

to 25 ↑

to 25 ↑

River

CATTAIL CHORUS
NATURAL AREA

POUDRE RIVER TRAIL

P

KINGFISHER POINT
NATURAL AREA

Start/End

E. Vine Dr.

Lincoln Ave.

14

Poudre

NIX
NATURAL
AREA

WILLIAMS NATURAL AREA

Lemay Ave.

SPRINGER
NATURAL AREA

GUSTAV SWANSON
NATURAL AREA

Linden St.

River

UDALL NATURAL AREA

RIVERS EDGE
NATURAL AREA

1

287

College Ave.

287

Prospect Rd.

SALYER NATURAL AREA

P

Fort
Collins

McMURRAY
NATURAL AREA

Poudre

LEE MARTINEZ PARK
NATURAL AREA

Mulberry St.

Colorado
State
University

Shields St.

N. SHIELDS
NATURAL
AREA

W. Vine Dr.

Laporte Ave.

CITY
PARK

POUDRE RIVER TRAIL

P

Taft Hill St.

to Cathy Fromme Prairie →

FEET

8500
8000
7500
7000
6500
6000
5500
5000
4500

→

1.73          3.46          5.19          6.94
MILES

Along the shores of a quiet Poudre River, the author's kids, Anna and Alex Lipker, strike a pose.

bodies of water that dot the Poudre River Trail. The Cattail Chorus provides habitat for migrant and resident songbirds and waterfowl. The cottonwoods provide a winter roosting site for great blue herons. Yellow-headed blackbirds nest in the cattails.

A section of the Poudre River in the canyon has been designated by the National Park Service as a National Wild and Scenic River. The river was named in the 1820s by French fur trappers who were forced to hide (cache) gunpowder (poudre) on the river's banks in order to survive a harsh winter snowstorm.

The trail continues past the Cattail Chorus Natural Area. A picnic table beckons hikers to sit and enjoy the view of the river. This area opens to a meadow that can be high with native grasses or recently mowed, but always frames a view of the foothills to the west.

More than 150 bird species have been reported along the Poudre River Trail, including bald eagles, white pelicans, and great horned owls. The most common birds in this area are waterfowl, warblers, and forest birds. Beavers, muskrats, and other small mammals are also frequently seen among the cottonwoods lining the river.

Many tributary trails feed into the main Poudre River Trail. Most are unmarked access points from neighborhood sidewalks and streets. The trail at this point alternates between concrete and asphalt and is marked with a center line down the middle.

Pass the Kingfisher Point Natural Area, the Bignall Natural Area, the NIX Natural Area, and then the City of Fort Collins Parks and Recreation offices. After passing the Springer Natural Area, climb a long hill and double back onto a sidewalk. The trail is well marked, so just follow the trail signs. At Mulberry West, you may use the pedestrian-bicycle bridge to cross. Once across, pass a billboard, take a left before the City of Fort Collins Golf Course, and enter the Springer Natural Area again, another excellent site for wildlife viewing.

The Poudre River is on your left now, and the trail passes by the unsightly Mulberry Water Reclamation Facility. Continue past the Old Pickle Plant and the Udall Natural Area.

Turn left on Linden Street and pick up the trail about 200 feet on the right. This area is home to the Gustav Swanson Natural Area, with key habitats that include the river, ponds, riparian forest, and grasslands.

The Poudre River is to the right of the trail before it leaves the river for a short time. It cuts directly through Lee Martinez Park Natural Area, which is open to the public and home to a playground and a popular farm operated by the City of Fort Collins. The trail crisscrosses to allow for merging traffic, but you'll stay on the main thoroughfare.

Pass Shields Street and begin the last portion of the trail, which is a wide, exposed expanse of land that travels along the Poudre River and through the North Shields Pond Natural Area. The trail ends at the trailhead parking lot at North Taft Hill Road. If transportation has not been arranged, turn around and start back.

▶ **NEARBY ATTRACTIONS**

Check into the Environmental Learning Center, an outdoor classroom that showcases the importance of the Poudre River to the surrounding wildlife and vegetation, as well as the agricultural and municipal uses it supports. For more information, City of Fort Collins: **www.fcgov.com.**

# GLEN HAVEN: CROSIER MOUNTAIN TRAIL

## ▶ IN BRIEF

Crosier Mountain Trail is near the mountain town of Glen Haven. It's a cute little place and a miniature of neighboring Estes Park, with one bed-and-breakfast, one general store, one great gift shop, and a real estate office. Crosier Mountain is a small version of the massive trails that dominate neighboring Rocky Mountain National Park. It's a great workout with spectacular views and smaller crowds than are found in Estes Park.

## ▶ DESCRIPTION

From the Rainbow Pit (gravel pit) trailhead for Crosier Mountain, leave the parking lot and the hillside that is eroding nearby. Pass through a wood gate. At first the trail is eroding, with large cracks and gullies formed by water. The path narrows and ascends at a steady incline through a forest of evergreen and aspen trees. Continue up and navigate the loose gravel and rocks.

Take the large switchback to the right and continue. You can still hear the noise from CR 43 here. The trail levels out for a short distance and then switchbacks again to begin a new ascent. Views from the trail open up to the left as trees thin out and meadows appear. Travel into low bushes and scattered trees on the packed-dirt path with exposed tree root and scattered rocks.

Continue through a series of switchbacks and walk over rose quartz that now dots the trail. Look across the valley to views of mountainsides lined with homes. Rose quartz, fool's gold, and

### ⓘ KEY AT-A-GLANCE INFORMATION

**LENGTH:** 8 miles

**CONFIGURATION:** Out-and-back

**DIFFICULTY:** Difficult

**SCENERY:** Views of Estes Park, Rocky Mountain National Park; forested, meadows

**EXPOSURE:** Mostly shaded

**TRAFFIC:** Moderate

**TRAIL SURFACE:** Hard-packed dirt

**HIKING TIME:** 4 hours

**SEASON:** All year

**ACCESS:** Free; sunrise to sunset

**MAPS:** USGS Glen Haven

**FACILITIES:** Trailhead kiosk

**SPECIAL COMMENTS:** Dogs must be leashed. Signs warn that this is bear country and ask hikers to stay on the trail.

## ▶ DIRECTIONS

From Denver, take I-25 north to US 34 west through Loveland. Travel to Drake, continuing on US 34, turn right onto CR 43. Pass the Garden Gate trailhead at 2.2 miles and at 5.5 miles, reach the Rainbow Pit trailhead on the left. A large gravel pit cuts the south side of the road.

**Glen Haven: Crosier Mountain Trail**

**UTM Zone (WGS84)   13T**

**Easting   463940**

**Northing   4478350**

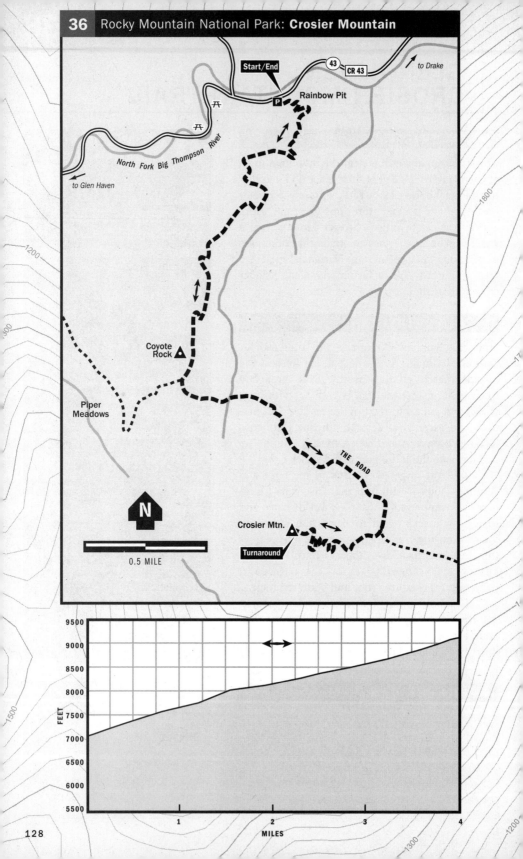

Start/End

43 CR 43

to Drake

Rainbow Pit

North Fork Big Thompson River

to Glen Haven

Coyote Rock

Piper Meadows

THE ROAD

N

0.5 MILE

Crosier Mtn.

Turnaround

9500
9000
8500
8000
7500
7000
6500
6000
5500

FEET

1
2
3
4
MILES

loose rock now make up the trail. Trees provide a nice canopy in this early section. Other trailheads leading to Crosier Mountain are widely exposed and very hot in the summer months.

The trail levels out, descends for a section, and then rises again. Cross over a small gully; the trail levels out one more time and then makes a quick switchback. You see your first views of Rocky Mountain National Park from here. The trail is again eroded and very steep. As you cross the ridge, you'll see more views of Drake and the Big Thompson Canyon. The trail levels out again, passes boulder formations, then descends for a while. Pass through a short lip and then travel up. The trail is wide here and a little overgrown in spots. Pass a sign to the left marking Coyote Rock.

At the intersection of Crosier Mountain, Glen Haven, and The Road, turn left. This route originates from The Road. After the turn, head down into a cool, small gully, then back up again. If legs and lungs are a little tired here, be assured that the intersection has marked the halfway point to the summit.

Hiking buddies, Suellen May and Wyatt Lymber, descend into a meadow along the Crosier Mountain Trail.

The trail widens a little and enters a forest of lodgepole pines, where it levels out fairly well and provides a nice respite. But just as quickly, the trail goes back into rougher terrain, with rocks and loose gravel.

At the intersection of Crosier Mountain, North Fork of the Big Thompson, and Glen Haven, turn right. The trail is steep and tiring from this point on. Social trails spur off the main trail, so keep to the left when there is a right turnoff. The trail finally levels out and travels through a small meadow with views of Longs Peak straight ahead, behind the dead trees. At the top of Crosier Mountain, the trail ends. The summit is characterized by a large drop-off and views of Estes Park and Rocky Mountain National Park. Rest on the welcoming, large boulders, then turn around to start the long walk back to the trailhead.

## ▶ NEARBY ATTRACTIONS

Miller Fork, Storm Mountain and West Creek Trails (Canyon Lakes Ranger District): **www.fs.fed.us/arnf.** Estes Park and Rocky Mountain National Park: Estes Park Chamber of Commerce, **www.estesparkresort.com** or Rocky Mountain National Park.

# HORSETOOTH MOUNTAIN PARK:
## HORSETOOTH FALLS AND HORSETOOTH ROCK

## KEY AT-A-GLANCE INFORMATION

**LENGTH:** 7.2 miles

**CONFIGURATION:** Loop

**DIFFICULTY:** Moderate

**SCENERY:** Open meadow, forest; views of Horsetooth Reservoir and Fort Collins

**EXPOSURE:** Mostly shaded

**TRAFFIC:** Heavy near Horsetooth Falls; moderate around Horsetooth Rock

**TRAIL SURFACE:** Dirt, loose rocks

**HIKING TIME:** 4 hours

**SEASON:** All year

**ACCESS:** $6 (exact change required); open sunrise to sunset

**MAPS:** At trailhead; USGS Horsetooth Reservoir

**FACILITIES:** Restroom, water, emergency call box, information kiosk, picnic table under shelter, grill

**SPECIAL COMMENTS:** Some rock scrambling is required to get to the top of Horsetooth Rock. Larimer County Parks and Open Lands Department offers a pass ($65 resident, $74 nonresident), which is available for the calendar year.

Horsetooth Mountain Park:
Horsetooth Falls and Horsetooth Rock

UTM Zone (WGS84)   13T

Easting   484700

Northing   4485720

## IN BRIEF

Horsetooth Rock is an important Front Range landmark and is affectionately known as The Tooth to locals. This trail combines a short walk through wildflowers to Horsetooth Falls with a longer hike through dense forest to Horsetooth Rock.

## DESCRIPTION

The trailhead is a confusing mix of mountain bike and foot traffic, so be careful to pass the service road and miscellaneous gates and go right on the Soderburg Trail. Be sure to carry a map of Horsetooth Mountain Park trails because the trails, albeit well marked, can be tricky to navigate.

The dirt trail, flanked on each side by seasonal wildflowers, starts with a slight grade but soon flattens and offers a view of CR 38. Trail workers have put a lot of loving care into this trail and placed flat rocks flush with the path. They act as walking stones on a part of the trail that becomes muddy in times of rain or runoff.

At the intersection of Soderburg Trail and Horsetooth Falls Trail, take a right. Crest the hill and take in views of Fort Collins homes and buildings, along with the neighboring meadow landscape that is brown and arid in the fall and green and lush in spring. The trail ascends and is fairly exposed to the elements. A small bench off of the trail offers hikers a small respite. Descend through scattered pine trees.

## DIRECTIONS

From Denver, take I-25 north to the Fort Collins/Harmony Road exit. Go left, traveling west on Harmony Road through Fort Collins until Harmony Road turns into CR 38E after the intersection with Taft Hill Road. Continue around the south end of Horsetooth Reservoir. Look for signs to Horsetooth Mountain Park and turn right into the parking lot.

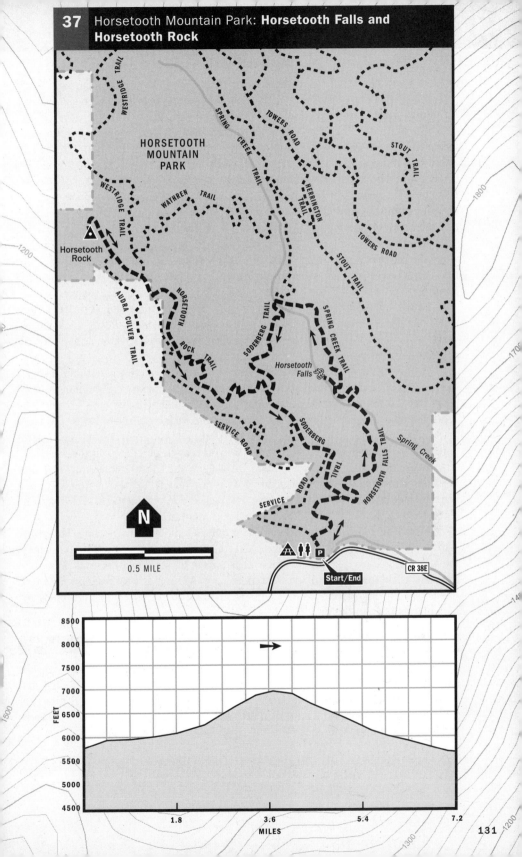

HORSETOOTH MOUNTAIN PARK

Horsetooth Rock

Horsetooth Falls

N

0.5 MILE

CR 38E

Start/End

**Trails labeled on map:**
- WESTRIDGE TRAIL
- SPRING CREEK TRAIL
- TOWERS ROAD
- STOUT TRAIL
- HERRINGTON TRAIL
- WATHREN TRAIL
- AUDRA CULVER TRAIL
- HORSETOOTH ROCK TRAIL
- SODERBERG TRAIL
- SERVICE ROAD
- HORSETOOTH FALLS TRAIL
- Spring Creek

**Elevation profile:**
FEET — 4500 to 8500
MILES — 1.8, 3.6, 5.4, 7.2

As the trail starts to ascend again, notice two large boulders to the right along a creek bed that is dry for most of the year. Cross a wooden footbridge and climb a set of man-made stairs.

Go straight at the intersection of Horsetooth Falls and Spring Creek Trail and locate Horsetooth Falls, which is only a few yards from the intersection. On the left, a trail sign indicates a side trail that leads to the falls, where granite cliffs tower over small pools. The Rocky Mountains are known for their finicky water supply, so the falls could be gushing or just trickling. There is always a guarantee of a small trickle of water from the spring for which Spring Creek is named. The cliffs' cool shadows and the allure of calming water make this a good resting place.

Return on the side trail, and turn left on Spring Creek Trail. Spring Creek runs along this serene portion of the trail, through intermittent forest and meadows. Continue on a series of steep switchbacks to an overlook with more views of the falls. From here, resume your forward course and use the man-made fence as your guide.

At the intersection of Spring Creek Trail and Soderburg Trail, turn left onto a wide, dirt service road that steadily climbs toward Horsetooth Rock. Look left for views of Horsetooth Reservoir, Fort Collins, the outskirts of Loveland, and, on a clear day, the northeastern plains.

At the sign for Horsetooth Rock, turn right off of Soderburg Trail and begin a steep climb. The narrow trail winds through ponderosa pines and granite outcroppings. As the trail climbs to the summit, traverse solid slabs of pink granite. The Tooth looms overhead. It is possible to ascend the rock by crossing below the landmark to its north side, though the trip up requires a bit of nontechnical rock scrambling. Views of the Bellevue Valley appear as you pass through gaps in the rock.

Horsetooth Rock looks just like it sounds, a horse's tooth—one large molar, to be exact. According to Arapaho legend, Horsetooth Rock is the heart of the Great Red Warrior slain by the Great Black Warrior in a long and ferocious battle in the sky. The blood shed in the battle is said to have colored the rimrock red.

From The Tooth, return along the summit trail and take a right onto Soderburg Trail. Look out for wildlife, since mule deer like to roam here. At a blind corner on the Soderburg Trail, take the left route that directs hikers down the trail. Mountain bikes are asked to go right, down the service road. A bench is also available for a rest. The Soderburg Trail continues to a T-intersection. Make a sharp right and follow the switchbacks back to the parking lot.

### ▶ NEARBY ATTRACTIONS

Horsetooth Mountain Park is a 2,772-acre park and open space located in the foothills of Fort Collins with 28 miles of trails for hiking, mountain biking, and horseback riding. Horsetooth Reservoir offers boating, waterskiing, and fishing. For further information on more outdoor activities in the area, visit Larimer County Parks and Open Lands Department's Web site at **www.larimer.org/parks.**

# LARIMER COUNTY: DEVIL'S BACKBONE TRAIL

## IN BRIEF

The Devil's Backbone is a small section of the hogbacks found up and down the Front Range. The hogbacks are remnants of an ancient exposed seafloor that has been honed by the elements over thousands of years. It's an easy, well-maintained trail right outside of Loveland on the way to Estes Park (Rocky Mountain National Park).

## DESCRIPTION

Start the hike by passing a large group of cottonwood trees and take a quick break here if you need to use the shelter of the trees and the picnic tables scattered throughout. At this point, the trail is smooth, hard-packed red dirt flanked by landscape rocks.

The hogback in view may be seen from many different vantage points throughout the area and is more ancient than the Rocky Mountains. That is one reason that the folks at the Larimer County Parks and Open Lands ask that you do not climb on the fragile rock formations.

## DIRECTIONS

From Denver, take I-25 north to CO 34 west toward Loveland and Estes Park (Rocky Mountain National Park). Still on CO 34, travel through Loveland (CO 34 is also known at West Eisenhower Boulevard in Loveland city limits), past Lake Loveland, and past all the shopping and strip malls and grocery stores. When you reach the western outskirts of town, you'll recognize the Devil's Backbone to the north of CO 34. Look for Hidden Valley Drive near the old water tank and for signs that mark Devil's Backbone. Turn right onto a good gravel road which is Hidden Valley Drive. Trailhead parking is a half-mile up the road on the left and marked by a beautiful metal sign that mimics the Backbone.

## KEY AT-A-GLANCE INFORMATION

**LENGTH:** 3.48 miles

**CONFIGURATION:** Balloon

**DIFFICULTY:** Easy

**SCENERY:** Severe rock outcrop (hogback) that makes up the Devil's Backbone, meadows, scrub bushes, raptor habitat, views of the Rocky Mountains

**EXPOSURE:** No shade or shelter except for a few trees just beyond the trailhead

**TRAFFIC:** Heavy

**TRAIL SURFACE:** Dirt

**HIKING TIME:** 2 hours

**SEASON:** All year. Please note that there may be seasonal trail closures for nesting birds; check with Larimer County Parks and Open Lands (www.larimer.org/parks) for more information.

**ACCESS:** Free, donation suggested at trailhead; open sunrise to sunset

**MAPS:** Open Space Trail Guide at trailhead; USGS Masonville

**FACILITIES:** Restroom, picnic area, doggy pick-up bags, emergency call box

**SPECIAL COMMENTS:** If there is no parking at the trailhead, a sign suggests that you come back at another time. This is to reduce the overuse of this heavily traveled trail. We suggest that you do this easy hike on a weekday—perhaps as a beginning or an end to a trip up the Big Thompson Canyon. Dogs must be leashed. Do not climb on the rock formations.

**Larimer County: Devil's Backbone Trail**

**UTM Zone (WGS84)    13T**

**Easting    487500**

**Northing    4472900**

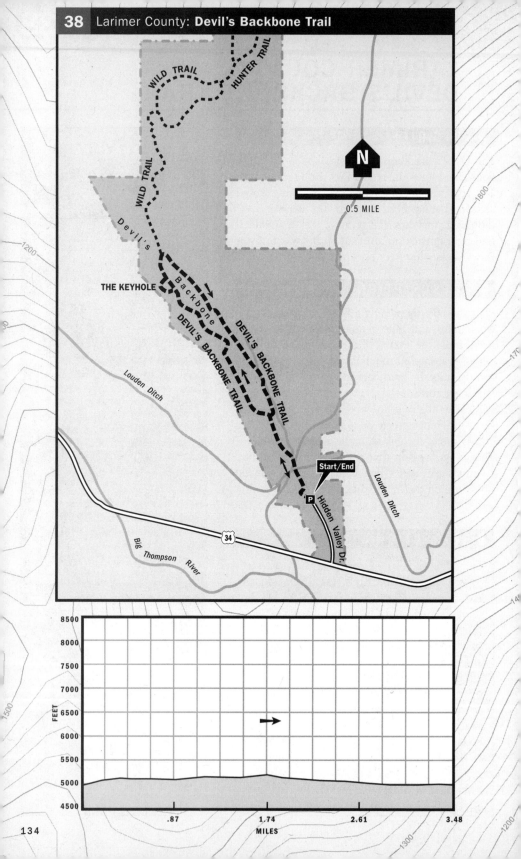

A portion of the "vertebrae" of the Devil's Backbone, seen throughout the length of the trail.

Pass an old mine shaft and Louden Ditch, an irrigation ditch circa 1878 that originally watered 12,000 acres of farmland. They are both fenced off and posted as private property.

This trail is shared by many mountain bikers, so the signs along the trail ask riders to take different routes than hikers. Other signs on the trail are single numbers that correlate with an interpretive brochure published by Larimer County Parks and Open Lands and available at the trailhead. These numbered markers point out areas of natural and historical interest from bird habitat to dinosaur fossil discoveries.

A staircase early in the trail is designed for foot traffic, so continue up the staircase and across the footbridge. Be very cautious on these wooden pieces of stair and bridge. While hiking the trail with my friend Shannon in a pelting rain of ice, I fell on the slick staircase. A second footbridge goes over a streambed that's dry in the fall but full of water in the spring.

A subdivision is going up to the east of the trail and sounds of construction often echo off the hogback. Focus on the beauty of the area and the sounds of the many raptors and other birds that nest in the cavities of the Backbone. Red-tailed hawks, prairie falcons, golden eagles, ravens, and a colony of swallows all make their homes here.

Turn left at the first trail bench and continue as the trail gradually ascends to the base of the Backbone. From a marked overlook, take in incredible views of the Backbone and the Rocky Mountains. The overlook is a small detour to the left of the trail; take it and come right back to the main path. Again, views are nice, despite development on the west side of the Backbone.

In the 1800s, hops cultivator Alfred Wild bought the southern portion of the Devil's Backbone. Wild is noted as one of the area's pioneer industrialists. Larimer County bought The Backbone in 1998 opened it to the public in 1999.

Cross a large piece of rock in the trail and pass the signpost labeled "5." This gray rock, which is part of the Morrison Formation, dates back approximately 150 million years. Dinosaur bones and footprints have been found in the Morrison Formation all along the Front Range, but none are visible from this trail. A prehistoric elephant and a jawbone with seven teeth were discovered in a nearby gypsum mine.

Follow the trail to Keyhole Bypass, a special window carved directly through the Backbone. The Keyhole was formed by erosion of coarse-grained rocks and is only one of the geological attractions of this hike. The region that the trail traverses is so rich in geological interest—with rock outcrops from the Morrison, Entrada, and Triassic Lykins Formations—that local fourth graders often visit the trail to study geology.

Turn back around and continue north on the main trail to the Backbone Trail and Wild Trail intersection. You have been on a foot-travel-only section of the trail (along the eastern ridge of the Backbone) until this point, but will go back on the multiuse trail back to the trailhead. This gives you the opportunity to complete a perfect loop and experience different vantage points of the Backbone. To do this, take a right at this intersection. Many bikers continue on to the left at this point and add another 7 miles to the route.

The vistas of the Backbone drop down to a lower level where views of the area mountains are limited. However, a sunset hike rewards you with an amazing light show: mahogany-colored brush hills, purple alpenglow sky, and a fiery red hue along the hogback, which may be attributed to the Backbone's namesake. The loop reconnects at the footbridge. Continue down the stairs, across to the trees, and back home again. There is a donation box at the trailhead that benefits Larimer County Parks and Open Lands. For good karma's sake, we deposited $5.

## ▶ NEARBY ATTRACTIONS

Big Thompson Canyon and the Dam Store are a short drive west of the trailhead. Loveland has commendable shopping, dining, and lodging. A cute bed-and-breakfast, The Wild Lane Inn, is less than 1 mile from the trailhead. Loveland is famous for its sculpture artists, the annual Sculpture in the Park, and the Loveland re-stamp Valentine program.

For further information, Larimer County Parks and Open Lands: **www. larimer.org/parks.**

# LORY STATE PARK: ARTHUR'S ROCK

## ▶ IN BRIEF

Arthur's Rock, named for an early settler, is a granite outcropping in Lory State Park. At an elevation of 6,780 feet, summit hikers are rewarded with breathtaking views of Lory State Park, Horsetooth Reservoir, and the Fort Collins area. Arthur's Rock is a good, short hike for Fort Collins residents and an easy hike for someone in Denver who wants to spend the day in the Fort Collins area.

## ▶ DESCRIPTION

Arthur's Rock Trail begins to the right of the restrooms and trailhead kiosk. Formerly ranchland, Lory State Park is a 2,400-acre parcel that was purchased in 1967 and named in honor of Charles Lory, president of Colorado State University in Fort Collins from 1909 to 1940. Lory's diverse terrain is home to mule deer, wild turkey, black bear, mountain lion, coyote, squirrel, cottontail rabbit, blue grouse, mourning dove, songbirds, and many reptiles.

The trail is characterized by rocks and smooth, hard-packed dirt. Cross two bridges and then head up Arthur's Rock gulch, a harrowing slot

## ▶ DIRECTIONS

From Denver, take I-25 north to the CO 14 exit in Fort Collins. Travel west through Fort Collins; CO 14 is also Mulberry Road in Fort Collins city limits. Turn right onto College Avenue/CO 287. Continue through northern Fort Collins toward La Porte. Do not take 287 toward Laramie; instead, continue on CR 54G. Follow signs to Lory State Park. Turn left on CR 52E at Vern's Restaurant and then turn left on CR 23 in Bellevue. Turn right on CR 25G, then left onto the gravel road (marked Lory State Park) that leads inside the park boundary. Pay at the visitor center and then drive to the very end of the road. The trailhead is visible from here.

## ⓘ KEY AT-A-GLANCE INFORMATION

**LENGTH:** 3.62 miles

**CONFIGURATION:** Out-and-back

**DIFFICULTY:** Difficult

**SCENERY:** Meadow, forest, views of Horsetooth Reservoir

**EXPOSURE:** Sunny in meadow, shaded in alpine portion

**TRAFFIC:** Moderate, only open to foot travel

**TRAIL SURFACE:** Hard-packed dirt, loose rocks

**HIKING TIME:** 2.5 hours

**SEASON:** All year

**ACCESS:** Park fee, $5 per vehicle, $2 for individual; park passes must be posted on windshield. A daily pass is valid from the day purchased until noon the following day. Open sunrise to sunset.

**MAPS:** Lory State Park map at visitor center; USGS Horsetooth Reservoir

**FACILITIES:** Kiosk and restroom at trailhead. Purchase park passes, learn about the park environment, view interpretive displays, and buy souvenirs at the visitor center.

**SPECIAL COMMENTS:** Arthur's Rock is inside Lory State Park, which is part of the Colorado State Parks system. This area is well patrolled and park rules are strictly enforced. Look for rules in the Lory State Park map, at the trailhead, and at the visitor center. Be aware that controlled hunting is allowed in Lory State Park—check at the visitor center for more information.

Lory State Park: Arthur's Rock

UTM Zone (WGS84)  13T

Easting  485260

Northing  4490200

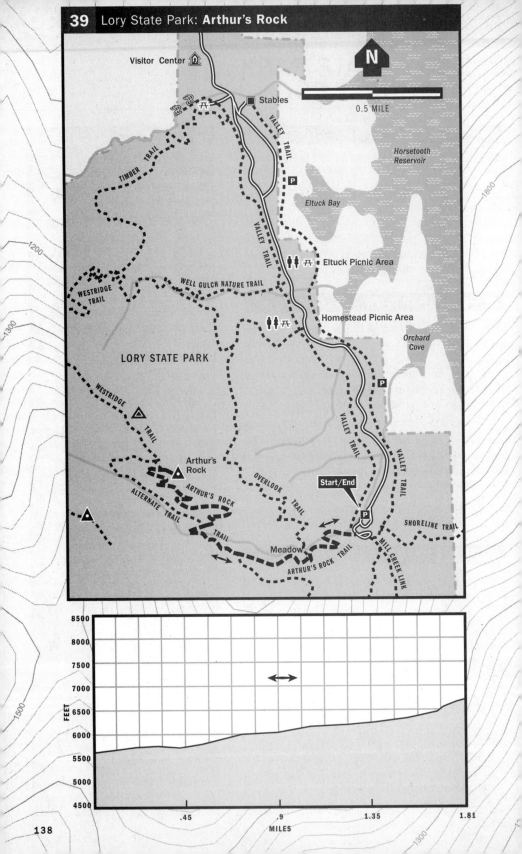

Visitor Center

Stables

N

0.5 MILE

TIMBER TRAIL

VALLEY TRAIL

Horsetooth Reservoir

P

Eltuck Bay

VALLEY TRAIL

WELL GULCH NATURE TRAIL

Eltuck Picnic Area

WESTRIDGE TRAIL

Homestead Picnic Area

Orchard Cove

LORY STATE PARK

WESTRIDGE TRAIL

P

Arthur's Rock

VALLEY TRAIL

OVERLOOK TRAIL

VALLEY TRAIL

ARTHUR'S ROCK TRAIL

Start/End

P

ALTERNATE TRAIL

SHORELINE TRAIL

Meadow

ARTHUR'S ROCK TRAIL

MILL CREEK LINK

-1200

-1300

-1800

-1500

-1300

FEET

8500
8000
7500
7000
6500
6000
5500
5000
4500

.45    .9    1.35    1.81
MILES

between rock cliffs. The path is narrow with boulder outcroppings on both sides and well maintained with man-made staircases, natural staircases, and man-made bridges. The incline is steady with manageable switchbacks. The first views from the trail include a bit of the Horsetooth Reservoir and Lory State Park scenery, which includes unique rock outcroppings, sandstone hogbacks, grassy open meadows, shrubby hillsides, and ponderosa pine forests.

If you're afraid of heights or are subject to vertigo, there are short portions at the beginning of this trail that may trigger a minor sweat. After crossing the ridge and coming around from the switchbacks and views, the path lands you into an expansive meadow complete with a quaint bridge. Sunflowers grow tall in the late summer and early fall; grass sways back and forth at hip level. The gentle rocking is soothing as the meadow passes quickly and the first views of Arthur's Rock appear to the right. Until now, this massive rock structure has been hidden from view.

Pass a sign that marks Arthur's Rock Trail and Mill Creek Link Trail. Mill Creek Link Trail is a sharp left behind you, so continue straight on the Arthur's Rock Trail. Mill Creek Link Trail accesses Horsetooth Mountain Park. Subsequently, there are many connector trails throughout Horsetooth Mountain Park and Lory State Park.

Cottonwood trees line the creek that runs to your right, but soon the trail leaves the creek and enters a forest. Reach a sign that splits the trail and offers an Arthur's Rock alternate route to the left and Arthur's Rock Trail straight ahead. Continue straight on Arthur's Rock Trail. This route takes you to the top of the massive, sun-kissed rock formation, but does so with many forgiving switchbacks. This trail has many signs, and the next one points to the summit of Arthur's Rock and a scenic overlook. Take a second to go off trail on a small footpath to the right and sneak a preview of the scenery. Back on the trail, come face to face with the vertical body of Arthur's Rock. Glowing red at dusk, this smooth, towering, vertical rock is at arm's length. The trail, with exposed roots and rocks, is wide enough at this point for one hiker.

Don't be alarmed if you hear voices on the trail. Arthur's Rock is massive and effectively echoes the faintest sounds. Go up, up, and up, and once your quads are in full burn, the trail levels. I promise. There is a lot of poison ivy along this trail, so please remember: "Leaves of three, let them be." Signs posted along the trail remind you of the poison ivy dangers. One park perk: Wildflowers, animals, and birds can all be studied with the aid of a guided hike available to groups by reservation.

At this point, you have ascended the south face of Arthur's Rock and are now ready for the remaining challenge of the trail, one major reason why I've rated this hike as difficult. Continuing, reach a small saddle on the hill and come to the intersection of Timber Trail and Arthur's Rock Summit. Bear right toward the summit. There is a sign here that reads ROUTE TO SUMMIT, DIFFICULT TRAIL, USE CAUTION. A little bouldering is required here, so be prepared to turn back if you are not comfortable with scrambling over large rocks. No technical equipment is required, though, except the use of both hands and steady feet. Trail volunteers have obviously put many meticulous hours into this portion of the trail, making sure it is safe and easy to navigate. Move on to the summit and look to the east. The view pans from the waters of Horsetooth Reservoir to the trees and buildings of Fort Collins and then expands to the vast flatland of the Colorado prairie. Turn around and head back down again the way that you came.

# RABBIT MOUNTAIN: EAGLE WIND TRAIL

Rabbit Mountain: Eagle Wind Trail

UTM Zone (WGS84)  13T

Easting  480950

Northing  4454900

## IN BRIEF

Rabbit Mountain is an excellent hike on an exposed plateau that offers views of the Colorado prairie and three amazing mountain ranges: Indian Peaks, Rocky Mountain National Park, and the Continental Divide. It's easy enough for families, yet interesting enough for seasoned hikers.

## DESCRIPTION

From the parking area, veer left and then immediately head right at the first fork up the trail toward Eagle Wind Trail. The hard-packed dirt trail with loose rocks ascends slightly at first. Cut across the hill via trail switchbacks and take a right at the junction of Little Thompson Overlook Trail, Indian Mesa Trail, and Eagle Wind Trail. Prairie dogs and their burrows line the edges of the trail and raptors are often seen flying overhead, scouting these dogs. Signs at the trailhead warn of rattlesnakes, since they are common around Rabbit Mountain and like to sun themselves on warm boulders and sunny slopes. Be aware of their possible presence.

Continue over the bridge that traverses the Saint Vrain Supply Canal and crosses the service road. Indian Mesa Trail runs parallel to this route for a few more yards. Head south and pass a memorial bench on the left. This resting spot was appropriately picked because views of Mount Meeker and Longs Peak to the west are prevalent here. Views of civilization, such as homes and a gravel pit, can also be seen.

Rabbit Mountain is a transition zone since it divides the Saint Vrain drainage basin from the

## DIRECTIONS

From Denver, take I-25 north to CO 66 exit. Turn left, traveling west on CO 66 through Longmont almost to the town of Lyons. Turn right on 53rd Street, which turns into 55th Street, and follow signs to Rabbit Mountain.

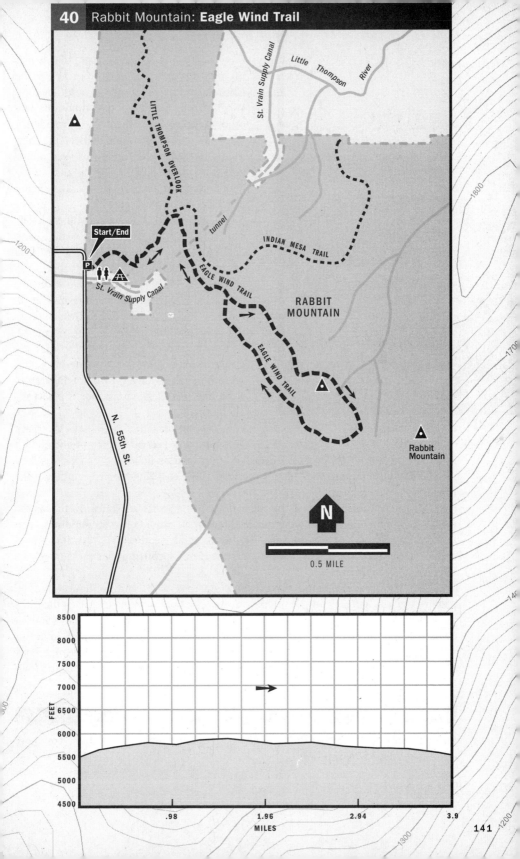

A view from Rabbit Mountain and the Eagle Wind Trail of the neighboring bluffs and prairie.

Big Thompson drainage basin. Geologists say that this area was once tropical lowland covered by rivers, swamps, and lagoons. Where hikers wander today, dinosaurs and other reptiles did their own wandering through lush vegetation. Historians also point out that Native Americans lived in this area for at least 5,000 years because of the abundant game, natural springs, and shelter from the strong west winds.

Eagle Wind Trail is a balloon, so hikers start the loop portion of this trail after approximately 1 mile of hiking. At an obvious split in the trail, take the left route. The nesting fine area mentioned before begins here, so be sure to stay on the trail at all times. There are great views of Twin Peaks to the west and the plains to the northeast. Views of Rabbit Mountain to the east are obscured here by low-lying ponderosa pines, but not to worry since the mountain summit is not the final destination, nor is it accessible by this hike.

Modern-day trail trivia says that Jack Moomaw, the second owner of the Rabbit Mountain property, was Rocky Mountain National Park's first forest ranger. His family sold Rabbit Mountain to Boulder County in 1984, ensuring the preservation of the land it its natural state.

On the upper portion of this plateau, you may hear airplanes overhead, the chirping of prairie dogs, or the buzz of insects. Rabbit Mountain is an important winter feeding area for large herds of deer due to mild weather and plentiful prairie grasses. Deer also attract mountain lions, so it is not surprising that these large cats have been spotted here.

The trail enters a stand of fragrant ponderosa pines and continues through patches of cacti, yucca, and tall prairie grasses. The trail is flat as it crosses the hill's plateau before it takes a wide turn and loops back to the right as it passes Rabbit Mountain on the left. The trail drops slightly and then climbs a short hill. Cut through a small open meadow, head through more ponderosa pines, and then back to the starting point of the loop. From this point, retrace your route back to the trailhead.

## ▶ NEARBY ATTRACTIONS

Little Thompson Overlook Trail at Rabbit Mountain; Indian Mesa Trail. For more information: **www.osmp.org.**

# ROCKY MOUNTAIN NATIONAL PARK: GEM LAKE

## ▶ IN BRIEF

Gem Lake, if you'll pardon the pun, is a jewel. Located on the eastern edge of Rocky Mountain National Park, this trailhead is one of the closest to the town of Estes Park.

## ▶ DESCRIPTION

To begin this hike, walk through the parking lot to the east, pass the National Park Service residence on the left, and enter the grove of aspen trees at the end of the parking lot. A sign clearly marks the beginning of the Gem Lake/Twin Owls Trail. Estes Park is home to retirees, families, and other outdoor enthusiasts, so both the very old and very young use this trail. It is a mix of gravel, small rocks, and dirt.

Continue through the aspen trees and the small meadow landscape that characterize the beginning of this trail. The aspen trees will be green in summer, bare in winter, and golden in the fall. For the best fall colors, time your hike around the last two weeks of September.

In a few yards a steady climb begins, supplemented by man-made log staircases. An intersection marks access for rock climbers to Twin Owls. The Twin Owls are the massive rock formations to

## ⓘ KEY AT-A-GLANCE INFORMATION

**LENGTH:** 3.64 miles

**CONFIGURATION:** Out-and-back

**DIFFICULTY:** Moderate

**SCENERY:** Views of Estes Park, Rocky Mountain National Park, Twin Owls, alpine lake

**EXPOSURE:** Mostly shaded

**TRAFFIC:** Heavy

**TRAIL SURFACE:** Hard-packed dirt, some loose rocks and exposed tree roots

**HIKING TIME:** 2.5 hours

**SEASON:** All year

**ACCESS:** Free; open sunrise to sunset

**MAPS:** Estes Park Chamber of Commerce or Rocky Mountain National Park; USGS Estes Park

**FACILITIES:** Trailhead kiosk

**SPECIAL COMMENTS:** Dogs are not allowed here or on any trail in Rocky Mountain National Park. No horses, no bikes. A backcountry permit is required for fires or overnight camping.

## ▶ DIRECTIONS

From Denver, take I-25 north to CO 34. Stay on CO 34 until it intersects Big Thompson Avenue/Elkhorn Avenue and turns into Wonderview Avenue. Pass the Stanley Historic District and take the first right onto MacGregor Avenue. Turn left into MacGregor Ranch; it looks like a private ranch, but it is an easement through the ranch. The one-lane road is full of potholes. (The car traveling uphill has right-of-way.) Follow the signs to Twin Owls Trailhead. Pass signs to MacGregor Ranch Museum. The trailhead parking lot is to the left after the Ranger's Cottage on the right.

**Rocky Mountain National Park: Gem Lake**

**UTM Zone (WGS84)    13T**

**Easting    455590**

**Northing    4472290**

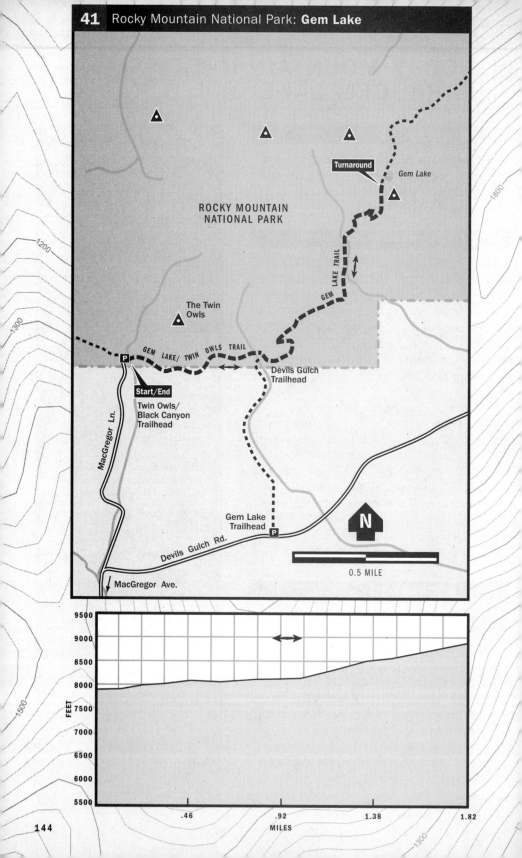

Turnaround

Gem Lake

ROCKY MOUNTAIN
NATIONAL PARK

GEM LAKE TRAIL

The Twin
Owls

GEM LAKE / TWIN OWLS TRAIL

Devils Gulch
Trailhead

Start/End
Twin Owls/
Black Canyon
Trailhead

MacGregor Ln.

Gem Lake
Trailhead

Devils Gulch Rd.

MacGregor Ave.

N

0.5 MILE

9500
9000
8500
8000
7500
7000
6500
6000
5500

FEET

.46    .92    1.38    1.82
MILES

the left that resemble two giant owls resting on the crest of the hill. The Twin Owls are extremely popular with climbers, who make up most of the initial traffic on the trail. Climbing here is very technical, and a strict code of conduct is enforced by other climbers.

Staying on the Gem Lake Trail, the next intersection is Gem Lake Trail and Climber's Access to Upper Twin Owls, Bowels of the Owls, and Gollum's Arch. Continue straight on the Gem Lake Trail.

To the right, catch the first views of Rocky Mountain National Park and one of its more famous mountains and a popular fourteener (a peak higher than 14,000 feet): Longs Peak. This peak can be found by looking for the silhouette of a beaver climbing up the side of a hill. The peak is at the beaver's nose.

Gem Lake, Twin Owl Trailhead, and Devil's Gulch Parking Area meet at the next intersection you will encounter. Many hikers come from the Devil's Gulch parking area, but that route omits views of the Twin Owls. Continue straight through this intersection, follow the footpath through the meadow and forest setting, and then cross a small stream lined with aspens. Heavy foot traffic has cut many random paths to scenic overlooks, but staying on the trail reduces unnecessary erosion.

Continue over smooth rock outcroppings and drink in the views of Lake Estes and Estes Park. The trail veers to the left and becomes a soft, sandy footpath. On this hike, I saw a young, racked buck, a rare sight this close to town. Continue up the many switchbacks past a precariously placed outhouse. This portion of the trail is quite narrow and navigates a boulder field.

Gem Lake comes into view at the base of granite cliffs with boulders and a small beach at the water's edge. This mountain lake is a bit cold for the body, but a few minutes' respite here will cleanse the soul. When the sun hits the water, you'll see the mix of jewel tones—emerald, sapphire, ruby, and diamond—that give the lake its name.

To return to the trailhead, head back the way you came. If you have more time, there are plenty of hikes that continue past Gem Lake and venture for hours, if not days, into Rocky Mountain National Park.

## ▶ NEARBY ATTRACTIONS

The Stanley Historic District houses the famous Stanley Hotel, where Stephen King supposedly got his inspiration for *The Shining*. It's fun to walk around the hotel, and the food is excellent. Estes Park has a nice mix of shopping, dining, historic attractions, and lodging. Rocky Mountain National Park is a treasure that offers hiking, picnicking, camping, fishing, rock climbing, snowshoeing, cross-country skiing, birding, and photography in the 74 mountain peaks that reach elevations of 14,000 feet.

For further information, Estes Park Chamber of Commerce, **www.estesparkresort.com** or Rocky Mountain National Park (National Park Service): **www.nps.gov.**

# ROCKY MOUNTAIN NATIONAL PARK: LILY MOUNTAIN

Rocky Mountain National Park:
Lily Mountain

UTM Zone (WGS84)   13T

Easting   454560

Northing   4462470

## ▶ IN BRIEF

Lily Mountain is ideal for Estes Park visitors who don't have the time or money to hike Rocky Mountain National Park. This is a classic alpine hike with rewarding views and a steady climb. Lily Mountain is often passed over for other hikes in the vicinity, such as Twin Sisters, and the hike is often confused with the small walk around Lily Lake. In addition, it is usually kept a secret and out of brochures, making this hike one of the least crowded around Estes Park.

## ▶ DESCRIPTION

Leave the parking area and begin to climb directly from the trailhead. Pass a National Park Service boundary post and a Lily Mountain sign. The first half-mile parallels CO 7 as the trail begins its ascent along the ridge. Large pines and boulder clusters dominate the landscape here. The hard-packed dirt trail has loose rocks and some exposed tree roots. Expect snow on the trail if you hike outside of the recommended seasons. We hiked in early winter and encountered packed snow from the trailhead on.

　　Early in the trail the landscape also includes aspen trees and consistent light filtering through the trees. The trail takes an uncharacteristic dip

## ▶ DIRECTIONS

From Denver, take I-25 north to CO 66. Travel west through Longmont on CO 66 and then through Lyons. Take a right at the dead-end stoplight in Lyons and go west on CO 36 to Estes Park. Turn left off of CO 36 onto CO 7 before the first stoplight in Estes Park. Go south on CO 7, past Mary's Lake. The road curves sharply. After 4.8 miles from the turn onto CO 7, look for small parking area on the right shoulder of the road and Lily Mountain trail marker.

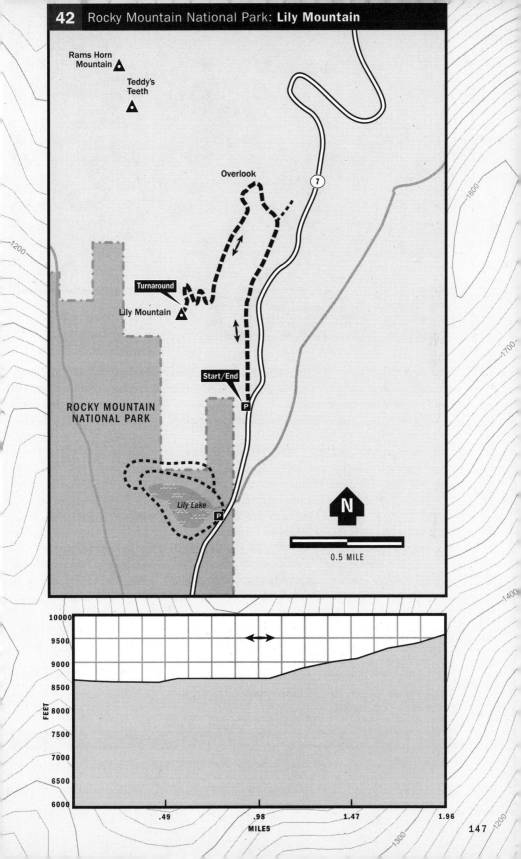

Rams Horn Mountain

Teddy's Teeth

Overlook

7

Turnaround

Lily Mountain

**Start/End**

P

ROCKY MOUNTAIN NATIONAL PARK

Lily Lake

P

N

0.5 MILE

1800

1700

1200

1300

1400

1200

FEET

10000
9500
9000
8500
8000
7500
7000
6500
6000

.49    .98    1.47    1.96

MILES

The author and her sister, Karen Lipker, wave at a fellow hiker as they descend Lily Mountain on a snowy but sunny December day.

and then flattens out before ascending a small man-made staircase and starting a series of small switchbacks. As the trail crests, the Estes Park Valley, Mary's Lake, and the southern portion of the town of Estes Park come into view. Pass a natural break in the trail that has been carved by hikers going off of the trail to the right and continue to the left. This boulder-shaded spot is a nice place for a rest. From this junction, start another gradual climb toward Lily Mountain. The summit is not yet in view. Continue on the trail and pass more large rocks and a picturesque dead tree that stands as a sentinel on the right after a large switchback.

At a large outcropping of boulders, you'll see an overlook on the right. Look to the left for views of Rocky Mountain National Park and right for more views of the Estes Park Valley and the town of Estes Park. Get back on the trail and continue to climb. The trail becomes dark and shaded, with a forest of large pine trees clustered together.

As the trail continues to ascend with switchbacks, there are built-in erosion control devices, mainly logs and landscaping materials, along the path. This side of the ridge can be very windy, and you will hear the wind whipping through the dense lodgepole pines. You will also hear the sounds of the highway far below.

Pass a trail marker at the crest of the hill. Continue to the right toward Lily Mountain's Peak, which consists of a large rock pile. Cairns mark the route to the top and hikers must scramble up this last part of the trail.

Views from the top are extraordinary and include Longs Peak, Twin Sisters, and the Mummy Range. After photographs, maybe lunch, and a rest, turn around to retrace the same route.

## ▶ NEARBY ATTRACTIONS

Twin Sisters, Longs Peak, and all Rocky Mountain National Park hikes. For more information: **www.estesparkresort.com** or **www.nps.gov**.

# ROCKY MOUNTAIN NATIONAL PARK: LONGS PEAK

## ▶ IN BRIEF

The excursion up this awe-inspiring mountain blurs the lines between a hike and a climb. The 15 miles will likely rank among the most spectacular, yet hard-earned miles you have ever hiked. This mountain displays both imposing stature and magnificent beauty that validate its popularity. Longs Peak is the tallest mountain in Rocky Mountain National Park and the fourteener that sits farthest north in Colorado. It is also the easternmost point of the Continental Divide.

## ▶ DESCRIPTION

Leave the trailhead and follow the East Longs Peak Trail (Keyhole Route) and begin an enchanting jaunt through the trees. Pass a small campground named Goblins Forest. At 1.9 miles, reach a well-constructed bridge crossing over a small cascading waterfall. This is a beautiful place to take a break.

Your first views of Longs Peak are here as the trees transition to shorter vegetation. At 2.5 miles, there is a fork in the trail. Follow the sign left toward the summit. After another mile, you'll reach the junction of the Chasm Lake Trail. This is another great spot to rest, as there is a pit toilet and a vista of the east Diamond face of Longs Peak. Head northwest as the trail skirts up Mount Lady Washington to Granite Pass.

## ▶ DIRECTIONS

From Denver, take I-25 north to CO 66. Travel west through Longmont on CO 66 and then through Lyons. Take a left at the dead-end stoplight in Lyons and go west on CO 36 to Estes Park. Turn left off of CO 36 onto CO 7 before the first stoplight in Estes Park. Go south on CO 7, past Mary's Lake. The road curves sharply and travels to the Longs Peak Trailhead turnoff. Turn right here and travel 1 mile to the Longs Peak Trailhead.

## ℹ KEY AT-A-GLANCE INFORMATION

**LENGTH:** 15 miles

**CONFIGURATION:** Out-and-back

**DIFFICULTY:** Difficult

**SCENERY:** Evergreen forest, spectacular mountain views, tundra

**EXPOSURE:** Shaded at beginning, no shade at end, high alpine exposure

**TRAFFIC:** Heavy

**TRAIL SURFACE:** Dirt, loose rock, talus, large boulders, large flat slate

**HIKING TIME:** 12 hours

**SEASON:** June–October

**ACCESS:** Free; open sunrise to sunset

**MAPS:** USGS Longs Peak

**FACILITIES:** Ranger station with ranger usually on duty, restrooms, camping sites, and picnic facilities; museum, plentiful information on hikes and Rocky Mountain National Park.

**SPECIAL COMMENTS:** Dogs are not allowed on any trail in Rocky Mountain National Park. A backcountry permit is required for fires or overnight camping. See additional notes at the end of hike description regarding other considerations.

**Rocky Mountain National Park: Longs Peak**

**UTM Zone (WGS84)   13T**

**Easting   452659**

**Northing   4457866**

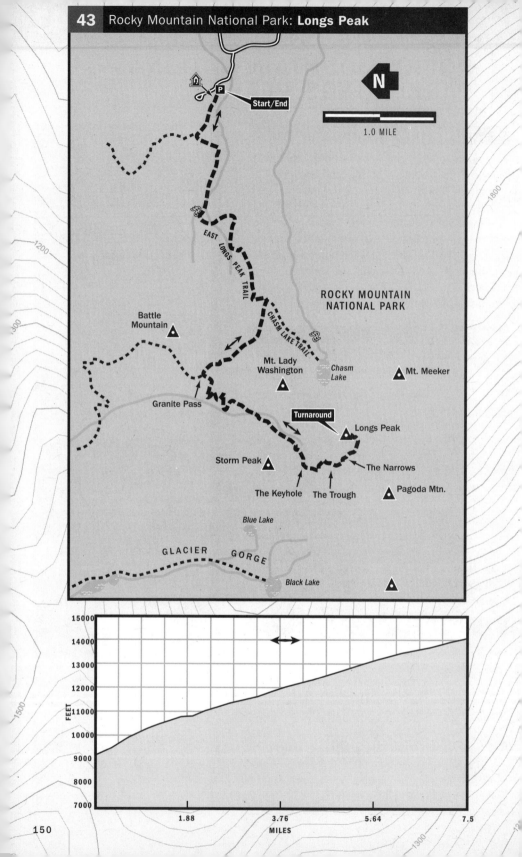

Start/End

N

1.0 MILE

EAST LONGS PEAK TRAIL

CHASM LAKE TRAIL

ROCKY MOUNTAIN
NATIONAL PARK

Battle
Mountain

Mt. Lady
Washington

Chasm
Lake

Mt. Meeker

Granite Pass

Turnaround

Longs Peak

Storm Peak

The Narrows

The Keyhole

The Trough

Pagoda Mtn.

Blue Lake

GLACIER    GORGE

Black Lake

15000
14000
13000
12000
11000
10000
9000
8000
7000

FEET

1.88          3.76          5.64          7.5
MILES

Stay left and hike southwest for 1.7 miles to the Boulder Field. Within this Boulder Field is another pit toilet and several rock shelters that act as a windbreak for tents. The boulder field consists of car-sized boulders. Begin to scramble your way straight up toward the keyhole. At the base of the Boulder Field, the top of Longs Peak, the Keyhole and the expanse of the boulder field are visible.

Many people choose to backpack this far to make for a shorter climb the next day. All campers must obtain a Backcountry Wilderness Use Permit. Be warned that you are camping well above tree line and the surface area is 100 percent rock.

The impressive view of the Longs Peak summit is highlighted here by a rock formation aptly dubbed the Keyhole. At the Keyhole is a small, stone shelter. The terrain becomes significantly more difficult beyond the Keyhole, so take a moment to evaluate the time, the weather, and your physical condition. There is no shame in turning back if the conditions aren't right; don't let pride get in the way of wisdom.

Cross through the Keyhole to the west side of the ridge and glance at an expansive view of Glacier Gorge. The trail is now marked by bull's eyes painted on the rocks. The remainder of the trail is extremely slick when wet and very exposed to the elements. A fall here could be fatal. Follow the exposed ledge for just over a quarter-mile to a large couloir called the Trough. Ascend the Trough to the top of the west ridge.

Now the trail will traverse east across Longs Peak's south face using a ledge called the Narrows. This ledge is narrow—only one hiker wide—and exposed. Take your time and stay calm.

Beyond the Narrows lies the Homestretch. The Homestretch leads you northeast by a series of steep, slick, angled slabs. Be mindful of loose rock; tread lightly, and watch for rock kicked loose by other hikers. In a short time, the summit of Longs Peak seems to just magically appear. This airy pinnacle is large and flat. The commanding panorama is well-deserved compensation for your sweat and tired legs. At 14,255 feet, there are plenty of photo opportunities.

After celebration of your lofty accomplishment, turn around and head back the way that you came. The ascent will most likely be crowded, which can be a problem on the narrow ledges where hikers cannot pass each other.

Note: Hiking time and terrain warrant extra consideration when preparing for this outing. A headlamp is useful for an early start, which is essential for a successful completion of this hike. Many hikers begin as early as 2 a.m. Equip yourself with ample layers of clothing and extra food and water; this is a long one. As always, tell someone where you are going and when you expect to be back. An average of 60 search-and-rescue incidents occur per year on this peak alone. Crowds of hikers fill this trail every day. Be prepared for a lot of human contact. Snow is often found on this hike, especially through the Trough portion, at any time during the hiking season.

## ▶ NEARBY ATTRACTIONS

Twin Sisters, Storm Pass Trail, and all Rocky Mountain National Park hikes. For more information: **www.estesparkresort.com** or **www.nps.gov.**

# ROCKY MOUNTAIN NATIONAL PARK: STORM PASS TRAIL TO ESTES CONE

## KEY AT-A-GLANCE INFORMATION

**LENGTH:** 6.72 miles

**CONFIGURATION:** Out-and-back

**DIFFICULTY:** Difficult

**SCENERY:** Evergreen forest with spectacular mountain views at the top

**EXPOSURE:** Shaded

**TRAFFIC:** Moderate

**TRAIL SURFACE:** Dirt with loose rock and tree roots

**HIKING TIME:** 3.5 hours

**SEASON:** May–October (open all year)

**ACCESS:** Free; open sunrise to sunset

**MAPS:** USGS Longs Peak

**FACILITIES:** Ranger station with ranger usually on duty, restrooms, campsites, and picnic facilities; museum, plentiful information on hikes and Rocky Mountain National Park.

**SPECIAL COMMENTS:** Dogs are not allowed on any trail in Rocky Mountain National Park. A backcountry permit is required for fires or overnight camping. This hike shares a trailhead with Longs Peak Trail, a very popular hike. Many people start Longs Peak Trail at 4 or 5 a.m., finishing in early evening. Parking is limited, sometimes freeing up in the afternoon. However, an early start is recommended because lightning storms are common after 12 p.m.

**Rocky Mountain National Park: Storm Pass Trail to Estes Cone**

**UTM Zone (WGS84)　13T**

**Easting　452734**

**Northing　4457899**

## ▶ IN BRIEF

Estes Cone is an inactive volcano cone. In this book we will profile the trail from Longs Peak Trailhead, even though there are two other access points to Estes Cone. This mostly shaded trail is a nice hike in the summer. It is also a good hike early or late in the season, when some other nearby hikes are thick with snow or impassable due to snow. Estes Cone is a Rocky Mountain National Park hike that can be accessed here without an entrance fee.

## ▶ DESCRIPTION

Follow Longs Peak Trail from behind the little ranger's display and miniature museum at the parking lot. Please stop to sign in at the trail register right by the trailhead. Immediately ascend well-maintained man-made stairs. Since the trail is in Rocky Mountain National Park, hikers can expect a well-kept path throughout this hike, although the last half-mile is rocky, steep, and hard to navigate.

The first half-mile of trail is a steady, moderate grade that intersects with Storm Pass Trail. Take a right here onto Storm Pass Trail and follow the signs to Estes Cone.

The trail slowly gives way to loose rock and exposed tree roots. The grade varies as well,

## ▶ DIRECTIONS

From Denver, take I-25 north to CO 66. Travel west through Longmont on CO 66 and then through Lyons. Take a left at the dead-end stoplight in Lyons and go west on CO 36 to Estes Park. Turn left off of CO 36 onto CO 7 before the first stoplight in Estes Park. Go south on CO 7, past Mary's Lake. The road curves sharply and travels to the Longs Peak Trailhead turnoff. Turn right here and travel 1 mile to the Longs Peak Trailhead.

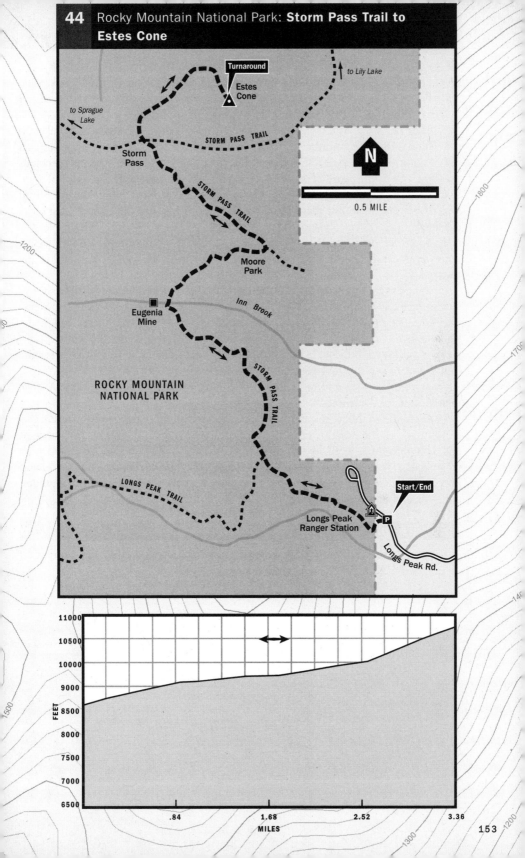

Turnaround

Estes Cone

to Lily Lake

to Sprague Lake

STORM PASS TRAIL

Storm Pass

STORM PASS TRAIL

**N**

0.5 MILE

Moore Park

Inn Brook

Eugenia Mine

ROCKY MOUNTAIN NATIONAL PARK

STORM PASS TRAIL

LONGS PEAK TRAIL

Start/End

Longs Peak Ranger Station

P

Longs Peak Rd.

including some short descents and traverses below Pine Ridge. Cross Inn Brook using a log bridge and continue to the right of an abandoned log cabin site with a rusted boiler and tailings. This is all that remains of the Eugenia Mine.

The trail starts a descent that seems a little out of place, since our goal is to travel to a summit. Continue to drop down and cross a small meadow as the trail opens up to views of Twin Sisters and our destination, Estes Cone. The trail becomes sandy and smooth. Pass the Moore Park campsites and at mile 2 reach a trail spur. Take a left, follow the signs to Estes Cone, and begin a sharp ascent toward Storm Pass. It is from this point that the trail makes up for lost time and gains most of its elevation.

To the left are spectacular views. The mountain to your far left is Mount Meeker. Longs Peak can be spotted poking above the ridge, with the peak's diamond facing the trail.

Lungs begin to tire as the elevation climbs and the trees become visibly shorter and stunted. At 2.5 miles, you reach the pass, marked by large rock cairns and signs. The Storm Pass Cutoff, to the right, is accessed at the Lily Lake Trailhead. Follow the signs to Estes Cone Trail, bearing right up through rock cairns and the stunted evergreens that dot the hillside. Estes Cone is straight ahead and once out of the trees the trail begins to ascend the cone's southwest flank.

The trail is steep and rocky, with twisted and stunted wind-worn trees. A close look at some of these trees will show lightning damage.

Continue to follow the cairns as you pick your way through a vertical rock garden for the last half-mile. Eventually, reach a small flat area, then head up and right and scramble through rocks to the summit of Estes Cone. You are rewarded with magnificent views of Estes Park, Rocky Mountain National Park, Longs Peak, and Mount Meeker. But you should head down, back to the trailhead, before afternoon lightning storms return as they do most of the summer.

## ▶ NEARBY ATTRACTIONS

Twin Sisters, Longs Peak and all Rocky Mountain National Park hikes. For more information: **www.estesparkresort.com** or **www.nps.gov.**

# ROCKY MOUNTAIN NATIONAL PARK: TWIN SISTERS

## ▶ IN BRIEF

The Twin Sisters sit at the easternmost edge of Rocky Mountain National Park and are accessed without entering the park. The trail winds through forest with some of the best panoramic views of Longs Peak. This is a great conditioning climb for those wanting to tackle considerable elevations.

## ▶ DESCRIPTION

Start at Lily Lake Visitor Center. Get on the road right behind the visitor center and follow it away from the highway. At the official trailhead for Twin Sisters, take a left onto the trail. Start out on a small service road bordered on both sides by a new evergreen tree growth. Immediately on the left is a small wooden bridge, Twin Sisters Trail information, and a trail marker.

Start a steady ascent on a trail comprised of loose rock and dirt. Enter a pine forest and then enter Forest Service land as the trees crowd and condense around the trail. Hikers ascend rather quickly and must scramble across some early rocks. The trail takes a deep right switchback and continues up the face of the mountain. The ascending path is aided in spots, not only by switchbacks, but also by man-placed rock staircases. Continue to climb as scenery stays the same. Cross a rock slide and enter into Rocky Mountain National Park. The trail becomes much steeper here, with a large staircase looming in the distance.

## ▶ DIRECTIONS

From Denver, take I-25 north to CO 66. Travel west through Longmont on CO 66 and then through Lyons. Take a left at the dead-end stoplight in Lyons and go west on CO 36 to Estes Park. Turn left off of CO 36 onto CO 7 before the first stoplight in Estes Park. Go south on CO 7, past Mary's Lake. The road curves sharply and travels to Lily Lake Visitor Center on the left. Turn in here and park.

## ⓘ KEY AT-A-GLANCE INFORMATION

**LENGTH:** 8 miles

**CONFIGURATION:** Out-and-back

**DIFFICULTY:** Difficult

**SCENERY:** Views of Estes Park, Rocky Mountain National Park; optimal views of Longs Peak

**EXPOSURE:** Mostly shaded

**TRAFFIC:** Heavy

**TRAIL SURFACE:** Hard-packed dirt, some loose rocks

**HIKING TIME:** 4 hours

**SEASON:** May–October (open all year)

**ACCESS:** Free; open sunrise to sunset

**MAPS:** USGS Longs Peak

**FACILITIES:** Trailhead kiosk

**SPECIAL COMMENTS:** Dogs are not allowed on any trail in Rocky Mountain National Park. A backcountry permit is required for fires or overnight camping. The former Twin Sisters Trail, which began directly west of the summit in Tahosa Valley, has been abandoned by the National Park Service. Park at the Lily Lake Visitor Center and hike the extra 0.3 miles to avoid the nightmare parking along the road, right before the true trailhead.

**Rocky Mountain National Park: Twin Sisters**

**UTM Zone (WGS84)    13T**

**Easting    454440**

**Northing    4461730**

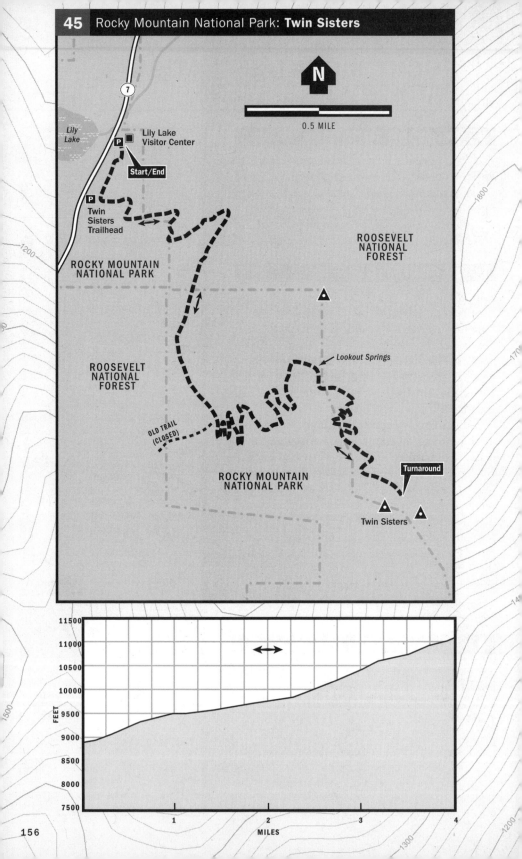

N

0.5 MILE

Lily Lake

Lily Lake Visitor Center

Start/End

Twin Sisters Trailhead

ROCKY MOUNTAIN NATIONAL PARK

ROOSEVELT NATIONAL FOREST

ROOSEVELT NATIONAL FOREST

*Lookout Springs*

OLD TRAIL (CLOSED)

ROCKY MOUNTAIN NATIONAL PARK

Turnaround

Twin Sisters

1200

1800

1700

1500

1400

1300

1200

A view of Longs Peak and the Tahosa Valley from a coveted spot on the Twin Sisters trail.

Turn and look to the right to capture the first amazing views of Longs Peak as it rises up over the Tahosa Valley. Pass through a second rockslide. Reach a small overlook and take in the view. Continue on as trail starts a gradual descent, which is welcome since the previous steps have been straight uphill.

Pass a huge, five-story-tall boulder and then take artificially carved rock stairs up. The trail switches back again to the left and continues an uphill climb. Aspen trees have now begun to mix in with the tall, dense evergreens. Smaller switchbacks continue, and the trail is very rocky with exposed tree roots.

The trail continues its upward journey and then reaches an area where there are fewer trees, more shrubs, and small aspens. The trail is narrow and hard to navigate due to huge rocks in the path. Climb away from the hillside and leave the view of Longs Peak. Enter Forest Service land again and continue. After passing through timberline, keep going to the summit area and head past the communications tower. The true Twin Sisters summit is not directly accessible by trail, but can be reached by a brief scramble heading east from the communications tower. Take in the views and head back the way that you came.

## ▶ NEARBY ATTRACTIONS

Lily Mountain, Lily Lake, Longs Peak, and all Rocky Mountain National Park hikes. For more information: **www.estesparkresort.com** or **www.nps.gov**.

# ROUND MOUNTAIN: SUMMIT ADVENTURE TRAIL

## KEY AT-A-GLANCE INFORMATION

**LENGTH:** 9.84 miles

**CONFIGURATION:** Out-and-back

**DIFFICULTY:** Difficult

**SCENERY:** Subalpine, dense pine trees, large boulders, views of Big Thompson Canyon

**EXPOSURE:** Shaded, cool; exposed, hot. (Be prepared to be hot in the spring/summer and cold in fall/winter)

**TRAFFIC:** Mild

**TRAIL SURFACE:** Loose dirt and rock, exposed tree roots

**HIKING TIME:** 6 hours

**SEASON:** May–October

**ACCESS:** Free; open dawn to dusk

**MAPS:** USGS Drake, maps for Foothills Nature Trail available at trailhead

**FACILITIES:** Restroom, trailhead register

**SPECIAL COMMENTS:** The Foothills Interpretive Nature Trail and the Summit Adventure Trail both originate from the Round Mountain trailhead. The main Round Mountain hike is the Summit Adventure Trail and is the hike featured here. The Foothills Nature Trail is an interpretive, 1-mile nature hike. A significant portion of the trail lies directly above CO 34, so expect traffic noise from the canyon.

Round Mountain:
Summit Adventure Trail

UTM Zone (WGS84)   13T

Easting   475840

Northing   4474232

## IN BRIEF

Round Mountain is a difficult hike to the summit of Sheep Mountain above the Big Thompson River and Canyon. The trail is a steady uphill grade with a forgiving and welcome descent after the summit. It is easy to navigate, with mile markers and informational signs full of trail trivia.

## DESCRIPTION

This challenging hike begins on the Foothills Nature Trail, an interpretive trail that is part of the Round Mountain National Recreation Trail. From the parking area, walk past the restroom, sign in at the hiking register, and continue up a wide gravel road. Do not be deceived by the undemanding beginning; the first 0.25 miles overlaps with the easy interpretive trail, but the majority of this hike takes hikers up the side of the Big Thompson Canyon, over the Continental Divide, and to the top of Sheep Mountain. The Summit Adventure Trail also serves as an interpretive trail, with several information plaques. When I hiked with my friends Sarah and Shannon, we found that the plaques were spaced just right, giving us time to stop and catch our breath if we needed to, while learning about the natural history of the area.

The two trails split at a well-marked fork. Take a left onto the Summit Trail and begin an immediate climb on a dirt-and-rock trail that runs parallel to the Big Thompson River and the highway below. As the trail climbs, it narrows and

## DIRECTIONS

From Denver, take I-25 north to CO 34 west through Loveland. Travel 4 miles on CO 34 west of the Dam Store in the Big Thompson Canyon. Turn left into the small dirt parking lot across the highway from the entrance of Vistenz-Smith Park. You will pass the Loveland Power Plant on the right.

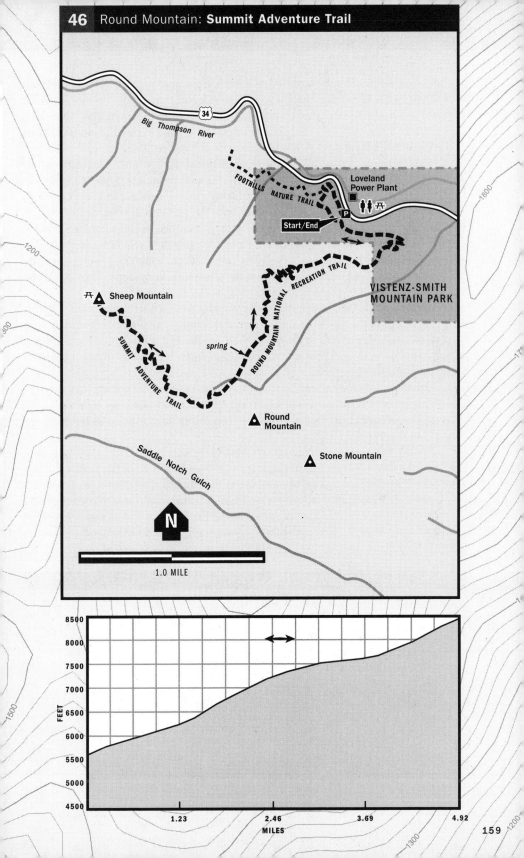

34

Big Thompson River

FOOTHILLS NATURE TRAIL

Loveland
Power Plant

P

Start/End

VISTENZ-SMITH
MOUNTAIN PARK

ROUND MOUNTAIN NATIONAL RECREATION TRAIL

Sheep Mountain

SUMMIT ADVENTURE TRAIL

spring

Round
Mountain

Stone Mountain

Saddle Notch Gulch

N

1.0 MILE

FEET

8500
8000
7500
7000
6500
6000
5500
5000
4500

1.23     2.46     3.69     4.92
MILES

produces steep drop-offs and exposed tree roots. Continue climbing and climbing and climbing. Instead of cutting directly across the ridge of the canyon, the trail begins a series of unforgiving switchbacks that route hikers up the mountainside. This steep incline, in addition to being a lung-buster, is heavily eroded in places. Natural erosion has even carved magnificent rock sculptures out of boulders along the trail.

The first mile takes hikers through National Forest land, and the trail is extremely narrow, rocky, and shaded. Already, the trail meanders through a variety of vegetation: yucca, Spanish bayonet or small soap weed, fringed sagebrush, ponderosa pine trees, and Rocky Mountain juniper. Once the trail reaches the canyon top, it breaks onto exposed hillsides that can be quite sunbathed in the summer. Continuing on the second mile of the climb are more drop-offs and new views of the northeastern plains. It is necessary to have some nontechnical bouldering skills, since you must maneuver through chasms between towering rock formations. These rock formations jettison out of the mountain like mythical guardians of the trail.

Once through the passage, the trail opens up to aspen trees and a small spring that gurgles out of the mountainside. The trail descends a bit after the third mile, and views of Round Mountain's top are prevalent for the last mile or so. A small aspen forest lines the path and then the trail ascends again into a less exposed forest of Douglas fir and various pines.

Although Round Mountain is the hike's namesake, this is not the final destination. The Summit Adventure Trail takes hikers to the top of Sheep Mountain. The hike is also referred to as Dome Mountain, but locals have never wavered from the Round Mountain title.

The summit of the trail, approximately 8,500 feet above sea level (and 2,250/2,750 feet from where you began) is sheltered by a halo of trees. Take a deep, long breath and be sure to sign the trail log at the summit. The summit is marked by a six-foot-high, man-made stack of rocks. There is a nice picnic area to relax and rest.

Round Mountain is a hike of extremes, so the strain of the ascent is remedied by the sloping descent. After a respite at the summit, head downhill and sign out at the hike register.

## ▶ NEARBY ATTRACTIONS

Foothills Nature Trail, part of the Round Mountain National Recreation Trail.

# SOUTH OF DENVER
*Including*
*Colorado Springs*

# BEAR CREEK CAÑON PARK: PALMER RED ROCK LOOP

Bear Creek Cañon Park:
Palmer Red Rock Loop

UTM Zone (WGS84)   13S

Easting   509520

Northing   4296910

## IN BRIEF

Many of the hikes in Colorado Springs are great, but also short and easy. At 6 miles and with a difficult rating, the Palmer Red Rock Loop is a break from the norm. The trail takes hikers on a loop in the foothills on the western edge of Colorado Springs. The first half of the loop ascends and the second half descends.

## DESCRIPTION

Start at the Section 16 trailhead and take the Palmer Red Rock Loop. The single-track trail goes through miniature oak trees that are a little bigger than the area's scrub oak, but definitely not full trees. The path switchbacks up the hillside and provides great views of downtown Colorado Springs. Follow the trail north. As you climb, you'll see bigger views, including a small portion of Bear Creek Cañon Park. Here, the oaks start giving way to yuccas. Social trails abound in the first stretch of this hike, but the main trail is always obvious. The trail turns to red dirt, descends, and levels out for awhile with views toward Garden of the Gods.

About 0.75 miles into the hike, you come to an intersection with the Intenman Nature Trail. Continue straight. (A right turn here takes hikers to the east edge of Manitou Springs, while a left turn leads to the Forest Overlook.) A map is posted at this intersection. The trail continues on

## DIRECTIONS

From Denver, take I-25 south to Colorado Springs. Take exit 141, which is CO 24, and go left. Take a left on 26th Street and drive up into the foothills a little bit. At the stop sign, turn right on Gold Camp Road and go a mile to the trailhead and parking area on the right. If that parking lot is full, continue another 100 yards and there is a parking area on the left.

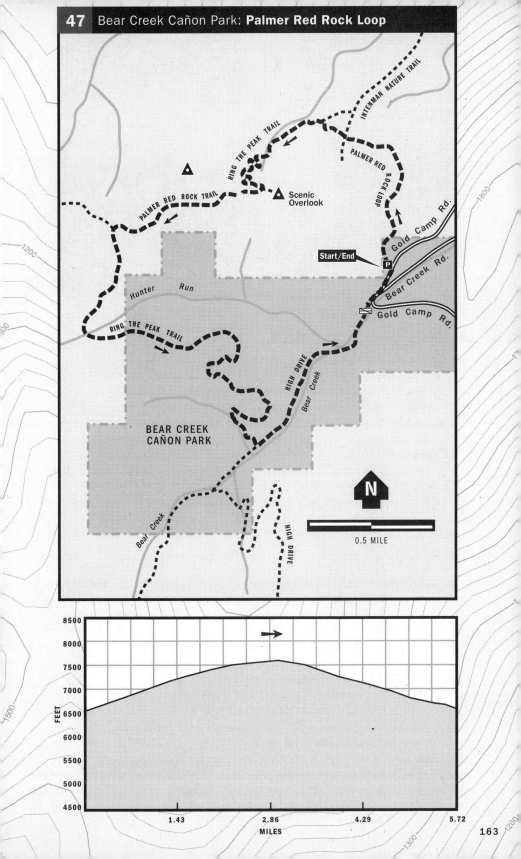

Views of the plains and of Colorado Springs can be seen from the trail in Bear Creek Cañon Park.

Palmer Red Rock Trail and is also marked as Ring the Peak Trail. In 300 yards, you'll see an alternate right turn to the Intenman Trail; keep going straight.

While steep, the trail offers shade as you enter the evergreen trees. Come to a T; take a left. After eight switchbacks and a lot of steep climbing, come to a well-defined line where the trees thin. A left here goes to a scenic overlook, but the main trail switchbacks to the right and continues climbing. When you come to the top of the ridge, you'll be treated to a scenic view of tree-covered foothills and a glimpse of The Broadmoor, a historic, landmark hotel. A left here goes to several scenic overlooks; a right will keep you on the main trail. This is a noticeable change of direction heading west, traversing the mountainside. Continue to follow the Ring the Peak signs. As the trail starts to descend, you cross open, yucca-covered areas with wide sun exposure.

As the trail curves to the left, starting to loop back toward the trailhead, you enter an obvious change in ecological zones. There is a notably cool, dense spruce forest right after the yuccas. The steep hillside doesn't allow for much sun here except the morning eastern sun. To the left you see Colorado Springs across the plains.

The trail travels downward gradually and steadily, traversing the surrounding mountains. You are actually doing a big U-turn, always turning to the left, eventually pointing east on the other side of the valley. Continue going east in a straight line for 0.75 miles and the trail will start to wind around again. Continue a very gradual descent and drop down into Bear Creek Cañon. At the trail intersection in Bear Creek Cañon, take a left and continue downhill on Ring the Peak Trail. Another 200 yards down the trail, the trail forks. Go right and stay on the main trail.

When you reach a dirt road, High Drive, turn left and walk down the single-lane, dirt road. The last mile of this hike is on the road, used mostly by bikes and closed to cars. Proceed through the gate, where the road is now paved, and come to a stop sign. Turn left onto Gold Camp Road and go uphill, noting the rock formations above and to the left. Another few minutes' walk will take you back to the car.

# BLODGETT PEAK OPEN SPACE: WATER TANK TRAIL

▶ **IN BRIEF**

Once part of the Blodgett Ranch, the Blodgett Peak Open Space area offers 167 acres of open space, trails, and wildlife habitat. The Water Tank Trail takes hikers along an old utility road and past unique geological rock features. Most of the land and rock formations are visible from numerous points around Colorado Springs. A pair of peregrine falcons was released at Eagle Peak, located north of Blodgett Peak.

▶ **DESCRIPTION**

The utility road begins at the eastern boundary between two drainage basins. Leave the parking lot and pass the gate and the portable toilet. The trail begins to wind through scrub oak until it reaches the water tank. The property's lowest elevation is 7,054 feet, and the elevation rises sharply at the water tank on its western boundary at 8,184 feet at the end of this trail.

The trail curves to the left; follow it around the hillside. The path is a wide, dirt utility road that stays consistent and smooth through the entire hike. At the fork, stay right on the main trail. A smaller, jogging trail has been cut into the grass along the utility road.

Much of the property is dominated by gambrel oak and ponderosa pine. On the north-facing slopes, Douglas fir is prevalent because of the cooler temperatures and greater moisture available. As the trail continues to ascend, the trees become dense.

▶ **DIRECTIONS**

From Denver, take I-25 south to Colorado Springs. Take exit 149 and turn right, going west on Woodmen Road. At the intersection of Woodmen Road and Rockrimmon Road, turn right. Travel 5 miles through residential area until you reach the trailhead on the right, at 3898 West Woodmen Road.

**KEY AT-A-GLANCE INFORMATION**

**LENGTH:** 2 miles

**CONFIGURATION:** Out-and-back

**DIFFICULTY:** Easy

**SCENERY:** Pine trees, thick scrub oak, cliff views

**EXPOSURE:** No shade

**TRAFFIC:** Moderate

**TRAIL SURFACE:** Wide, dirt utility road

**HIKING TIME:** 50 minutes

**SEASON:** All year

**ACCESS:** Free; daylight hours

**MAPS:** USGS Cascade

**FACILITIES:** Portable toilet

**SPECIAL COMMENTS:** Dogs must be leashed. A city ordinance stresses the importance of dog refuse removal. No model rocket launches.

**Blodgett Peak Open Space: Water Tank Trail**

**UTM Zone (WGS84)  13S**

**Easting   509880**

**Northing   4310630**

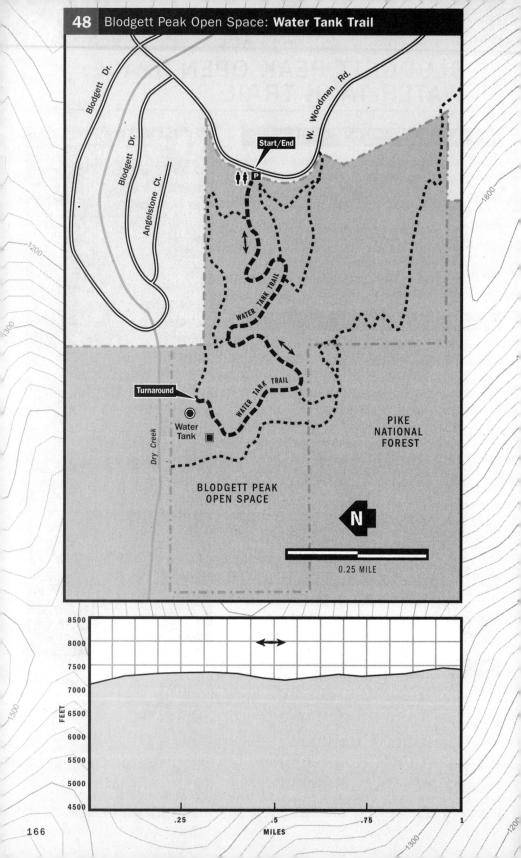

A peek at the Water Tank that serves as this hike's namesake and the surrounding peaks

The trail continues to ascend and curves gently up the hillside. Views to the west, directly in front of hikers, are the nesting cliffs of Blodgett Peak and Eagle Peak. You don't have to look close to see the falcons playing above. Behind you, to the east, are views of Colorado Springs.

At the water tank, turn around and head back the way you came. Future trails are planned in this new open space that will travel beyond the water tower and connect to Pike National Forest and other trails. Pike National Forest borders Blodgett Peak Open Space on three sides.

## ▶ NEARBY ATTRACTIONS

Other Colorado Springs area hikes, including the Foothills Trail and the Woodmen Trail, plus the nearby Oak Valley Ranch Park: **www.SpringsGov.com/Parks.**

# CASTLEWOOD CANYON STATE PARK: INNER CANYON LOOP

## KEY AT-A-GLANCE INFORMATION

**LENGTH:** 1.8 miles

**CONFIGURATION:** Loop

**DIFFICULTY:** Easy

**SCENERY:** Ponderosa pine, piñon pine, scrub oak, high plains, canyon overlooks, distant view of the mountains

**EXPOSURE:** Little shade

**TRAFFIC:** Moderate

**TRAIL SURFACE:** Hard-packed dirt, smooth

**HIKING TIME:** 1 hour

**SEASON:** All year

**ACCESS:** $5 State Park fee; only open during daytime hours; park opens at 8 a.m. and closing time varies by season

**MAPS:** USGS Russellville Gulch and South Castle Rock

**FACILITIES:** Visitor center, restroom, playground, covered picnic area, amphitheater

**SPECIAL COMMENTS:** Dogs must be on a leash that cannot exceed six feet in length. Most areas in the park are handicap accessible. No horses.

---

Castlewood Canyon State Park:
Inner Canyon Loop

UTM Zone (WGS84)   13S

Easting   522010

Northing   4353570

## IN BRIEF

Castlewood Canyon is the northernmost portion of the Black Forest. Largely surrounded by grassland, the canyon is home to dam ruins. The Inner Canyon Loop takes hikers through a lush corridor where ponderosa pines thrive along Cherry Creek as it flows to Denver. There are 12 miles of hiking trails in Castlewood Canyon State Park, including the handicap accessible Canyon View Nature Trail.

## DESCRIPTION

Leave the parking area and go to the Lake Gulch Trailhead. Pass by the restrooms, picnic area, and the playground. Concrete at the beginning, the wide path's surface then turns into dirt and loose rocks. On the left is the turnoff for the Pikes Peak Amphitheater.

The trail begins to gradually descend, and views to the left open up to the valley below.

Ranches and residential areas become visible. The trail now skirts over large boulders, but is still easy to navigate. Here, the path is narrow and foliage hugs the sides. Start to wind downward. The trail is cut into the hillside here: If you reach your right hand out, you can touch the hillside; on your left, the hill drops down.

Erosion-control devices such as hand-laid logs can be found throughout the descent. The trail begins to curve to the right. To the left is a small gully and canyon walls. Forest still dominates the right.

## DIRECTIONS

From Denver, take I-25 south to Castle Rock, turn east on CO 86, going right, and go 6 miles to Franktown. Turn right, going south on CO 83 (South Parker Road) and go 5 miles south to the park entrance on the right. Pay at the visitor center drive-through window and proceed to the east facilities, Canyon Point.

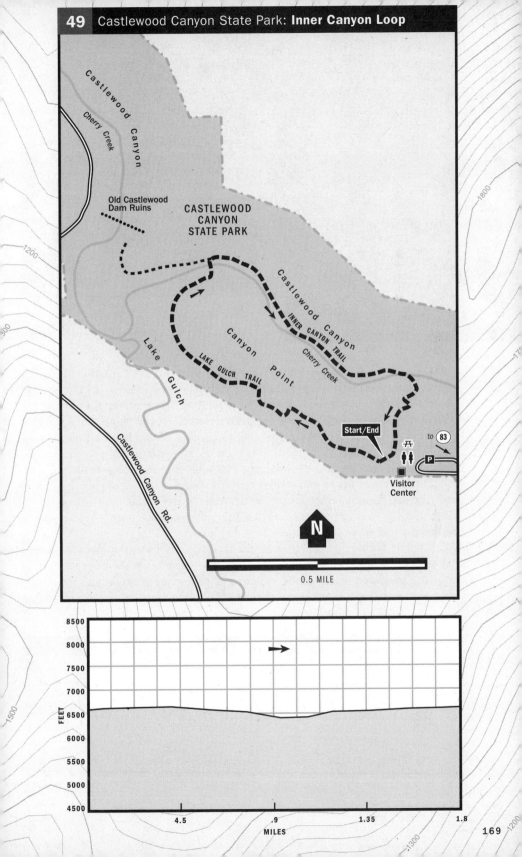

Castlewood Canyon

Cherry Creek

Old Castlewood
Dam Ruins

CASTLEWOOD
CANYON
STATE PARK

Castlewood Canyon

INNER CANYON TRAIL

Cherry Creek

Canyon Point

LAKE GULCH TRAIL

Lake Gulch

Castlewood Canyon Rd.

Start/End

to 83

P

Visitor
Center

**N**

0.5 MILE

8500

8000

7500

7000

6500

6000

5500

5000

4500

FEET

4.5    .9    1.35    1.8

MILES

A sign that greets visitors at the turn-off to Castlewood Canyon State Park

Next, the trail narrows, with grass on both sides. Cherry Creek fills the gully; cross the stream via a wooden footbridge. Climb stairs and come to the intersection of Lake Gulch Trail, Inner Canyon Trail, and Dam Ruins. Continue straight up the hill on Inner Canyon Trail, which then begins to descend. As you climb through rocks, you'll hear the sound of trickling from Cherry Creek. The trail levels a little, crosses a small wooden bridge, then another. Stay on the designated trail and there is no scrambling required on the large boulders. Just walk over or through them.

Climb another set of man-made stairs and begin a set of switchbacks. Pass a dead tree and cross another bridge. Walk over the dry streambed, cross another bridge, and start another ascent through high scrub oak. Canyon ledges and boulders line the dirt trail.

Come to a little erosion area near the creek that looks like theater seating and pass behind it. Cross two more bridges over Cherry Creek. On the other side of the creek, the trail ascends via gentle switchbacks. There are stairs in steeper places. Reach an actual staircase and at the top, pass an Inner Canyon trailhead sign and go right. The trail is now concrete and heads directly back to the car.

## ▶ NEARBY ATTRACTIONS

Try the other Castlewood Canyon State Park hikes. The longest trail is the Rimrock Loop at 2.14 miles: **www.parks.state.co.us.**

# COLORADO TRAIL: LITTLE SCRAGGY TRAIL

## IN BRIEF

The Little Scraggy Trail features 11.5 miles of Colorado's landmark 475-mile-long Colorado Trail and part of Colorado Trail Segment 3. This winding, wooded trail has great views and rock formations. Hikers encounter a naturally smooth trail surface that is easy to navigate. This moderate hike will not leave you the least bit scraggy.

## DESCRIPTION

From the parking lot, cross over toward the restroom. Turn left on the single-track trail near the information kiosk. Start hiking as the trail winds through a lush pine forest. Eventually come to Forest Service Road 550 and cross straight over the road as the trail continues its twists and turns. The trail is memorable for its smooth path lined with ponderosa pines and a smattering of lodgepole pines. It remains relatively level as it travels through the Buffalo Creek Area. The namesake Little Scraggy Peak is always to the left, although it is never quite visible.

Pass an overlook with striking rock formations where you can see for miles in all directions. On a clear day, the southern views may open up to Pikes Peak. Pass the intersection with Shinglemill Trail. Bear left, go downhill, and stay on the main Colorado Trail. This is a gradual hill and halfway down, you'll access wide-open views. At the bottom of the descent, you'll find aspen groves and a little lush gully. Cross a tiny creek. The trail veers to the right and parallels the creek

## KEY AT-A-GLANCE INFORMATION

**LENGTH:** 11.5 miles

**CONFIGURATION:** Out-and-back

**DIFFICULTY:** Moderate

**SCENERY:** Forested, rock formations, distant views of mountains

**EXPOSURE:** Mostly shaded

**TRAFFIC:** Moderate

**TRAIL SURFACE:** Extremely smooth and hard-packed dirt

**HIKING TIME:** 5 hours

**SEASON:** All year

**ACCESS:** $4; open sunrise to sunset

**MAPS:** USGS Green Mountain

**FACILITIES:** Restroom

**SPECIAL COMMENTS:** Dogs must be leashed. This is a short section of the Colorado Trail, which runs more than 400 miles from Denver to Durango. Hikers may encounter large mountain-bike crowds as well as backpackers doing long trips.

## DIRECTIONS

From Denver, take C-470 south to US 285 west. Travel 21 miles to Pine Junction, turn left on CO 126, and go south for 13 miles until you see a sign for the Colorado Trail on the right side of CO 126 at FS 550. Take a quick right into the parking lot at the trailhead.

**Colorado Trail: Little Scraggy Trail**

**UTM Zone (WGS84)**   **13S**

**Easting**   **477870**

**Northing**   **4354860**

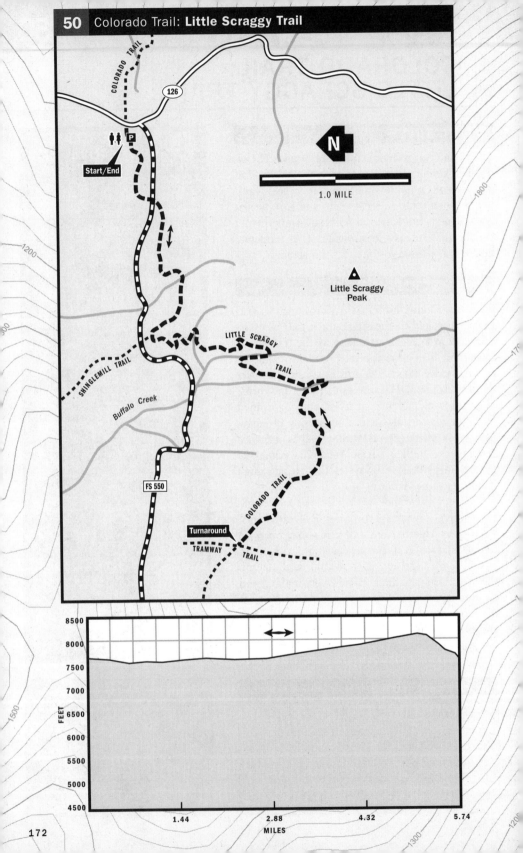

COLORADO TRAIL

126

Start/End

P

N

1.0 MILE

Little Scraggy
Peak

SHINGLEMILL TRAIL

LITTLE SCRAGGY

TRAIL

Buffalo Creek

FS 550

COLORADO TRAIL

Turnaround

TRAMWAY TRAIL

FEET

8500
8000
7500
7000
6500
6000
5500
5000
4500

1.44    2.88    4.32    5.74
MILES

for a while. After the lush section, emerge into a familiar wildflower meadow with pine trees. Be sure to stay on the main trail here as it continues to wind around and loop in a circle to the right. Other, less-used trails cut through the meadow.

Continue on this trail, through the forest, and up through meadows. Eventually, you will parallel another creek and then intersect with Tramway Trail, where we end our hike. Turn around here and go back the way you came.

You may continue on the Colorado Trail for hundreds of miles or travel one-way the entire 13.5-mile length to the Rolling Creek trailhead and the Lost Creek Wilderness.

### ▶ NEARBY ATTRACTIONS

Colorado Trail: **www.coloradotrail.org**. Other Pike National Forest trails: **www.fs.fed.us/r2/psicc/recreation/trails**.

Little Scraggy Trail rock outcroppings typical of those seen throughout most of the hike

# DOUGLAS COUNTY OPEN SPACE: GLENDALE FARM TRAIL

## KEY AT-A-GLANCE INFORMATION

**LENGTH:** 1.5 miles

**CONFIGURATION:** Loop

**DIFFICULTY:** Easy

**SCENERY:** Foothills and rolling plains

**EXPOSURE:** No shade

**TRAFFIC:** Moderate

**TRAIL SURFACE:** Hard-packed dirt, some loose rocks

**HIKING TIME:** 40 minutes

**SEASON:** All year

**ACCESS:** Free; open sunrise to sunset

**MAPS:** USGS Castle Rock North

**FACILITIES:** Portable restrooms, picnic facilities, horse-hitching rails, emergency phones

**SPECIAL COMMENTS:** A fenced, five-acre off-leash dog park is located southwest of the main trailhead and is perfect for letting the dog run before hiking the trail. Once on the trail, dogs must be leashed. Rattlesnakes live in this area. Climbing on the rocks is not allowed.

---

Douglas County Open Space: Glendale Farm Trail

UTM Zone (WGS84)   13S

Easting   511220

Northing   4371097

## ▶ IN BRIEF

Glendale Farm Trail sits in a region called Happy Canyon. So think of this as a happy hike. It's a great first-time hike for kids or novices because of the short length and easy navigation. There is no shade, so the midsummer heat can be unbearable. Douglas County Open Space does an amazing job on these new trails. They are usually complete with benches and picnic tables placed along the way. Color information and history brochures are available at the trailhead.

## ▶ DESCRIPTION

From the end of the parking lot, go straight through the fence, hike 50 feet and take a right turn. Travel counterclockwise on the loop and begin hiking among scrub oak, prairie grasses, and sagebrush. Glendale Farm consists of short-grass prairie and shrubs. Pronghorn antelope, coyotes, cottontail rabbits, prairie dogs, mule deer, black bears, red foxes, and rattlesnakes all make this land their home.

The loop winds uphill a little at first. Once hikers arrive at the back corner, the easternmost part of the trail, the grade levels out and gets a easier as the trail continues north. From here, you'll enjoy views of Glendale Farm's 160 acres and distant panoramas of the mountains. Although the farm buildings no longer stand, remnants on this trail, like the barnyard and orchard, remind hikers of the dedicated spirit of early pioneers.

Continue along the trail and know that one such pioneer was so happy, he could always be

## ▶ DIRECTIONS

From Denver, take I-25 south to the Surrey Ridge exit (number 190). Travel east under the highway, take a quick left, and you'll see the parking lot from there.

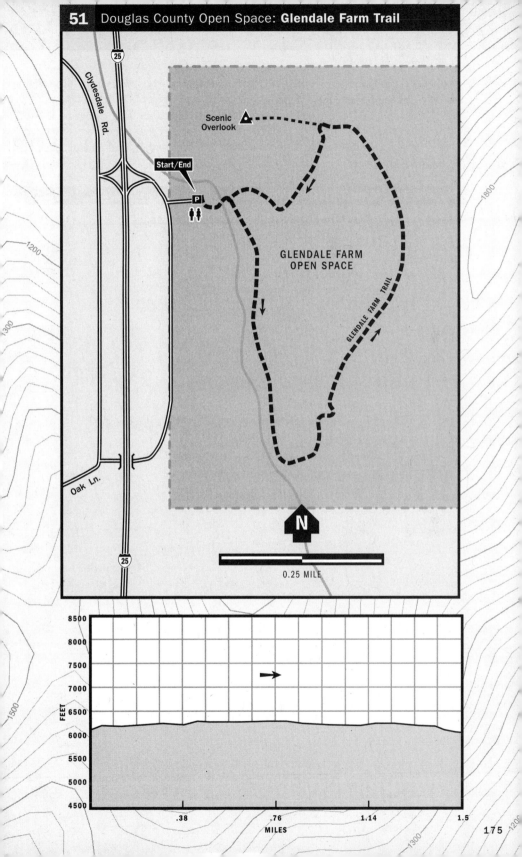

25

Clydesdale Rd.

Scenic
Overlook

Start/End

P

GLENDALE FARM
OPEN SPACE

GLENDALE FARM TRAIL

Oak Ln.

25

1200

1300

1500

1800

N

0.25 MILE

8500

8000

7500

7000

6500

6000

5500

5000

4500

FEET

.38

.76

1.14

1.5

MILES

1300

1200

heard singing as he rode over these hills. His happiness echoed through the valley and gave this region its name, Happy Canyon.

Approaching a barbed-wire fence, the trail curves to the left, going west, and then meets a fork. The right fork goes to a scenic overlook that is not recommended because of the proximity of I-25, so take a left, wind downhill, and end up back at the trailhead.

## ▶ NEARBY ATTRACTIONS

Other Douglas County Open Space trails: **www.douglas.co.us**.

# DOUGLAS COUNTY OPEN SPACE: GREENLAND TRAIL

## ▶ IN BRIEF

The Greenland Trail, within roughly 3,000 acres of Greenland Open Space, winds through rolling grasslands, a pond, scrub oak, and pine forests. This scenic hike is right off of I-25 and offers easy access.

## ▶ DESCRIPTION

Leave the parking area and proceed past the picnic shelter, heading south. The trail is wide, smooth-packed dirt. After the trail travels alongside the Old Territorial Trail, it will intersect with the Kipps Loop portion of the Greenland Trail. Take a left turn at this intersection and begin to travel clockwise around the loop. All turns along the trail are well marked.

The trail ascends and the trail surface softens for the next mile. As you climb, the sights and sounds of I-25 begin to disappear behind the ridge to the left. Take a short respite under the trees here, as they provide rare shade along the trail. Pass a small burn area from 2002, along with a picnic table and a horse-hitching rail.

The trail descends for a short time and then begins another gradual uphill climb. As it gets close to the low scrub oaks, you soon reach the highest point in the path. Start a small descent and pass another group of trees, a picnic table and a hitching rail.

A 19th-century grave marker also marks the farthest point in the loop. This large spherical

## ⓘ KEY AT-A-GLANCE INFORMATION

**LENGTH:** 8.5 miles

**CONFIGURATION:** Loop

**DIFFICULTY:** Easy

**SCENERY:** Mountain views, plains, Pikes Peak

**EXPOSURE:** No shade

**TRAFFIC:** Light

**TRAIL SURFACE:** Smooth, hard-packed dirt

**HIKING TIME:** 3 hours

**SEASON:** All year

**ACCESS:** Free; open sunrise to sunset

**MAPS:** USGS Greenland, Larkspur

**FACILITIES:** Portable restrooms, picnic shelter, covered horse-hitch rails, water spigot, emergency telephone

**SPECIAL COMMENTS:** Dogs must be leashed. Take plenty of water and know your limitations. Water is available at the trailhead. The land outside the fences is privately owned. An accessible group picnic shelter, patterned after Greenland's old mercantile building, seats up to 48 people. Benches, hitch rails, and picnic tables can be found along the trail.

## ▶ DIRECTIONS

From Denver, take I-25 south (south of Larkspur and north of Palmer Lake) to the Greenland exit, number 167. Take a right, going west on CR 74, travel 0.75 miles and continue straight into the parking lot.

**Douglas County Open Space: Greenland Trail**

**UTM Zone (WGS84)   13S**

**Easting   512710**

**Northing   4336590**

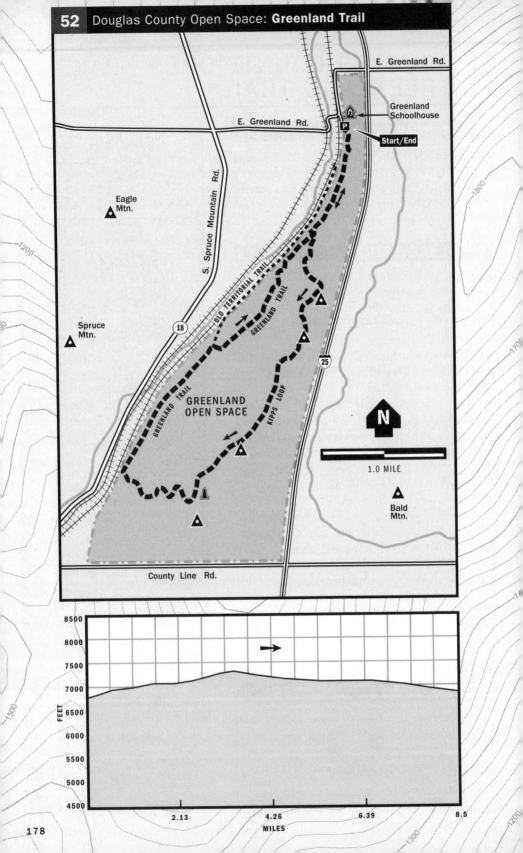

A reproduction of Greenland's old mercantile building is an accessible group picnic shelter.

monument, which is fenced among the trees and very elaborate, pays tribute to Edward Kipps, an area pioneer.

Greenland was once a bustling village with two general stores, a post office, a school, and a saloon. In 1871, the Denver & Rio Grande Railroad extended to this site and the two railroad stations shipped out everything from livestock to pottery. The ranching industry continued after the town's decline in the 1930s.

The next few miles descend and the trail is in plain sight as hikers cross the prairie. At the bottom of the hill, with the railroad tracks straight ahead, take a right turn as the trail forks. Continue straight on the easy road for a mile to the intersection with Old Territorial Road. Bear right and go uphill, staying on the Greenland Trail and getting off the road. Wind up and over a small hill, past a pond, and continue back in the direction of the trailhead.

## ▶ NEARBY ATTRACTIONS

The new Spruce Meadows Trail is nearby, along with other Douglas County Open Space hikes: **www.douglas.co.us.**

# GARDEN OF THE GODS:
# PERKINS CENTRAL GARDEN TRAIL

**LENGTH:** 0.9 miles

**CONFIGURATION:** Loop

**DIFFICULTY:** Easy

**SCENERY:** Giant red-rock formations, some grasses, short shrubs

**EXPOSURE:** Full exposure; some shade in rock formations

**TRAFFIC:** Heavy

**TRAIL SURFACE:** Paved

**HIKING TIME:** 50 minutes

**SEASON:** All year

**ACCESS:** Free; open dawn to dusk

**MAPS:** USGS Cascade

**FACILITIES:** Restrooms, picnic facilities; visitor center nearby with interpretive nature displays, classes, tours, and activities. Trail is lined with benches and resting spots and loaded with information kiosks that could easily extend a visit here.

**SPECIAL COMMENTS:** Dogs must be leashed. Bikes and equestrians are only permitted on designated trails. Rangers urge visitors not to climb rocks. Climbing is prohibited because, throughout the years, several fatal accidents have occurred.

Garden of the Gods:
Perkins Central Garden Trail

UTM Zone (WGS84)   13S

Easting   510420

Northing   4303340

## ▶ IN BRIEF

Garden of the Gods is a must-see for any visitor to Colorado Springs, ranking up there with Pikes Peak and the U.S. Air Force Academy. There are 19 significant rock formations found in Garden of the Gods, and the Perkins Central Garden Trail passes around more than half. This easy 0.6-mile round-trip trail is accessible to wheelchairs and strollers and located in the heart of the park, at the base of the highest rock formations.

## ▶ DESCRIPTION

Leave the parking area, pass the restrooms on the left, and travel south along the Central Garden Trail. Several side trails lead directly to the unusual rock formations, and others lead away from the main trail, but the route is never too far. It is hard to get lost in this park.

Pass the Kissing Camels on the left, defined by a large wall of red rock topped by two formations making the shape of a heart and appearing to kiss. The next rock is to the right, usually blazing in the sun with its white walls: White Rock. To the left is North Gateway Rock. Pass a circular meeting point on the left and save its information kiosks and ample resting spots for the return.

The paved Central Garden Trail's concrete is a subtle mix of reds. At the first fork in the trail, bear right. Pass Signature Rock, then Sentinel Rock (also known as Twin Spires) and move through the unique blend of juniper trees, small spruce trees, brush, and prairie grasses. Loop

## ▶ DIRECTIONS

From Denver, take I-25 south to Colorado Springs. Take exit 146, turn right onto Garden of the Gods Road, then turn left onto 30th Street into Garden of the Gods Park. Turn right on Gateway Road, right again on Juniper Way Loop, and left into the north main parking lot.

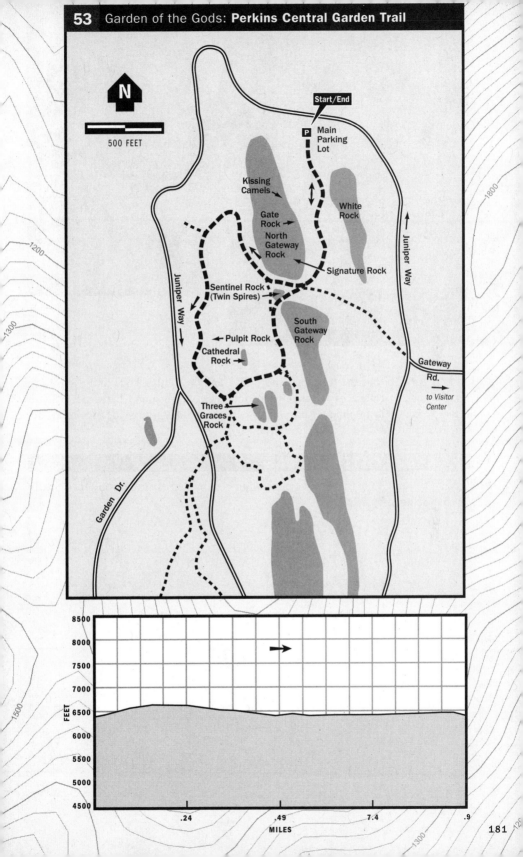

N

500 FEET

Start/End

P Main
Parking
Lot

Kissing
Camels

Gate
Rock

North
Gateway
Rock

White
Rock

Signature Rock

Juniper Way

Sentinel Rock
(Twin Spires)

South
Gateway
Rock

Pulpit Rock

Cathedral
Rock

Gateway
Rd.

to Visitor
Center

Three
Graces
Rock

Juniper Way

Garden Dr.

8500

8000

7500

7000

6500

6000

5500

5000

FEET

4500

.24          .49          7.4          .9

MILES

Kids of all ages appreciate the beauty and vastness of the Garden of the Gods. Here, the author's kids wave as they take a break.

around, travel beside the road for a short time, and pass Pulpit Rock to the left. Keep right to pass Three Graces and then Cathedral Rock. On the immediate right is South Gateway Rock. Turn right after traveling the length of the western side of South Gateway Rock and head back to the trailhead.

## ▶ NEARBY ATTRACTIONS

Other Colorado Springs area hikes, including nearby Red Rock Canyon Open Space: **www.SpringGov.com/Parks**.

# NORTH CHEYENNE CAÑON PARK: LOWER COLUMBINE TRAIL

## ▶ IN BRIEF

The Lower Columbine Trail makes its way up the canyon from behind the Starsmore Discovery Center to the Middle Columbine Trail (near the road) to Upper Columbine Trail (near Helen Hunt Falls). The Lower Columbine Trail, featured here, leaves behind the tranquil Starsmore Discovery Center and makes its way 1 mile up the road from the main park gate.

## ▶ DESCRIPTION

Leave behind the Starsmore Discovery Center. You can either go through the building or take either trail around the perimeter. The trail follows North Cheyenne Cañon Road well into the park. On the left, pass covered picnic tables and restrooms. The trail eventually meets up with a dirt road; continue straight.

Views of Cheyenne Cañon State Park are dominated by massive red-rock formations similar to those seen at the Garden of the Gods.

Continue and pass a water-storage unit to the right. Also on the right—within hearing distance—is a small creek with a waterfall. Social trails lead down to the creek, but stay on the wide, well-maintained main trail, which is heavily wooded with tall scrub oak and pine trees. Pass a series of man-made waterfalls and continue a steady ascent.

In the afternoon, the trail becomes shaded because the canyon walls hide the sun. Pass another picnic area on the right. To the left is a

## ▶ KEY AT-A-GLANCE INFORMATION

**LENGTH:** 2 miles

**CONFIGURATION:** Out-and-back

**DIFFICULTY:** Easy

**SCENERY:** Canyon, scrub oak, red-rock formations, pine trees

**EXPOSURE:** Shaded

**TRAFFIC:** Moderate

**TRAIL SURFACE:** Dirt

**HIKING TIME:** 50 minutes

**SEASON:** All year

**ACCESS:** Free. Park hours: May 1–October 31; 5 a.m. to 11 p.m.; November 1–April 30; 5 a.m. to 9 p.m.

**MAPS:** USGS Colorado Springs and Manitou Springs

**FACILITIES:** Restrooms, picnic facilities, Starsmore Discovery Center with nature displays, classes, tours, and activities.

**SPECIAL COMMENTS:** Dogs must be leashed. Bikes and equestrians are allowed.

## ▶ DIRECTIONS

From Denver, take I-25 south to Colorado Springs. Exit onto CO 24 going west, then turn left onto 21st Street, which turns into Cresta Road. Turn right on Cheyenne Boulevard, drive to the entrance of Cheyenne Cañon Park, and park at the Starsmore Discovery Center.

North Cheyenne Cañon Park:
Lower Columbine Trail

UTM Zone (WGS84)   13S

Easting   511723

Northing   4293378

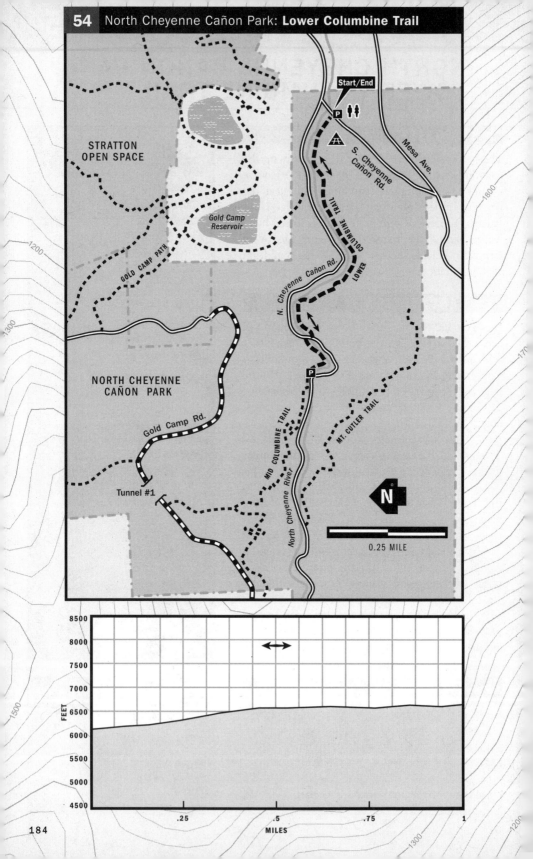

STRATTON
OPEN SPACE

Gold Camp
Reservoir

Start/End

S. Cheyenne
Cañon Rd.

Mesa Ave.

GOLD CAMP PATH

N. Cheyenne Cañon Rd.

LOWER COLUMBINE TRAIL

NORTH CHEYENNE
CAÑON PARK

Gold Camp Rd.

Tunnel #1

MID COLUMBINE TRAIL

North Cheyenne River

MT. CUTLER TRAIL

N

0.25 MILE

8500
8000
7500
7000
6500
6000
5500
5000
4500

FEET

.25    .5    .75    1

MILES

This hike begins right behind the Starsmore Discovery Center. Be sure to visit their interpretive displays or visit with a volunteer.

small cave where fires have obviously been stoked, because there are ash burns all along the rock ceiling. At the sign that points the trail to the left, be sure to go left. A wider trail goes right, but it is a gated entrance to a picnic area. The trail steadily ascends. In steeper areas, there are stairs placed into the hillside and some small switchbacks.

You'll travel along the main road for most of this hike, but it never really feels like you are on the road. The trail crests and follows along an area where the hillside is very steep with drop-offs on the right. A missed step here can be dangerous. After the crest, the trail begins to descend before it climbs once more. You'll be able to see the road now. You're still pretty secluded, though, and the hillside is heavily forested. Cross the concrete bridge over the stream and then cross the road to the Middle Columbine Trail, or turn around and head back.

## ▶ NEARBY ATTRACTIONS

Try the other North Cheyenne Cañon Park trails and other Colorado Springs area hikes, including nearby Stratton Open Space: **www.SpringsGov.com/Parks.**

# PIKE NATIONAL FOREST: DEVIL'S HEAD FIRE LOOKOUT

## KEY AT-A-GLANCE INFORMATION

**LENGTH:** 3 miles

**CONFIGURATION:** Out-and-back

**DIFFICULTY:** Moderate

**SCENERY:** Evergreen and aspen forest; fire lookout tower, views

**EXPOSURE:** Mostly shaded

**TRAFFIC:** Heavy

**TRAIL SURFACE:** Dirt; tree roots, loose rocks; large staircase

**HIKING TIME:** 1.5 hours

**SEASON:** April–November

**ACCESS:** Free; open sunrise to sunset

**MAPS:** USGS Devil's Head

**FACILITIES:** Picnic tables, water spigot, outhouse

**SPECIAL COMMENTS:** Dogs must be leashed. Foot traffic only; no bikes; horses allowed, but discouraged. Do not climb stairs to the tower during lightning. Forestry officials limit the number of people in the tower at one time. On most days from April to November, the tower is staffed from 9:30 a.m. to 6 p.m. There is a campground at the trailhead and the ranger says that bears are sighted every night.

Pike National Forest:
Devil's Head Fire Lookout

UTM Zone (WGS84)   13S

Easting   491000

Northing   4346530

## IN BRIEF

The steep staircase that leads to the Devil's Head fire lookout tower is the highlight of the hike. The 143 steps get the best hikers huffing and puffing. The reward at the top is a unique glimpse at a working lookout, one of only 18 that remain in Colorado; the only one staffed by a paid employee. (The remaining 17 are not all in use, and one is available for rent.) Forest Service rangers, such as Billy Ellis, have scanned for fires in Pike National Forest—looking through binoculars for smoke—since 1912. Billy has been at it for 21 summers and spotted 11 fires last year.

## DESCRIPTION

When you leave the parking lot, pass the benches and concrete patio, and climb the concrete stairs that mark the beginning of the hike. Pine and aspen trees and plenty of places to sit and relax line the trail. Nearby Rampart Range Recreation Area and the 100 miles of off-road motorcycle trails supply the occasional buzz of motorcycles.

Dense trees along the trail create an enchanting effect. Pass a bench. Begin a switchback that includes a small, sturdy footbridge about ten feet long. Continue up another switchback and pass two large benches.

At the halfway mark, just beyond the large rock, look toward the plains for expansive views of the open prairie. Pass another set of benches; take in the view. Switchback again and pass another set of large rock outcroppings.

## DIRECTIONS

From Denver, take C-470 to US 85 and travel south to Sedalia. In Sedalia, turn right off of US 85 onto CO 67 and head west 10 miles on CO 67 to Rampart Range Road. Go left, traveling south 9.25 miles on this well-maintained dirt road to the trailhead parking lot.

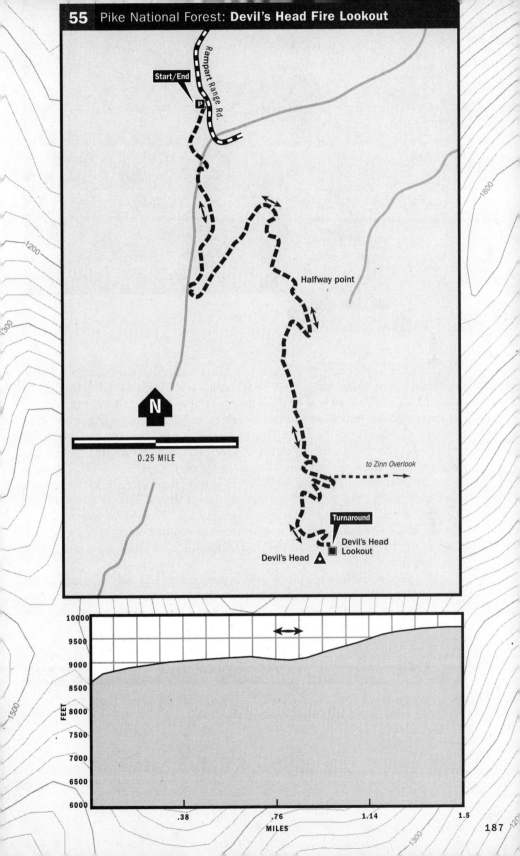

Start/End

Rampart Range Rd.

Halfway point

N

0.25 MILE

to Zinn Overlook

Turnaround

Devil's Head
Lookout

Devil's Head

10000
9500
9000
8500
8000
7500
7000
6500
6000

FEET

.38          .76          1.14          1.5
MILES

A unique sight indeed—the
Devil's Head Fire Lookout

Look out for the many "road apples" in the trail left by mules used to pack sup-plies to the Forest Service ranger. Pass more benches and a forest-fire information sign.

At 1.2 miles, bear right at a fork in the road and head toward Devil's Head look-out tower. The left turn is an optional, adventurous 0.75-mile side trip to the Zinn Overlook. Continue past the ranger's cabin, more benches, an outhouse, and infor-mation signs. The ranger and his wife live in the cabin at the base of the tower. They get groceries once a week and have no running water or sewer.

A steep staircase takes you the final 143 steps to the tower. The lookout tower, which is named on the National Register of Historic Places, perches at 9,748 feet. The massive granite rock outcropping that Devil's Head is named for cannot be seen from the tower because the tower actually sits on top of the outcrop, at the highest point of Devil's Head mountain. The best views of Devil's Head are actually from Woodland Park.

Once at the tower, chat with the ranger about his curious statistics, such as the youngest (2) to the oldest (90) visitors to reach the tower. On a clear day, the visibil-ity extends more than 100 miles in every direction. The panorama includes Denver, Castle Rock, Sedalia, and 11 of Colorado's fourteeners. From here, turn around and head down the stairs, back to the trailhead.

## ▶ NEARBY ATTRACTIONS

Pike National Forest Trails and Dutch Fred Trail, Jackson Creek Road, Flat Rocks Overlook: **www.fs.fed.us/r2/psicc/recreation/trails.**

# PIKE NATIONAL FOREST: WIGWAM TRAIL

## ▶ IN BRIEF

The drive to the trailhead takes hikers through massive square miles of burned forest that were torched in Colorado's largest wildfire, the Haymen Fire (2002). In contrast, the Wigwam Trail testifies to what did survive. Lush, green, heavy vegetation and tall evergreen trees are quite a relief. Off of the beaten path, the trail is lightly used and hikers do not encounter many other humans.

## ▶ DESCRIPTION

The official trailhead (Wigwam Trail #609) can be found at the end of the lower parking lot where the road turns around. Sign in at the trailhead log sheet. Hike across Wigwam Creek and then cross it again. Here, you officially enter the Lost Creek Wilderness Area. Cross primitive rock bridges as you follow the Wigwam Creek drainage uphill.

The trail heads northwest along Wigwam Creek and rises with a moderate ascending grade. Evergreen trees and low growth mark the landscape for several miles, following the creek's drainage, before the trail opens up. Travel into lush meadows as the creek flows into numerous beaver ponds. Some of these beaver ponds are

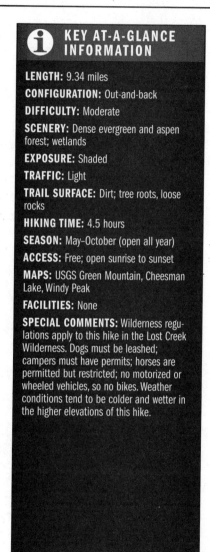

### ⓘ KEY AT-A-GLANCE INFORMATION

**LENGTH:** 9.34 miles

**CONFIGURATION:** Out-and-back

**DIFFICULTY:** Moderate

**SCENERY:** Dense evergreen and aspen forest; wetlands

**EXPOSURE:** Shaded

**TRAFFIC:** Light

**TRAIL SURFACE:** Dirt; tree roots, loose rocks

**HIKING TIME:** 4.5 hours

**SEASON:** May–October (open all year)

**ACCESS:** Free; open sunrise to sunset

**MAPS:** USGS Green Mountain, Cheesman Lake, Windy Peak

**FACILITIES:** None

**SPECIAL COMMENTS:** Wilderness regulations apply to this hike in the Lost Creek Wilderness. Dogs must be leashed; campers must have permits; horses are permitted but restricted; no motorized or wheeled vehicles, so no bikes. Weather conditions tend to be colder and wetter in the higher elevations of this hike.

## ▶ DIRECTIONS

From Denver, take I-70 west to C 470 to US 285, traveling west for 23 miles to Pine Junction. Turn left at the town of Pine Junction onto CO 126, toward Pine and Buffalo Creek. Drive 21.8 miles on CO 126. Turn left, traveling south on FS 211, which leads toward Cheesman Reservoir. Travel 2 miles and bear right at the sign pointing to Goose Creek. Drive 1.1 miles until you reach a fork, bear right on FS 560, and bear right at the next fork staying on FS 560. Drive 4 miles to the trailhead signs, turn left at the signs, and drive 1.3 miles to the trailhead.

Pike National Forest: Wigwam Trail

UTM Zone (WGS84)   13S

Easting   469510

Northing   4343920

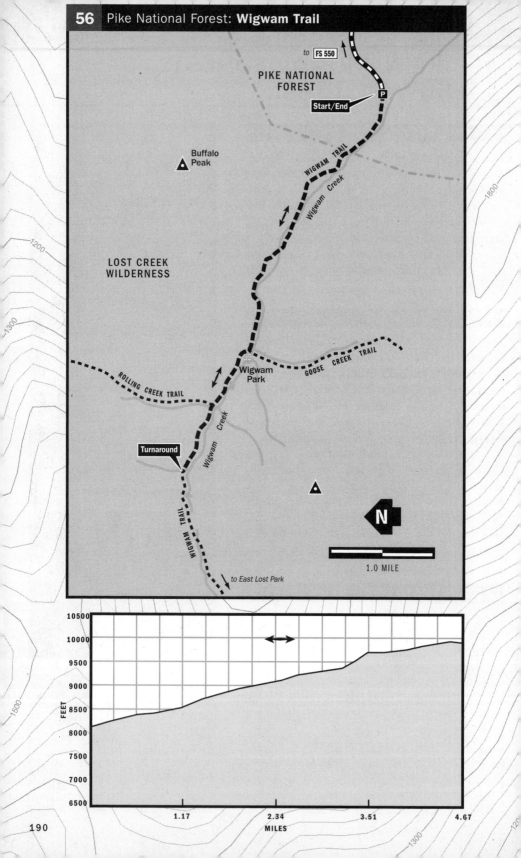

to FS 550

PIKE NATIONAL
FOREST

Start/End

WIGWAM TRAIL

Buffalo
Peak

Wigwam Creek

LOST CREEK
WILDERNESS

Wigwam
Park

GOOSE CREEK TRAIL

ROLLING CREEK TRAIL

Wigwam Creek

Turnaround

WIGWAM TRAIL

N

1.0 MILE

to East Lost Park

Lush landscape is found frequently along the Wigwam Trail.

rather large. Small aspen trees along the trail have been gnawed down by beavers used to dam up Wigwam Creek.

This area is called Wigwam Park. The last stretch to the park has several short, steep, rocky sections. Continue straight at the intersection with Goose Creek Trail, and just to the west of there, pass the intersection with Rolling Creek Trail. Continue, cross the creek again, and enter a grove of tall aspens.

The hike ascends, crosses the creek one last time, and ends in a high saddle at the end of the mountain valley, after the meadows and before the descent into East Lost Park. Turn around here and retrace your steps back to the trailhead. You can continue on from the turnaround point, since Wigwam Trail has approximately 6 more miles of trail.

## ▶ NEARBY ATTRACTIONS

Pike National Forest Trails, Goose Creek Trail (# 619), Rolling Creek Trail (# 663), Brookside-McCurdy Trail: **www.fs.fed.us/r2/psicc/recreation/trails.**

# PINE VALLEY RANCH PARK:
# PINE VALLEY RANCH LOOP

## KEY AT-A-GLANCE INFORMATION

**LENGTH:** 3.2 miles

**CONFIGURATION:** Loop

**DIFFICULTY:** Moderate

**SCENERY:** Scenic vistas, forest, lake, river

**EXPOSURE:** Mostly shaded

**TRAFFIC:** Moderate

**TRAIL SURFACE:** Dirt, loose rocks

**HIKING TIME:** 1.5 hours

**SEASON:** All year

**ACCESS:** Free; open 1 hour before sunrise to 1 hour after sunset

**MAPS:** USGS Pine

**FACILITIES:** Restrooms, group picnic shelters, "Pine Valley Ranch Depot" information kiosk, observatory

**SPECIAL COMMENTS:** Dogs must be leashed. Portions of the trail are "hiker only." The park has some handicap-accessible facilities and hiking areas. Observatory programs are scheduled through the Lookout Mountain Nature Center at (303) 526-0594. Reserve a shelter for an event at (303) 271-5925.

Pine Valley Ranch Park:
Pine Valley Ranch Loop

UTM Zone (WGS84) 13S

Easting 470127

Northing 4361946

## IN BRIEF

Visitors to Pine Valley Ranch Park can hike the trails, fish from the pond piers, ice-skate in the winter, enjoy observatory programs, and connect to Pike National Forest for additional recreation. Pine Valley Ranch Park enjoys a unique blend of historic and natural features, like the fact that the Narrow Gauge Trail, part of the Loop, follows the original railroad bed.

## DESCRIPTION

At the trailhead is the Pine Valley Ranch Depot. Stop here to read the information signs and pick up a park map. Start hiking west on the Narrow Gauge Trail. The wide trail leads you through dense willows along the North Fork of the South Platte River. Turn left onto Buck Gulch Trail and cross over the river via a wooden bridge.

Continue south on Buck Gulch Trail; pass the North Fork View Trail turnoff. There is a set of restrooms and a covered picnic area here. You can now see Pine Lake on the left. Follow the trail as it narrows and begins to climb into the hills away from the lake. Turn left onto Strawberry Jack Trail and travel into Pike National Forest, continuing the steady ascent.

The trail shows evidence of the destruction of forest fires. Burned trees and telltale signs of new growth signify the rebirth of a forest. At 1.25 miles, you reach the Park View Trail. Turn left and reach the highest point of this hike, just beyond the intersection. Begin to descend and pass a

## DIRECTIONS

From Denver, take I-70 west to C-470 south to US 285 south to Pine Junction. Turn left off of US 285, going southeast onto Pine Valley Road (CR 126), and continue 5.8 miles to the town of Pine. Turn right onto Crystal Lake Road and follow it 1.22 miles to the trailhead.

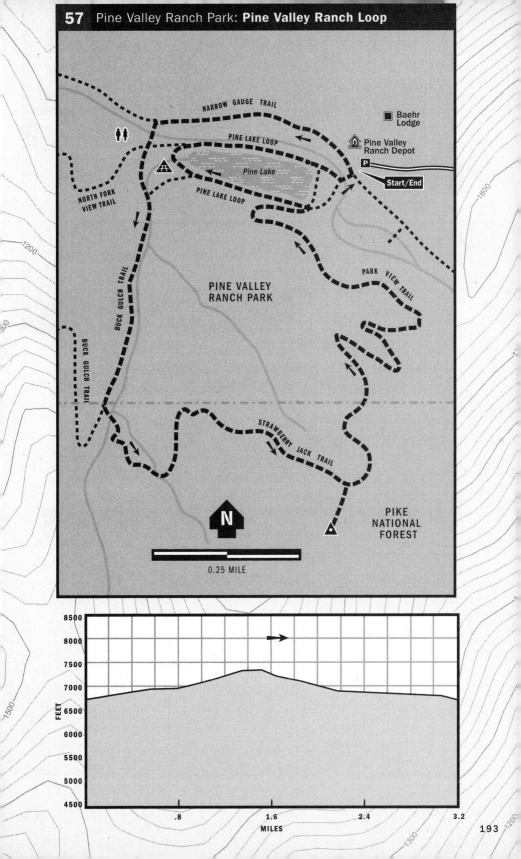

NARROW GAUGE TRAIL

Baehr Lodge

PINE LAKE LOOP

Pine Valley Ranch Depot

P

Start/End

Pine Lake

PINE LAKE LOOP

NORTH FORK VIEW TRAIL

PARK VIEW TRAIL

BUCK GULCH TRAIL

PINE VALLEY RANCH PARK

BUCK GULCH TRAIL

STRAWBERRY JACK TRAIL

N

PIKE NATIONAL FOREST

0.25 MILE

A hiker reading an information
sign in Pine Valley Ranch Park.

bench halfway down the hill. This is a good place to take in the view: Pine Lake, the observatory, and Baehr Lodge, with a large rock outcropping as a backdrop. The Lodge was built in 1927 and is now listed on the National Register of Historic Places.

Well-constructed stairs make the steep descent a little easier as the trail winds toward the lake. Turn left onto the Pine Lake Loop Trail. Keep your eyes open for wildlife that may include beaver, especially as you approach the wetlands at the west edge of the lake. Complete the Pine Lake Loop, going clockwise, and cross back over the river to the trailhead.

## ▶ NEARBY ATTRACTIONS

Other Jefferson County area hikes and Pine Valley Ranch Park connector trails: **www.co.jefferson.co.us/openspace.**

# REYNOLDS OPEN SPACE PARK: RAVEN'S ROOST OXEN DRAW LOOP

## IN BRIEF

Raven's Roost Oxen Draw Loop is a straightforward up-and-down hike with an additional steep climb to the Eagle View Trail Overlook. There is a great view of the South Platte area from this vantage point. An interpretive trail identifies plants along this diverse trail.

## DESCRIPTION

From the parking area, begin to hike on the Raven's Roost Trail and turn right when the outhouse comes into sight. Raven's Roost Trail and Elkhorn Interpretive Trail merge for a short time. Pick up an interpretive trail guide at a post along the trail. Follow Elkhorn Interpretive Trail and climb several switchbacks until the Raven's Roost Trail breaks off to the right. Raven's Roost turns into a Forest Service road for a while as the route follows the steep roadbed along the ridgeline.

Follow Raven's Roost Trail as it separates from the Forest Service road and begins to descend, dropping down to a small creek crossing. At the next trail intersection, turn right onto Eagle's View Trail. This trail is steep and leads hikers to a ridgeline and small meadow with a marvelous vantage point. To the south are views of Pikes Peak and Rampart Range. Turn around and head back on Eagle's View Trail, to the intersection of Eagle's View, Raven's Roost, and Oxen Draw Trails. Turn right onto the Oxen Draw Trail and cross the stream a number of times. This trail

## KEY AT-A-GLANCE INFORMATION

**LENGTH:** 3.7 miles

**CONFIGURATION:** Loop

**DIFFICULTY:** Moderate

**SCENERY:** Wide variety of evergreens: ponderosa, blue spruce, Douglas fir, alpine fir

**EXPOSURE:** Mostly shaded

**TRAFFIC:** Moderate

**TRAIL SURFACE:** Dirt, rocky in sections

**HIKING TIME:** 1.75 hours

**SEASON:** All year

**ACCESS:** Free; open 1 hour before sunrise to 1 hour after sunset

**MAPS:** USGS Platte Canyon and Pine

**FACILITIES:** Outhouse, picnic tables

**SPECIAL COMMENTS:** Dogs must be leashed. No bikes.

## DIRECTIONS

From Denver, take I-70 west to C-470 south to US 285 south to Conifer. Travel through Conifer to Foxton Road. Go left on Foxton Road for 5.3 miles to Reynolds Open Space and the large, dirt parking lot on the south side of the road.

**Reynolds Open Space Park: Raven's Roost Oxen Draw Loop**

**UTM Zone (WGS84)   13S**

**Easting   479481**

**Northing   4368386**

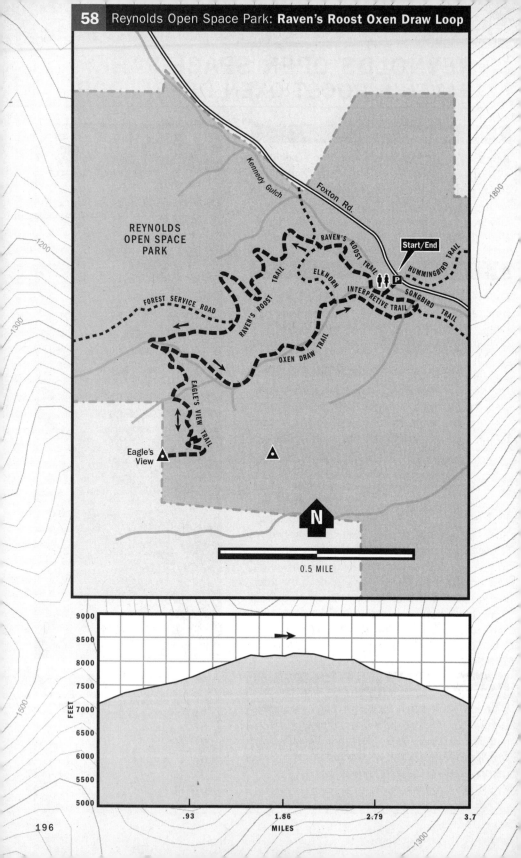

REYNOLDS
OPEN SPACE
PARK

Kennedy Gulch

Foxton Rd.

RAVEN'S ROOST TRAIL

Start/End

HUMMINGBIRD TRAIL

RAVEN'S ROOST TRAIL

ELKHORN

INTERPRETIVE TRAIL

SONGBIRD TRAIL

FOREST SERVICE ROAD

OXEN DRAW TRAIL

EAGLE'S VIEW TRAIL

Eagle's
View

**N**

0.5 MILE

FEET

9000
8500
8000
7500
7000
6500
6000
5500
5000

.93     1.86     2.79     3.7
MILES

follows the ravine through dense forest and brings hikers back to the Elkhorn Interpretive Trail. Turn right onto Elkhorn Interpretive Trail and continue past the next intersection. Come to a bench placed at the edge of a relaxing meadow filled with wildflowers in the summer. Turn left onto Songbird Trail and head back to the trailhead.

## ▶ NEARBY ATTRACTIONS

Other Jefferson County area hikes, including Songbird Trail and Hummingbird Trail in Reynolds Open Space. Visit their Web site at **www.co.jefferson.co.us/openspace.**

A lone hiker strolls along and can see the trail ahead in Reynolds Open Space Park.

# ROXBOROUGH STATE PARK: SOUTH RIM TRAIL

Roxborough State Park:
South Rim Trail

UTM Zone (WGS84)   13S

Easting   494577

Northing   4364232

## IN BRIEF

Roxborough State Park is a Colorado Natural Area and a National Natural Landmark. The park offers two main hiking areas: Fountain Valley and South Rim. The Fountain Valley Trail has a dramatic trailhead and a big parking lot. The South Rim Trail has the same scenery and fewer people. The remarkable geology of this area is largely represented by the Fountain Formation. These red rocks jettison from the earth, erupting from the green valley.

## DESCRIPTION

From the parking area, drop down below the road, go 100 yards, and cross a bridge, starting out on Willow Creek Trail going southeast. Take a left at the intersection with the Willow Creek Trail, onto South Rim Trail and start ascending. To the right you'll see some of the red-rock formations that dominate this area, primarily the Fountain Formation. As the trail climbs and the views expand, you will have constant views of these amazing rows of tilted rocks.

When the trail begins to switchback, hikers may begin to notice the scrub oak, yucca plants, sage brush, and cactus. The trail continues its gentle ascent, continually curving to the right.

## DIRECTIONS

From Denver, take C-470 south to the Wadsworth Boulevard (CO 121) exit, take Wadsworth Boulevard left, going south for 4.3 miles, then turn left on Waterton Road. After 1.7 miles, turn right on Rampart Range Road and travel 4 miles, then take a left on Roxborough Park Road. Follow the signs to the park. Pay your fee and cross through the official park gate and entrance. The South Rim parking lot has only about 10 spaces and is the first parking area on your left.

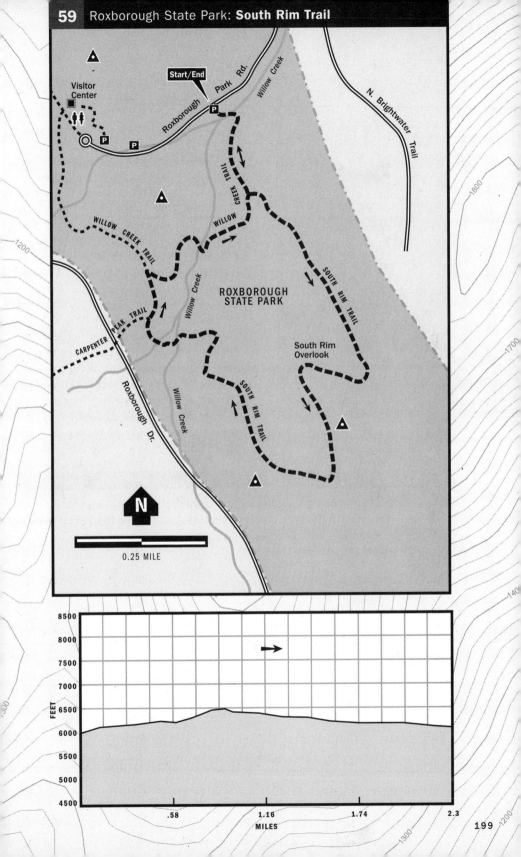

Start/End

Visitor
Center

Roxborough Park Rd.

Willow Creek

N. Brightwater Trail

WILLOW CREEK TRAIL

WILLOW CREEK TRAIL

ROXBOROUGH
STATE PARK

Willow Creek

SOUTH RIM TRAIL

South Rim
Overlook

CARPENTER PEAK TRAIL

Roxborough Dr.

Willow Creek

SOUTH RIM TRAIL

**N**

0.25 MILE

The single-track path of the South Rim Trail is a great way to see the rock formations of Roxborough State Park.

After reaching the ridgetop, the South Rim Overlook, the trail starts curving to the left instead. New red-rock formations dot the view. The light-yellow ridge east of the Fountain Formation is the Lyons Formation. The Dakota Hogback Ridge is another rock formation and can been seen in the distance with the same red rocks in a jettison row.

At the next intersection, with a social trail leading to a scenic overlook, keep going straight on South Rim Trail. Begin to descend as the trail starts to switchback, then deposits you into the rock formations. Continue straight at the intersection with Carpenter Peak Trail, staying on South Rim Trail. Look out for the intersection with Willow Creek Trail, which comes up fast and forks in from behind. You'll take a right here; a left turn will take you to the visitor center on the southwest portion of Willow Creek Trail. It's easy to miss if you are absorbed in the rock formations. At the next intersection with South Rim Trail, take a left, to complete the balloon, travel on familiar territory, and return to the trailhead.

## ▶ NEARBY ATTRACTIONS

Within Roxborough State Park are five additional hiking trails: Fountain Valley Overlook, Lyons Overlook, Willow Creek, Fountain Valley, and Carpenter Peak. Waterton Canyon and Sharptail Ridge Open Space are also close.

# WATERTON CANYON RECREATION AREA: WATERTON CANYON

Waterton Canyon serves as a trailhead for the 475-mile-long Colorado Trail. This is a long walk south to the Durango area, yet Waterton Canyon allows hikers to walk as far as they please and turn around. The featured hike travels 4 miles into the canyon as it follows the South Platte River into the mountains. This user-friendly hike is an enjoyable outing.

## ▶ DESCRIPTION

Cross Waterton Road and find the sign: "Colorado Trail Trailhead." The information board and trail marker are on a short dirt trail a few hundred feet beyond Waterton Road. Head west as the trail quickly turns into an asphalt road that carries you along the west side of the old Kassler water treatment facility. Almost immediately, the asphalt gives way to hard-packed dirt as the road continues beyond the treatment plant and toward the South Platte River. The trail passes through short bushes and tall grasses that line the river. Both covered and uncovered picnic tables as well as outhouses are plentiful along this portion of the trail, so finding a resting spot is never a challenge. The trail also serves as a road for the water department, although public vehicular access is restricted.

## ▶ DIRECTIONS

From Denver, take C-470 south to the Wadsworth Boulevard (CO 121) exit, take a left, going south on Wadsworth Boulevard, which quickly becomes South Platte Canyon Road. Continue south to West Waterton Road and turn left (east, the only way you can turn onto Waterton). The parking lot is immediately on the left (north) side of West Waterton Road. The trail marker and information post is several hundred feet south of the road.

### ⓘ KEY AT-A-GLANCE INFORMATION

**LENGTH:** 8 miles

**CONFIGURATION:** Out-and-back

**DIFFICULTY:** Moderate

**SCENERY:** Foothills, South Platte River, grassy areas, river habitat, cliff walls

**EXPOSURE:** Shaded by canyon walls and cottonwoods along the river

**TRAFFIC:** Heavy

**TRAIL SURFACE:** Smooth and hard-packed dirt

**HIKING TIME:** 4 hours

**SEASON:** All year

**ACCESS:** Free; open sunrise to sunset

**MAPS:** USGS Kassler and Platte Canyon

**FACILITIES:** Restrooms (handicap accessible), picnic facilities, bike rack, pay phone

**SPECIAL COMMENTS:** To protect wildlife, no dogs are allowed. The parking lot accommodates 150 cars and 20 horse trailers, so crowded conditions may exist, especially on the early portion of the trail.

Waterton Canyon Recreation Area: Waterton Canyon

UTM Zone (WGS84)   13S

Easting   491876

Northing   4370999

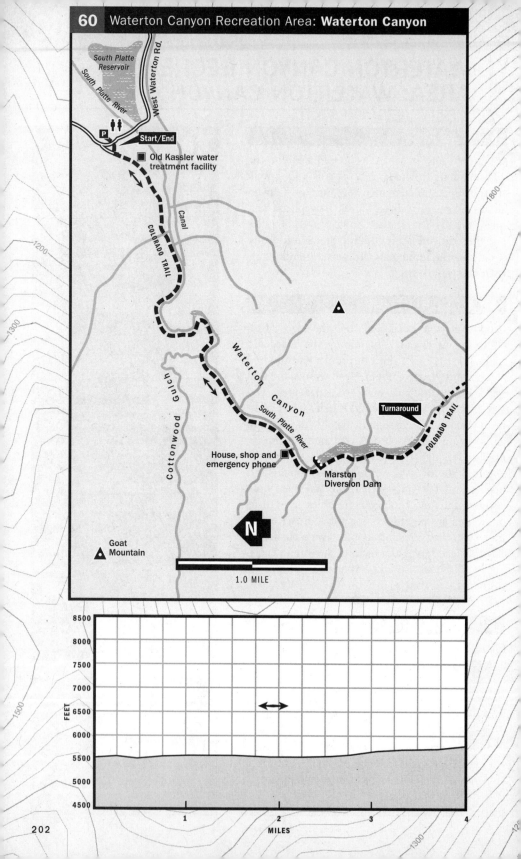

South Platte Reservoir

South Platte River

West Waterton Rd.

Start/End

Old Kassler water treatment facility

Canal

COLORADO TRAIL

Waterton Canyon

Cottonwood Gulch

South Platte River

Turnaround

COLORADO TRAIL

House, shop and emergency phone

Marston Diversion Dam

**N**

Goat Mountain

1.0 MILE

8500
8000
7500
7000
6500
6000
5500
5000
4500

FEET

1    2    3    4
MILES

Wildlife is plentiful in Waterton Canyon, as a crane gracefully demonstrates in a marshy wetland.

Continue on the trail, which is now a wide, two-lane dirt road with smooth and hard-packed surfaces, shaded by cottonwoods. Plenty of foot, bicycle, and horse traffic exist at this deservedly popular trail. Well maintained with a smooth, continuous slope, the trail closely follows the South Platte River as it winds its way into Waterton Canyon.

Each turn provides new interest to hikers as the trail continues. Beaver dams dot the waterways along the trail; some hikers may be lucky enough to see beavers swimming, especially later in the day. One of the many bends in the trail brings hikers underneath two large water-supply pipes to a small dam. Following the aqueduct are impressive cliffs that rise on the north side of the trail. At this point, the trail is in prime Rocky Mountain bighorn sheep territory. While scanning the rocks for bighorn sheep, don't forget to watch the riverbanks as well. Blue herons nest here and can be seen fishing for their next meal. Anglers regularly fly-fish in this part of the river.

The trail crosses through terrain that is less rocky and passes an unmarked trail that branches off to the northwest. Waterton Canyon tends to lure you from bend to bend, so it is important to be attentive to the time and weather. The canyon walls limit the amount of sky that can be seen, so storm clouds tend to surprise hikers. The walls also block the sun as it begins to set.

Continue along to another water diversion structure. At this point, there is an emergency phone, house, and mechanical shop used by water maintenance personnel. Eventually hikers arrive at the Marston Diversion Dam, where the sheet of water flowing over the dam highlights the hike. Turn around here and hike 4 miles back to the parking lot.

Some hikers may want to continue up the canyon to where the trail intersects

The South Platte River and the gentle
hills of Waterton Canyon

the beginning of the Colorado Trail. The
Colorado Trail stretches all the way to
Durango for those prepared and ambitious
overnight hikers who want to trek several
hundred miles.

▶ **NEARBY ATTRACTIONS**

Colorado Trail: **www.coloradotrail.org**.

# 60 Hikes
*within* 60 MILES

## DENVER AND BOULDER
### INCLUDING COLORADO SPRINGS, FORT COLLINS, AND ROCKY MOUNTAIN NATIONAL PARK

## APPENDIXES
## & INDEX

# APPENDIX A:
# OUTDOOR SHOPS

**Army and Navy Surplus Store–Denver**
www.armysurplusforless.com
3524 South Broadway in Englewood
(303) 789-1827
7560 Pecos in Denver
(303) 426-0488

**Arvada Army Navy Surplus**
www.arvadasurplus.com
(303) 424-5434

**Backpacker's Pantry**
6350 Gunpark Drive
Boulder, CO 80303
(303) 581-0581

**Bike–Hike**
1136 Main Street
Longmont, CO 80501
(303) 772-5105

**Boulder Army Store**
1545 Pearl Street
Boulder, CO 80303
(303) 442-7616

**Eastern Mountain Sports**
www.ems.com
Arapahoe Village Shopping Center
2550 Arapahoe Avenue
Boulder, CO 80302
(303) 442-7566

870 South Colorado Boulevard, Suite D
Glendale, CO 80246
(303) 759-3080

101 East Foothills Parkway
Fort Collins, CO 80525
(970) 223-6511

**Hiking Hut**
110 East Elkhorn Avenue
Estes Park, CO 80517
(970) 586-0708

**JAX Outdoor Gear**
www.jaxoutdoor.com
1200 North College Avenue

Fort Collins, CO 80524
(970) 221-0544
(800) 336-8314

**Little Mountain, Outdoor Gear for Kids**
1136 Spruce Street
Boulder, CO 80302
(303) 443-1757

**McGuckin Hardware**
www.mcguckin.com
2525 Arapahoe Avenue
Boulder, CO 80303
(303) 443-1822

**Mountain Miser LTD**
www.mountainmiser.com
209 West Hampden Avenue
Englewood, CO 80110
(303) 761-7070
(800) 841-0707

**Mountain Sports**
2835 Pearl Street
Boulder, CO 80302
(303) 442-8355

**Neptune Mountaineering**
www.neptunemountaineering.com
633 South Broadway, Suite A
Boulder, CO 80305
(303) 449-8866

**The North Face**
www.thenorthface.com
629-K South Broadway
Boulder, CO 80305
(303) 499-1731

**Outdoor Divas**
www.outdoordivas.com
1133 Pearl Street
Boulder, CO 80302
(303) 449-DIVA
(866) 449-DIVA

# APPENDIX A:
# OUTDOOR SHOPS *(continued)*

**Patagonia**
**www.patagonia.com**
1431 15th Street
Denver, CO 80202
(303) 446-9500

**REI**
**www.rei.com**
Denver Flagship
1416 Platte Street
Denver, CO 80202
(303) 756-3100

*Lakewood*
5375 South Wadsworth Boulevard
Lakewood, CO 80123
(303) 932-0600

*Englewood*
9637 East County Line Road
Englewood, CO 80112
(303) 858-1726

*Boulder*
1789 28th Street
Boulder, CO 80301
(303) 583-9970

*Fort Collins*
4025 South College Avenue
Fort Collins, CO 80525
(970) 223-0123

*Colorado Springs*
1376 East Woodmen Road
Colorado Springs, CO 80920
(719) 260-1455

**Trailridge Outfitters**
358 East Elkhorn Avenue
Estes Park, CO 80517
(970) 586-4595

**Large Sporting Goods Chain Stores:**

Christy Sports
**www.christysports.com**

Gart Sports
**www.gartsports.com**

# APPENDIX B:
# MAP SHOPS

**Boulder Army Store**
1545 Pearl Street
Boulder, CO 80303
(303) 442-7616

**Boulder Map Gallery**
www.bouldermapgallery.com
1718 13th Street
Boulder, CO 80302
(303) 444-1406

**City of Denver Bike Map**
200 West 14th Avenue, #301
Denver, CO 80204
(303) 640-2453

**DeLorme**
www.delorme.com

**EMS**
www.ems.com
All local EMS stores

**Golden Outfitters**
17211 West 16th Place
Golden, CO
(303) 279-4140

**Indian Peaks Ace Hardware**
74 Highway 119 South
Nederland, CO 80466
(303) 258-3132

**JAX Outdoor Gear**
www.jaxoutdoor.com
1200 North College Avenue
Fort Collins, CO 80524
(970) 221-0544

**Mapquest**
www.mapquest.com

**Maptech,Inc**.
www.maptech.com

**McVan Map Co.**
929 West Colorado Avenue
Colorado Springs, CO 80905
(719) 633-5757

**McGuckin Hardware**
www.mcguckin.com
2525 Arapahoe Avenue
Boulder, CO 80303
(303) 443-1822

**Microsoft Mapblast**
www.mapblast.com
National Geographic MapMachine
**www.nationalgeographic.com/
mapmachine**

**National Geographic Maps**
www.nationalgeographic.com/maps

**The North Face**
www.thenorthface.com
629-K South Broadway
Boulder, CO 80305
(303) 499-1731

**Offroute**
www.offroute.com

**REI**
www.rei.com
All local REI stores

**Tattered Cover**
2955 East 1st Avenue
Denver, CO
(303) 322-7727

**Timely Topos**
557 Burbank Street
Broomfield, CO
(303) 469-5022

**Topo USA**
www.topozone.com

**USDA Forest Service**
www.fs.fed.us

**Maps by Mail**
Visitor Map Sales
PO Box 25127
Lakewood, CO 80225

# APPENDIX B:
# MAP SHOPS *(continued)*

**Maps by Phone:**
(303) 275-5350
(303) 275-5367 (hearing impaired)
Maps available at all local agency offices

**United State Geologic Survey**
**www.usgs.gov**

**USGS Map Store**
**www.store.usgs.gov**

**GPS Manufacturers:**
Brunton
**www.brunton.com**

Garmin
**www.garmin.com**

Magellan
**www.magellangps.com**

Suunto
**www.suunto.com**

# APPENDIX C:
# AREA HIKING CLUBS

Access Fund
**www.accessfund.org**

Active.com
**www.active.com**

American Hiker
**www.americanhiker.com**

American Hiking Society
**www.americanhiking.org**

American Trails
**www.americantrails.org**

America Walks
**www.americawalks.org**

Climb the Rockies
**www.climbtherockies.com**

Colorado Fourteeners Initiative
**www.coloradofourteeners.org**

Colorado Mountain Club
**www.cmc.org**

Colorado Trail Foundation
**www.coloradotrail.org**

Continental Divide Trail Alliance
**www.cdtrail.org**

Fourteeners.org
**www.fourteeners.org**

Geocache Resources
**www.geocaching.com**

Happy Hikers Club
**www.membersaol.com/happyhikersclub**

Hiking and Backpacking
**www.hikingandbackpacking.org/
coloradoclubs**

Hiking in Colorado
**www.hikingincolorado.org**

Letterboxing
**www.letterboxing.org**

Mountain Peaks
**www.mountainpeaks.net**

Road Runner Club of America
**www.rrca.org**

Rocky Mountain Nature Association
**www.rmna.org**

Running Network
**www.runningnetwork.com**

Run Walk Jog
**www.runwalkjog.com**

Sierra Club
**www.rmc.sierraclub.org**
Rocky Mountain Chapter
1536 Wynkoop Street, 4th Floor
Denver, CO 80202
(303) 861-8819

Trails.com
**www.trails.com**

Volunteers for Outdoor Colorado
**www.voc.org**

# INDEX

# INDEX

# INDEX

# INDEX

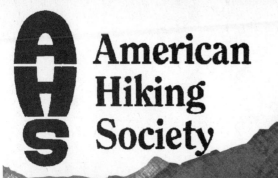